Vision

Books

Vision 2000 (... *Psalms Beyond 2000*

Mission 2000 (Year B)   *Jesus Beyond 2000*

Action 2000 (Year C)

Challenge 2000

Bible 2000   ### Booklets

Biblia 2000   *Spirit 2000*

Desafio 2000   *Lent 2000**

Psalms 2000   *Easter to Pentecost 2000**

Jesus 2000   *Advent/Christmas 2000**

                         *Cuaresma 2000**

                         *De Pascua a Pentecostés 2000**

                         Espíritu 2000

*Available for Years A, B, and C.

For further information call or write:
Thomas More Publishing
200 East Bethany Drive
Allen, Texas 75002-3804

Toll Free   800-264-0368
Fax   800-688-8356

Weekly Meeting Format

CALL TO PRAYER

> *The leader begins each weekly meeting*
> *by having someone light a candle*
> *and then three people pray the following:*

FIRST READER:

Jesus said,
"I am the light of the world. . . .
Whoever follows me
will have the light of life
and will never walk in darkness."

John 8:12

SECOND READER:

Lord Jesus, you also said
that where two or three
come together in your name,
you are there with them.
The light of this candle
symbolizes your presence among us.

THIRD READER:

And, Lord Jesus,
where you are,
there, too,
are the Father and the Holy Spirit.
So we begin our meeting
in the presence and the name
of the Father,
the Son,
and the Holy Spirit.

JESUS 2000

**A Contemporary
Walk with Jesus**

Mark Link, S.J.

ThomasMore®
Allen, Texas

IMPRIMI POTEST
Bradley M. Schaeffer, S.J.

NIHIL OBSTAT
Rev. Msgr. Glenn D. Gardner, J.C.D.
Censor Librorum

IMPRIMATUR
† Most Rev. Charles V. Grahmann
Bishop of Dallas

February 19, 1997

The Nihil Obstat and Imprimatur are official declarations
that the material reviewed is free of doctrinal or moral
error. No implication is contained therein that those
granting the Nihil Obstat and Imprimatur agree with the
contents, opinions, or statements expressed.

ACKNOWLEDGMENT

Unless otherwise noted, all Scripture quotations are
from Today's English Version text. Copyright © American
Bible Society 1966, 1971, 1976, 1992. Used by permission.

Some anecdotal material contained in this volume has
appeared in other publications by Mark Link.

Send all inquiries to:
Thomas More Publishing
200 East Bethany Drive   Toll Free   800-264-0368
Allen, Texas 75002-3804   Fax   800-688-8356

Printed in the United States of America

Product 7381   ISBN 0-88347-381-X

1 2 3 4 5   01 00 99 98 97

CONTENTS _____

How to Use *Jesus 2000*   5

Arrangement of *Jesus 2000*   11

Advent

Anticipation of Jesus   14

Special Note   30

Christmas

Coming of Jesus   44

Special Note   58

Special Note   65

Lent

Ministry of Jesus   66

Easter

Resurrection of Jesus   114

Special Note   167

Ordinary Time

Following of Jesus   168

Special Note   192

Vision 2000 Series on Internet:
http://v2000.org

HOW TO USE *JESUS 2000*

There are two ways to use this book:
on your own or as a member of a group.
If you use it on your own, simply devote
ten minutes a day to each meditation.
If you pray it as a member of a group,
you also meet with six to eight friends
once a week to share meditation thoughts.

Daily meditation guide

The Scripture readings in *Jesus 2000*
follow the gospel readings in the Lectionary
for weekdays and Sundays (Year A).
Begin each meditation by praying
the following prayer reverently:

*Father, you created me
and put me on earth for a purpose.*

*Jesus, you died for me
and called me to complete your work.*

*Holy Spirit, you help me
to carry out the work
for which I was created and called.*

*In your presence and name—
Father, Son, and Spirit—
I begin my meditation.
May all my thoughts and inspirations
have their origin in you
and be directed to your glory.*

Daily meditation procedure

The procedure for each meditation
is as follows:

- *Read* the meditation exercise slowly.
  When you finish, return to any
  phrase, sentence, or idea
  that struck you while reading.
  (Spend about one minute on this step.)

- *Think* about the phrase, sentence,
  or idea that struck you.
  Why did it strike you?
  (Spend about four minutes on this step.)

- *Speak* to God about your thoughts.
  Talk to God as you would to a close
  and trusted friend.
  (Spend about one minute on this step.)

- *Listen* to God's response.
  What may God wish to say to you?
  (Spend about four minutes on this step.)

End each meditation by reciting
the Lord's Prayer slowly and reverently.
Then jot down in a notepad
whatever struck you most
during your meditation.

N.B.: The "Daily Meditation Format,"
including the opening meditation prayer,
is printed on the inside front cover
of this book.

Weekly meeting guide

The purpose of the weekly meeting
is for *support* and *sharing*.
Meetings are 30 to 40 minutes long,
unless the group decides otherwise.
The meeting starts with a "Call to Prayer."
A member lights a candle and
the following prayer is said reverently:

FIRST READER

> *Jesus said,*
> *"I am the light of the world. . . .*
> *Whoever follows me*
> *will have the light of life*
> *and will never walk in darkness."*   John 8:12

SECOND READER

> *Lord Jesus, you also said*
> *that where two or three*
> *come together in your name,*
> *you are there with them.*
> *The light of this candle*
> *symbolizes your presence among us.*

THIRD READER

> *And, Lord Jesus,*
> *where you are, there too*
> *are the Father and the Spirit.*
> *And so we begin our meeting*
> *in the presence and the name*
> *of the Father,*
> *the Son,*
> *and the Holy Spirit.*

The meeting proper begins
with the leader responding briefly
to this question: Which daily meditation
was most meaningful for me and why?

When all have responded, the leader
opens the floor to anyone who wishes

- to elaborate on his or her response or
- to comment on another's response
  (not to take issue with it,
  but to affirm or clarify it).

The meeting ends with a "Call to Mission":
a charge to witness to Jesus and
to his teaching in daily life. It consists
in reverently praying the following:

FIRST READER

We conclude our meeting
by listening to Jesus say to us
what he said to his disciples
in his Sermon on the Mount:

SECOND READER

"You are like light for the whole world.
A city built on a hill cannot be hid.
No one lights a lamp
and puts it under a bowl;
instead it is put on the lampstand,
where it gives light
for everyone in the house.
In the same way
your light must shine before people,
so that they will see the good things
you do and praise your Father in heaven."

Matthew 5:14–16

Then a member extinguishes the candle
(lit at the start of the meeting).

FINAL READER
> *The light of this candle*
> *is now extinguished.*
> *But the light of Christ in each of us*
> *must continue to shine in our lives.*
> *Toward this end we pray together*
> *the Lord's Prayer: "Our Father . . ."*

For handy reference the "Call to Prayer"
and the "Call to Mission" are printed
on the end sheet and the inside back cover
of this book.

Two final points

First, the Lectionary readings vary
from year to year,
depending on what date Easter falls.
This leads to complications in some instances.
For simplicity's sake, therefore,
the sequence of Lectionary readings
has been altered in one or two cases.
Likewise, for simplicity's sake,
Lectionary readings for special days
are omitted.

Second, for the sake of visual grace, the author,
when quoting Scripture or other sources,
has capitalized words at the beginning
of sentences whose beginning has been pruned.

He has also added punctuation
at the end of edited sentences.

At times paragraphs have been broken up
or run together. All of this has been done
for reading ease and to better convey
the thought of quoted passages.

In making such minor changes in form,
the author has exercised the greatest care
to remain faithful to the thought
of all quoted sources.

For clarity's sake,
the name of Jesus or another proper name
has occasionally been inserted
in place of personal pronouns,
such as "he" or "they."

Finally, introductions to scriptural passages
have occasionally been added.
When this has been done, the added text
has been placed in brackets.
The one exception
is the brief introduction "Jesus said."

ARRANGEMENT OF *JESUS 2000*

Alvin Toffler's book *Future Shock*
deals with the impact of rapid change
on people in today's world.
This change often leaves them
with a feeling of uprootedness
and disorientation.

Today, more than ever, says Toffler,
we need a framework for our lives.
We need a pattern of holidays and
rotating seasonal events.
Without this pattern, we are like
a castaway at sea, adrift on a raft.

Toffler's observation
underscores one of the tremendous values
of the *liturgical year* of the Church.

Liturgical year

We may describe the liturgical year
as a reliving and celebration
of the key events of Jesus' life.
It is structured around two focal points:
Christmas, the minor one, and
Easter, the major one.
Each focal point
follows the same threefold structure:

- season of preparation,
- season of celebration,
- season of prolongation.

Christmas

The *preparation* for Christmas
is called Advent, meaning "coming."
The coming we prepare for is twofold:
Jesus' first coming in *history,* and
Jesus' second coming in *glory.*

The *celebration* of Christmas
focuses on the incredible mystery
that God, in the person of Jesus,
entered human history and lived among us.
The celebration extends from Christmas Eve
to, roughly, two weeks after Christmas.

The *prolongation* of Christmas
is called "Ordinary Time *after* Christmas"
(usually six to seven weeks in length,
depending on when Easter occurs that year).
This period sets the liturgical stage
for the celebration of the Easter cycle.

Easter

The *preparation* for Easter is Lent ("spring").
Lent begins with Ash Wednesday
and ends with Holy Week, which reenacts
the final week of Jesus' life on earth
(especially the Last Supper
on Holy Thursday
and the Crucifixion on Good Friday).

The *celebration* of Easter begins with
the Holy Saturday Easter Vigil service.
It ends fifty days later on Pentecost

with the celebration
of the coming of the Holy Spirit,
the birthday of the Church.

The *prolongation* of Easter
begins with "Ordinary Time *after* Easter."
It ends roughly four to eight weeks later,
depending on when Easter occurs that year.

And so *Jesus 2000* is arranged
according to the Church's liturgical year.

This arrangement enables us to telescope
and relive the life of Jesus
within a twelve-month period.

Let us now begin our "walk with Jesus"
through the liturgical year.

ADVENT

Anticipation of Jesus

Something strange began to happen
during Augustus Caesar's reign in Rome
(27 B.C.–A.D. 14).
There was a widespread feeling
of expectation among the masses.

"It was often associated with the figure
of a 'savior' or deliverer . . .
with something of divinity about him.
Millions . . . saw the emperor himself
as the divine deliverer."
C. H. Dodd, *The Founder of Christianity*

A similar expectation was stirring
among Jewish masses in Judea.
Unlike the Romans,
the Jews could pinpoint the reason for it.
The prophets spoke of the coming of a glorious
king who would inaugurate a glorious era.
To this king was given the title "Messiah."

It is this expectation of a Messiah
that we relive and celebrate
in the season of Advent. In retrospect
it is the expectation of the coming of Jesus,
the eternal Son of God.

*"The Son of Man will come at an hour
when you are not expecting him."* Matthew 24:44

The lyrics of an old Negro spiritual read:
"There's a king and captain high,
And he's coming by and by. . . .
You can hear his legions charging
in the regions of the sky.
And he'll find me hoeing cotton
when he comes.
There's a man they thrust aside,
Who was tortured till he died. . . .
He was hated and rejected,
He was scorned and crucified,
and he'll find me hoeing cotton
when he comes.
When he comes!
When he comes!
He'll be crowned by saints and angels
when he comes.
They'll be shouting out Hosanna!
to the man that men denied,
And I'll kneel among the cotton
when he comes."

When the Son of Man comes,
will he find me "hoeing cotton"?

*Endurance is
the ability to bear a hard thing
and to turn it into glory.* Philip Yancey

MONDAY
WEEK 1 _____ ADVENT

*Jesus said, "I have never found anyone
in Israel with faith like this."*
Matthew 8:10

When Lee's army entered Pennsylvania,
Lincoln knew that a defeat on northern soil
meant the loss of Washington and
the possible intervention of England and France
on the side of the confederacy.
He said:
"I went to my room
and got down on my knees.
Never before had I prayed
with so much earnestness.
I wish I could repeat my prayer.
I felt I must put all my trust
in Almighty God. He gave our people
the best country ever given man.
He alone could save it from destruction.
I had tried my best to do my duty
and had found myself unequal to the task.
The burden was more than I could bear.
I asked God to help us and give us victory. . . .
I was sure my prayer was answered.
I had no misgivings about the result
at Gettysburg."   Reported by General Daniel Sickles

What keeps me from putting all my trust
in God as Lincoln did?

Little love, little trust.   English proverb

*"You have shown to the unlearned
what you have hidden from the wise."* Luke 10:21

Legend says that
long ago a wonderful thing happened.
The angels in heaven decided to give
a special gift to the humans on earth.
It was the "key to happiness."
So they sent an angel down to earth
to make the presentation in a ceremony
on the morning of the next day.
But that night something terrible happened.
A bad angel stole the gift. The bad angel
thought and thought, asking himself,
"Where can I hide the key
so it will never be found?
Perhaps I could bury it deep in the ground.
Perhaps I could throw it into the sea.
Or perhaps I could hide it atop a mountain."
Then the bad angel got a brilliant idea!
"Ah! I know the perfect place to hide it—
a place no one will ever think of looking.
I'll bury it in the human heart."
And so he did.
Ever since, the human race has been searching
far and wide for the stolen "key to happiness."

What truth does the legend contain?
In what places have I been looking for happiness?

Jesus said, "I am the way." John 14:6

WEDNESDAY
WEEK 1 _____ ADVENT

Large crowds came to Jesus,
bringing with them the lame,
the blind, the crippled, the dumb, and
many other sick people, whom they placed
at Jesus' feet; and he healed them.
The people were amazed as they saw
the dumb speaking, the crippled
made whole, the lame walking,
and the blind seeing. Matthew 15:30–31

There's a touching scene
in Dickens's classic *A Christmas Carol*.
In it Mrs. Cratchit asks her husband, Bob,
"How did Tiny Tim behave in church today?"
Bob answers, "As good as gold. And better.
He gets thoughtful
sitting by himself so much
and thinks the strangest thoughts.
He told me, coming home,
that he hoped the people saw him in church,
because he was a cripple.
He said, 'It might be pleasant for them
to recall on Christmas day who it was who
made lame beggars walk and the blind see.' "

Tiny Tim's attitude was, in a sense,
a greater miracle than if he'd been healed.
What is my attitude toward my "crosses"?

Two men looked out through prison bars—
One saw mud, the other stars. Oscar Wilde

Jesus said,
"Not everyone who calls me 'Lord, Lord'
will enter the Kingdom of heaven,
but only those who do what my Father
in heaven wants them to do. . . .
But anyone who hears these words of mine
and does not obey them
is like a foolish man who built his house on sand.
The rain poured down, the rivers flooded over,
the wind blew hard against that house,
and it fell. And what a terrible fall that was!"

Matthew 7:21, 26–27

In his book *The Great Divorce,*
the British theologian C. S. Lewis
divides the world into two groups of people,
those who say to God, "Thy will be done,"
and those to whom God says,
"All right, then, have it your way."

Lewis's division of the world
invites me to reflect:
Into which of the two groups
do I most often find myself?
What is one area in which I find God's will
hard to accept?

I just want to do God's will. . . .
I'm happy tonight. . . .
I'm not fearing any man.
Martin Luther King Jr. in a speech on April 3, 1968,
the eve of his assassination

FRIDAY
WEEK 1 _____ ADVENT

Two blind men started following Jesus.
"Have mercy on us, Son of David!"
they shouted. . . . Then Jesus touched
their eyes . . . and their sight was restored.

Matthew 9:27, 29–30

Abraham Lincoln and Gilbert Greene
were walking outside of town one night.
Greene described what happened:
"As we walked on the country road . . .
Lincoln turned his eyes to the heavens
full of stars, and told me their names. . . .
He said, 'I never behold them
that I do not feel
that I am looking in the face of God.
I can see how
it might be possible for a man
to look down upon earth and be an atheist,
but I cannot conceive
how he could look up into the heavens
and say there is no God.'"

Emanuel Hertz, ed., *Lincoln Talks: A Biography in Anecdote*

How blind am I
to God's presence and God's wisdom
shining forth from our world?

He has decided the number of the stars
and calls each one by name.
Great and mighty is our Lord;
his wisdom cannot be measured. Psalm 147:4–5

*Jesus said, "The harvest is large,
but there are few workers to gather it in.
Pray to the owner of the harvest that he will
send out workers to gather in his harvest."*
Matthew 9:37–38

The Associated Press ran a feature story
on Father Richard Bozzelli, saying:
"He was poised to join Washington's
high-ranking legal circles when he heard
the call [to the priesthood],
and traded the executive offices at
the Federal Communication Commission
for two rooms in a rectory in a blue-collar
neighborhood of northeast Baltimore."
Ordained in 1994, he said his decision
was the result of a "slow turning to God"—
after treating religion "as a hobby."
While getting his degree
at Harvard Law School,
Bozzelli still found time to work
with disadvantaged kids and mop floors
and chop vegetables at a local soup kitchen.

How faithful am I in praying
that more people like Father Bozzelli
will answer God's call?
Am I in a position to answer the call?

*God calls . . . where your deep gladness
meets the world's deep hunger.* Frederick Buechner

John the Baptist . . . started preaching.
"Turn away from your sins. . . .
The Kingdom of heaven is near!"   Matthew 3:1–2

Dennis Alessi was walking down
a busy street in downtown Baltimore.
At an intersection stood an elderly man
calling out to the passersby,
"Turn from your sins!
Turn back to God!"
His pulpit was a clean metal trash can.
He was bald, wore glasses,
and was neatly dressed. Dennis said later:
"His pleas were dignified and sincere. . . .
I had no idea whether that man calling
into the crowd was heard by one
or a hundred others.
But he reached something in me. . . .
[I was moved to return] to the Church,
from which I'd been absent for seven years."
"The Open Door," *Catholic Digest* (Feb. 1996)

How do I explain the impact of this modern
"John the Baptist" on Dennis?
How relevant is his message for our day?

Mere sorrow, which weeps and sits still
is not repentance.
Repentance is sorrow
converted into action—into movement
toward a new and better life.   Marvin R. Vincent

Some men came carrying a paralyzed man. . . .
When Jesus saw how much faith they had,
he said to the man,
"Your sins are forgiven, my friend."

Luke 5:18, 20

Dr. Robert Healy wrote
a letter to *Psychology Today* magazine.
In it he told about a young man who entered
therapy after a brush with suicide.
The young man was on his way to a bridge
to leap off it to his death.
He stopped for a traffic light and
happened to glance toward the sidewalk.
On the curb stood an elderly woman.
She gave him the most beautiful smile
he'd ever seen. Then the light changed.
He drove off, but the smile haunted him.
He said later that he had no idea
who the woman was.
All he knows is that he owes his life to her.
She was the source of a blessing to him
at the most critical moment of his life.

Who was a source of blessing to me
at a critical moment in my life?

Shine through me and be so in me
that every soul I come in contact with
may feel your presence in my spirit.

John Henry Newman

TUESDAY
WEEK 2 _____ ADVENT

*Jesus said, "Your Father in heaven
does not want any of these little ones
to be lost."* Matthew 18:14

During the Great Depression,
Sue's family was desperately poor.
Meals often consisted of a bowl of oatmeal.
Her mother saved the coupons inside the boxes
to get needed things, like the cups pictured
on the box. What really attracted Sue,
however, was the picture of the doll on the box.
Just before Christmas she and her mother
saw the same doll as a display model
in a grocery store nearby.
Sue's mother could hardly get Sue
away from the window.
They walked home talking about the doll.
When Sue walked into the kitchen
on Christmas morning, there on the table,
next to the oatmeal box, was the doll.
Shortly afterward her mother died.
Years later Sue learned that her mother
had begged the store manager
to let her do work at the store
to earn the display model.

Can I recall a similar memory of my own
mother, father, or guardian?

*A mother's heart
is the child's schoolroom.* Henry Ward Beecher

Jesus said, "Learn from me. . . .
I am gentle and humble in spirit." Matthew 11:29

One day Lincoln was riding with friends.
Suddenly his friends found him missing.
One of the friends, Joshua Speed,
wrote later:
"We had passed through a thicket
of wild plum and crab trees,
and stopped to water our horses,
when Hardin came up alone.
'Where is Lincoln?' we all inquired.
'Oh,' replied he, 'when I saw him last
he had caught two young birds
which the wind had blown
out of their nest,
and he has been hunting
for the nest so as to put them back.'
In a short time
Lincoln came up having found the nest.
The party laughed at him, but he said:
'I could not have slept
if I had not restored
those little birds to the nest.'"
Emanuel Hertz, ed., *Lincoln Talks: A Biography in Anecdote*

What kind of reverence for life do I have?

By having reverence for life,
we enter into a spiritual relationship
with the world. Albert Schweitzer

THURSDAY
WEEK 2 _____ ADVENT

*[Just before John was beheaded by Herod,
Jesus eulogized him, saying,]
"John the Baptist is greater
than anyone who has ever lived."* Matthew 11:11

Charlie Ross was President Truman's
close friend and press secretary.
When Ross died suddenly,
the grief-stricken president
wrote out in long hand
a eulogy that he was to read
at a press conference.
It began: "The friend of my youth,
who became a tower of strength
when the responsibilities of high office
so unexpectedly fell to me, is gone."
At this point in the eulogy, Truman choked.
He said, "Ah hell, I can't read this thing.
You fellows know how I feel anyway."
With tears in his eyes,
he gave them the handwritten eulogy,
and walked sobbing to his office.

It was this kind of love that Jesus held
for John the Baptist. Is there someone
to whom I owe a great deal and ought to
express my appreciation now—rather than
wait and eulogize the person at death?

*The finger of God touches your life
when you make a friend.* Mary Dawson Hughes

*Jesus said, "Now, to what can I compare
the people of this day? They are like
children sitting in the marketplace.
One groups shouts to the other,
'We played wedding music for you,
but you wouldn't dance!
We sang funeral songs, but you wouldn't cry!'
When John came, he fasted and drank no wine,
and everyone said, 'He has a demon in him!'
When the Son of Man came,
he ate and drank,
and everyone said, 'Look at this man! He is
a glutton and wine drinker!'"* Matthew 11:16–19

The *Christian Science Monitor*
received this letter:
"When I subscribed a year ago,
you stated that if I was not satisfied
at the end of the year
I could have my money back.
Well, I would like my money back.
On second thought, to save you the trouble,
you may apply it to my next year's subscription."

When I meet the kind of people described
by Jesus and the *Christian Science Monitor*,
how do I usually react?

*People are unreasonable,
illogical and self-centered.
Love them anyway!* Theodore Roethke

SATURDAY
WEEK 2 _____ ADVENT

Jesus said,
"People did not recognize John the Baptist,
but treated him just as they pleased.
In the same way they will also mistreat
the Son of Man." Matthew 17:12

Watching a TV special on the Holocaust,
a woman was shocked to feel herself
becoming more irritated than moved by it.
Not until she read this passage
from Henri Nouwen's *Compassion*
did she realize why:
"Human suffering which comes to us
in a way and on a scale
that makes identification practically impossible
frequently evokes strong negative feelings.
It is therefore no wonder
that the diary of Anne Frank did more
for the understanding of human misery
than many of the films showing . . .
heaps of naked . . . corpses.
Anne Frank we can understand;
piles of human flesh only make us sick."

How might this explain why I may not be
so outraged by hunger and pain today?

Jesus said, "Whenever you did this
for one of the least important
of these followers of mine,
you did it for me!" Matthew 25:40

*Jesus said, "The deaf hear . . . and
the Good News is preached to the poor."* Matthew 11:5

A mother found a note written by her child,
who was deaf. It went something like this:
"Dear God: I don't want to hurt your feelings,
but I wish you hadn't made me deaf.
Could you change me back? [signed] Sue.
P.S. Say hello to my guardian angel."
The next day, Sue found a note.
It was written in gold ink
and went something like this:
"Dear Sue:
I am your guardian angel, and I asked God
to answer your note. You see,
God made me deaf, too. But God did give me
two fast legs, so I can run like the wind;
two lovely arms, so I can hug everybody;
and an imagination, so I can fly anywhere.
What I really like most, however,
is being able to turn off my hearing aid
when the other angels are yelling.
It makes things quiet so I can better hear God
singing love songs to me in my heart.
[signed] Your guardian angel.
P.S. We love more and more every day!"

What is the point of the angel's letter?

*Faith knows the way; hope points the way.
Love is the way.* Anonymous

SPECIAL NOTE _____

Starting today, the readings in the
Lectionary vary from year to year. To
determine which meditation to use today,

- find the current year,
- read across to the date listed,
- page ahead to that date and begin.

This will put you in a reading sequence
that will synchronize you with Christmas.
(For example, if the year is 1999,
page ahead to December 13 and begin.)

1997	December 15
1998	December 14
1999	December 13
2000	December 18
2001	December 17
2002	December 16
2003	December 15
2004	December 13
2005	December 12
2006	December 18
2007	December 17
2008	December 15
2009	December 14
2010	December 13

*[When Jesus asked Jewish leaders
if John's baptism was of divine or human origin,
they caucused privately, saying,]
"If we answer, 'From God,' he will say to us,
'Why, then, did you not believe John?'
But if we say, 'From human beings,'
we are afraid of what the people might do,
because they are all convinced that John
was a prophet."
So they answered Jesus,
"We don't know."*   Matthew 21:25–27

After the 1969 moon landing, a survey revealed
that many people in the inner city
believed it was staged on the back lot
of some studio in Hollywood.
NASA officials reported receiving letters
from persons and groups all over the world
calling the event a "big hoax."

Lies like the one by the Jewish leaders
in today's gospel continue to be repeated
by leaders in today's world. As a result,
there is great lack of trust today
in the very area where it is most needed.
How honest and straightforward am I
in my dealings with other people?

*What upsets me most is not
that you lied to me, but that from now on
I can no longer believe you.*   Friedrich Nietzsche

[Jesus told a story about a father
who said to his son,]
"'Go and work in the vineyard today.'
'I don't want to,' he answered,
but later he changed his mind and went."

Matthew 21:28–29

Years ago there was a Broadway play
about a young person
who was hopelessly hooked on drugs.
The young person dropped out of school
and rejected his family.
In an unforgettable scene in the play,
he looks up to heaven and cries out
in anguish and despair,
"How I wish life was like a notebook
so I could tear out the parts
where I've make all the mistakes
and throw them away."

Thanks to Jesus,
life is like a notebook.
And thanks to Jesus,
we can tear out the parts
where we've made all the mistakes
and throw them away.
What are two mistakes I would like to
"tear out" and throw away? How can I do it?

The confession of evil works
is the beginning of good works.   Saint Augustine

ADVENT _____

*Jesus said, "How happy are those
who have no doubts about me!"* Luke 7:23

Professor Howard Gardner
of Harvard's Graduate School of Education
said in an interview that he now believes
that certain people are in touch with reality
in a way that the rest of us are not.
"They have a sixth sense
of where things are coming from
and where they are going.
These people become leaders and inspirers."
Underscoring his point, Gardner says:
"If you asked me ten years ago,
I would have said that's just interpersonal
intelligence: Some people understand
other people better and can work with them.
I'm no longer persuaded that that's the case;
I think some people really are
tuned in to an aspect of the world—
the human and the non-human world—
that others of us aren't."
Christian Science Monitor (Sept. 9, 1993)

How firmly do I believe that Jesus
was someone who was "tuned in" to reality
in a way no other person ever was?
What keeps me from believing more firmly?

*"I do have faith, but not enough.
Help me have more!"* Mark 9:24

DECEMBER 15

_____ ADVENT

"When you went out to John in the desert,
what did you expect to see? . . .
A man dressed up in fancy clothes?
People who dress like that
and live in luxury are found in palaces!
Tell me, what did you go out to see?
A prophet? Yes indeed, but you saw
much more than a prophet." Luke 7:24–26

Dr. "Charlie" Mayo and his brother William
founded the famous Mayo Clinic
at Rochester, Minnesota.
Once he hosted a visitor from England.
Each night the visitor would put his shoes
outside his door to be shined—
expecting a servant to do it.
Dr. "Charlie" knew this was customary
in certain levels of British society.
So, rather than embarrass his guest,
he simply shined the shoes himself.

The greatest people have a simplicity
and spirit of service about them
that is hard for "not-so-great" people
to comprehend.
What kind of simplicity
and spirit of service do I have?

The greatest truths are the simplest;
and so are the greatest people.
Augustus and Julius Hare

_____

*Jesus said, "The deeds my Father gave me
to do . . . speak on my behalf and show
that the Father has sent me."* John 5:36

One morning Lincoln walked
into the bank with wet feet, explaining,
" 'I saw a little girl going to school.
She was drenched with the terrible storm,
and standing on the corner
unable to cross the street, which was flooded
with water more than ankle deep. . . .
I put my hands under her arms,
and wading across the street,
I set her down safely
on the other side.'
I have thought so many times since,
that Lincoln helping
the little colored school girl over
the flooded street was the type
and prophecy of Lincoln carrying four millions
of the same race over the Red Sea."
Emanuel Hertz, ed., *Lincoln Talks: A Biography in Anecdote*

What deed or person in my early life
has had the most impact
on shaping my later life?
Why would I pick that deed or person?

*I will study and get ready and
the opportunity will come.*
                              Abraham Lincoln

DECEMBER 17

*Jacob was the father of Joseph
the husband of Mary.
It was of her that Jesus
who is called the Messiah
was born.* Matthew 1:16 (NAB, 1970)

At the age of 22, Bernard entered
a Cistercian monastery in France.
He followed the rigid Rule of Saint Benedict:
silence, labor, and prayer.
Within a few years, Bernard was asked
to open at new monastery at Clairvaux.
After becoming its abbot,
he was catapulted into the public eye
as a great preacher, spiritual guide,
advisor to popes, and mediator of disputes
between European dignitaries.
A distinctive dimension of Bernard's
spirituality was his remarkable devotion
to Mary, the mother of Jesus.

What role does Mary
play in my spiritual life?
Should that role be greater?

*Imitating Mary, you will not go astray.
Praying to her, you will not despair.
Thinking of her, you will not err.
Supported by her, you will not fail. . . .
Embraced by her, you will be saved.*
Saint Bernard of Clairvaux

[Mary was betrothed to Joseph.]
An angel . . . appeared to him in a dream
and said, ". . . Take Mary to be your wife.
For it is by the Holy Spirit
that she has conceived.
She will have a son,
and you will name him Jesus." Matthew 1:20–21

Jewish "betrothals"
grew out of the ancient Jewish custom
of having parents
pick marriage partners for their children.
Conceivably,
two young people did not know each other
before the period of betrothal.
The betrothal period gave them a chance
to get acquainted; it lasted about a year.
Betrothal had the force of marriage.
A groom-to-be could not renounce
his bride-to-be except by divorce.
If he died during the betrothal period,
his bride-to-be became the legal widow.
Likewise, if a bride-to-be was unfaithful
during the betrothal period,
she could be punished as an adulteress.

If I were Joseph, what would be my thoughts
before the dream? After the dream?

If you judge people,
you have no time to love them. Mother Teresa

DECEMBER 19

Elizabeth and Zechariah had no children
because Elizabeth could not have any,
and she and Zechariah were both very old.　Luke 1:7

Dale Francis was teaching creative writing
in a state hospital for the mentally ill.
One student, named Mary,
had never spoken to anyone
since arriving at the hospital.
One day she gave him a note that read:
"Once I was on a train. It stopped.
I looked out the window of the train
into the window of a house.
There was a mother and father
sitting at a table,
their children at the table around them.
They were laughing and talking. I cried."
Dale was deeply moved.
He got Mary's permission to read the note
to the class at their next meeting.
Their warmth went out to Mary.
It was the beginning of her recovery.
Finally, she felt the love of a family,
which she had missed so sorely.

Why did the table scene make Mary cry?
How is it related to the story of Elizabeth
and Zechariah?

Every child comes with the message
that God is not discouraged with us.　Tagore

ADVENT _____

[An angel said to Mary,]
"You will . . . give birth to a son,
and you will name him Jesus. . . ."
Mary said to the angel, "I am a virgin.
How, then, can this be?" The angel answered,
"The Holy Spirit will come on you. . . ."
"I am the Lord's servant," said Mary;
"may it happen to me." Luke 1:31, 34–35, 38

A young person describes hearing God's
call and saying yes to it—as Mary did:
"I was raised in a small town
and my home overlooked the ocean. . . .
My mother would often take me to . . .
the harbor, and would teach me to sit still
and listen to God in the wind, in the sea,
in life. She would say,
'Be quiet and God will speak to you.'
God did speak to me, and for a long time . . .
I tried my best to run from God. . . .
I finally said 'Fiat' (So be it). . . .
At that moment my whole being
filled with a great inner peace and joy
which I shall never forget."
Vincent Dwyer, *Lift Your Sails*

Have I ever felt God was speaking to me,
but I did not want to follow? When? Why?

How can I ever be content to creep after
I have felt the impulse to fly? Anonymous

DECEMBER 21

[When Mary learned
that Elizabeth was about to give birth,
she went to visit her. At Mary's greeting,]
Elizabeth was filled with the Holy Spirit
and said . . . "You are the most blessed . . .
and blessed is the child you will bear!
Why should . . . my Lord's mother [come]
to visit me?"   Luke 1:41–43

A *Peanuts* cartoon
shows Lucy going to visit Charlie Brown.
Upon arriving,
she wishes him a cheery "Merry Christmas!"
Then, explaining the purpose of her visit
and her cheery greeting, she says,
"At this time of year, we should be kind."
Charlie looks somewhat puzzled and asks,
"Why at this time of year only?
Shouldn't we be kind all year long?"
Lucy looks equally puzzled and snaps at him,
"What are you? Some kind of religious nut!"

To what extent
does the point of the cartoon apply to me?

Kindness is the music of life.
It has a magical charm
that seems to have its origin in heaven—
perhaps some angel's song
that lost its way
and strayed down to earth.   Anonymous

ADVENT _____

Mary said, "My heart praises the Lord;
my soul is glad because of God my Savior."

Luke 1:46–47

It was Christmas Eve
on the campus of Princeton University.
Everything was quiet
and snow was falling.
Then carol singers could be heard coming.
Evelyn Woods Ulyat was walking her dog
when the carolers arrived on the scene.
They stopped at the home of Albert Einstein,
whose scientific genius revolutionized
our view of the universe. Evelyn writes:
"One of the boys started to sing,
'O little town of Bethlehem,
how still we see thee lie,'
and the others took it up.
The front door opened suddenly
and Dr. Einstein stood there a moment.
Then he turned back into the house
and reappeared with his violin. . . .
He started to play with the singers—
each verse through the hymn."

What does this tell us about Dr. Einstein?

Child, dear child, help me to discover
even in the most earnest and
the most severe people the child asleep
in their hearts.   Dom Helder Camara

[The remarkable circumstances
that marked the birth of John the Baptist
made people ask,] "What is this child
going to be?" For it was plain
that the Lord's power was upon him.   Luke 1:66

"Each newborn child arrives on earth
with a message to deliver to mankind.
Clenched in his little fist
is some particle
of yet unrevealed truth,
some missing clue, which may solve
the enigma of man's destiny. . . .
He must be treated as top-sacred."
Sam Levinson

It was this kind of awe—only much more so—
that marked John's birth. Luke concludes:
"John grew and developed in body and spirit.
He lived in the desert until the day when
he appeared publicly to the people."   Luke 1:80

What message did God give me to deliver?

John's father Zechariah was filled
with the Holy Spirit, and [said] . . .
"Let us praise the Lord, the God of Israel! . . .
He will cause the bright dawn of salvation
to rise on us and to shine from heaven
on all those who live in the dark shadow
of death, to guide our steps
into the path of peace."   Luke 1:67–68, 78–79

CHRISTMAS EVE _____

While they were in Bethlehem,
the time came for Mary to have her baby.
She . . . wrapped him in cloths and
laid him in a manger—there was no room
for them to stay in the inn.   Luke 2:6–7

Four days before the celebration
of Jesus' birth in 1968,
Apollo 8 lifted off from Cape Kennedy
carrying astronauts Frank Borman,
Bill Anders, and Jim Lovell.
On Christmas Eve,
Apollo 8 lost contact with earth
as it went behind the moon.
A billion people sat glued to their TV sets,
waiting for the spaceship to reappear.
As it emerged safely, its crew took turns
reading a "Christmas greeting" to earth.
The reading was the story of creation
from the Book of Genesis.
No one who watched that dramatic event
will ever forget the "specialness"
of that celebration of Jesus' birth.

Can I recall a "special" celebration
of Jesus' birth from my own life?
What made it special?

"Just a little while longer,
and he who is coming will come;
he will not delay."   Hebrews 10:37

CHRISTMAS

Coming of Jesus

Jesus was born and raised in a world
that was far from the dream
of the Kingdom of God
that he would eventually inaugurate.

It was a cruel world.
Human beings were sold
on the auction block and died
for the entertainment of others.

It was an pain-filled world.
Lepers, cripples, and the mentally ill
limped through life as best they could.
Suffering was as inevitable
as the sunrise and the sunset.

It was an ugly world.
Exploitation of the poor, racial prejudice,
and an "eye-for-an-eye" morality
were woven into the social fabric
of every nation.

It was into this world that Jesus was born—
not as a powerful prince
protected from many of these evils, but as
a poor peasant vulnerable to all of them.

CHRISTMAS _____

In the beginning the Word already existed;
the Word was with God,
and the Word was God. . . .
The Word became a human being. . . .
We saw his glory, the glory which he received
as the Father's only Son. John 1:1, 14

Sister Mary Coleman, a Maryknoll nun,
spent a good part of World War II
in a Japanese prison camp in the Philippines.
The prisoners set up a prayer room and
one of the Filipinos carved a wooden crucifix.
It proved to be a great aid to prayer.
When Christmas came, several prisoners
carved crib figures for the prayer room.
A guard who had watched the prisoners
meditate before Jesus on the cross
now watched them meditate with equal fervor
before the infant in the crib.
One day he pointed to the infant in the crib
and then to Jesus on the cross
and asked reverently, "The same one?"
Sister Coleman said softly, "The same one."
Then, looking at the crib and the crucifix again,
he said softly, "I'm sorry."

What does this story say to me?

O Christmas Sun! / What holy task is thine!
To fold a world in the embrace of God.

Guy Wetmore Carryl

*Jesus said, "You will be brought to trial
before rulers and kings, to tell
the Good News to them."* Matthew 10:17

From 1558 to 1829, Roman Catholics
in England were forbidden to worship publicly.
During this period the carol "The Twelve
Days of Christmas" was composed.
Catholics used it as a disguised form
of public worship and as an outline
for teaching their children the faith.
Slight variations in versions have come
down to us. Here is a widely accepted one:

1   partridge in a pear tree—1 Lord: Jesus;
2   turtle doves—2 Testaments: Old & New;
3   French hens—3 Virtues: faith, hope, love;
4   calling birds—4 Gospels: key NT books;
5   gold rings—5 Books of Moses:
    key OT books;
6   geese a-laying—6 Days of creation;
7   swans a-swimming—7 Gifts of Spirit;
8   maids a-milking—8 Beatitudes;
9   ladies dancing—9 Fruits of Spirit;
10 lords a-leaping—10 Commandments;
11 pipers piping—11 Faithful apostles;
12 drummers drumming—12 Articles of Creed.

Why are "trial" times often "graced" times?

*Christmas begins in God's heart and is
complete only when it enters my heart.*

[Mary Magdalene ran to tell the "good news"]
to Simon Peter and the other disciple,
whom Jesus loved. . . . Then Peter and
the other disciple went to the tomb . . .
saw and believed. John 20:2–3, 8

Mary Helen Gee says,
"When my kids were small,
I kept two sets of nativity figures:
an expensive set on the mantle
and a cheap set under the tree,
for the kids to play with—even take to bed
because 'Baby Jesus got cold during the night.' "
Jesus did something parallel to this
in the course of his own life on earth.
On Christmas morning
he revealed his *human* side
and invited us to relate to him
as our friend and companion.
On Easter morning
he revealed his *divine* side
and invited us to relate to him
as our Lord and Savior.

What do I find most attractive
about Jesus in his human side?
His divine side?

Jesus is
the condescension of divinity,
and the exaltation of humanity. Phillips Brooks

DECEMBER 28

After the wise men had left, an angel . . .
appeared in a dream to Joseph and said,
"Herod will be looking for the child
in order to kill him. . . . Take the child
and his mother and escape to Egypt."
[Joseph did as the angel said.]   Matthew 2:13

Kathryn Koob was one of 54 Americans
taken hostage by Shiite extremists
in Iran in 1979 and held for 444 days.
On Christmas of 1980 her captors
paraded her before the world on TV,
letting her send greetings to her family.
She turned the situation
into a moving spiritual experience
by singing a carol
she had learned as a child:
"Away in a manger, no crib for a bed,
the little Lord Jesus
laid down his sweet head. . . .
Bless all the dear children
in thy tender care,
And fit us for heaven to live with thee there."

Herod's violence and Iranian terrorism
marred the beauty of Christmas
but could not destroy it. What are some
early Christmas memories that I have?

The star of Bethlehem is a star
in the darkness of night even today.   Edith Stein

*[Mary and Joseph took the infant Jesus
to the Temple. A holy man named Simeon
saw Jesus in Mary's arms.
He went over to Mary.
Then, alluding to Jesus' future suffering,
he said to her,]*
*"And sorrow, like a sharp sword,
will break your own heart."*   Luke 2:35

Erma Bombeck was a journalist.
Her column appeared
in 900 papers across the country.
Like many columnists,
she received lots of letters from readers.
Typical is the following,
based on an actual letter from a mother:
"Even if the courts have given up on my son,
I have not. He's my son. How can I give up
on him? I pray for him; I cry for him;
I encourage him. And, above all, I love him."
This testimony of a mother's love for a son
helps us appreciate the pain of the sword
that would break Mary's heart
as she stood beneath the cross
when her son was so brutally crucified.

To what extent do I recognize
the role I played in Jesus' crucifixion?

*The recognition of sin
is the beginning of salvation.*   Martin Luther

There was a very old prophet,
a widow named Anna, daughter of Phanuel
of the tribe of Asher.
She . . . was now eighty-four years old.
She never left the Temple;
day and night she worshiped God.   Luke 2:36–37

Margery Williams's *Velveteen Rabbit*
has a scene in which a toy rabbit
is talking to a toy horse
that has lost most of its hair
from being handled so much by children.
The two animals are discussing
that "precious moment" in the life of a toy
when children start loving it as "real."
The horse explains that it usually happens
after most of your hair has been "loved" off.
"But the ugliness, caused by the loss of hair,"
says the horse, "doesn't matter,
because once you're 'real' to children,
you can never be ugly to them anymore."
The old Anna was like that.
She could never be ugly to God anymore.

What constitutes beauty in "old Annas"?

In every heart there is a spiritual antenna.
To the extent that it keeps picking up
messages of beauty, hope, and love,
to that extent
the heart is always young.   Anonymous

*The light shines in the darkness, and
the darkness has never put it out.* John 1:5

Austrian psychotherapist Viktor Frankl
was a prisoner in a Nazi concentration camp.
In *Man's Search for Meaning,* he recalls
digging a trench on a cold winter morning:
"Gray was the sky above;
gray the snow in the pale light of dawn;
gray the rags in which my fellow prisoners
were clad, and gray their faces. . . .
I was struggling
to find a reason for my sufferings. . . .
In a last violent protest against
the hopelessness of imminent death,
I sensed my spirit . . . say 'Yes'
in answer to my question
of the existence of ultimate purpose.
At that moment a light was lit in a distant
farmhouse, which stood on the horizon . . .
in the mist of the miserable gray
of a dawning morning in Bavaria."

Have I ever wondered about the purpose
of my life? What would I say it is?

*You yourselves used to be in the darkness,
but since you have become the Lord's people,
you are in the light.
So you must live
like people who belong to the light.* Ephesians 5:8

JANUARY 1 (Feast of the Mother of God)
_____ CHRISTMAS SEASON

[The shepherds] found Mary and Joseph
and saw the baby lying in the manger.
When the shepherds saw him,
they told them
what the angel had said about the child.
All who heard it were amazed. . . .
Mary remembered all these things
and thought deeply about them.   Luke 2:16–19

Sister Ann Catherine Ryan
was a member of a faith-sharing group
in Riberalta, Bolivia.
One day the group was reflecting upon Mary,
the mother of Jesus. After a little while,
a young woman spoke up
in confusion and frustration, saying,
"How can I identify with Mary?
Did Saint Joseph ever beat her . . . ?
Did she have to go to work in a factory
at 4 A.M. and work till 8 P.M.
cracking nuts for a meager wage
to support her child?"

How would I answer
the confused and frustrated young woman?
How well can I identify with Mary?

Two harmful excesses to be avoided:
excluding reason, and
admitting nothing but reason.
                                    Blaise Pascal

[People asked John, "Who are you?" He said,]
"I am 'the voice of someone shouting . . . :
Make a straight path
for the Lord to travel!' "   John 1:23

General Charles Gordon
was admired by all who knew him.
When England proposed to honor him
with money and titles, he refused.
He did agree, however,
to accept a lone gold medal
with a brief inscription etched on it.
After Gordon's death in 1885,
the medal could not be found anywhere.
It was later learned
that Gordon had melted the medal down,
sold the gold, and gave the cash to the poor.
On the date of the gift, his diary reads:
"The last earthly thing I had in this world
that I valued, I have given to the Lord."

How is Gordon's action a perfect response
to what John had in mind when he preached,
"Make a straight path for the Lord to travel!"
What is one concrete action I might take
in response to John's message?

When the soul
has laid down its faults
at the feet of God,
it feels as though it had wings.   Eugenie de Guerin

JANUARY 3

The next day John saw Jesus coming to him,
and said, "There is the Lamb of God,
who takes away the sin of the world!
This is the one I was talking about."

John 1:29–30

Harvey Mackay knows business inside out.
He calls Billy Graham the best salesman
he's ever met.
What makes him remarkable, he says,
is that he sells a product
that nobody has ever seen—eternal salvation.
What makes Billy even more remarkable,
says Mackay, is his mediocre style.
His delivery is pedestrian,
he's not entertaining or funny, and he doesn't
claim to be an outstanding biblical scholar.
Why is Billy the best? Mackay answers,
"His dedication to his 'customers.'
Every action he takes is designed to meet
their needs, not his own. And it shows."

John was like this, also. His dedication
was total. And every action he took
was designed to meet the needs of the people,
that is, to prepare them
to open their hearts to Jesus' salvation.
How dedicated am I to my "mission" in life?

I heard the Lord say, "Whom shall I send?". . .
I answered, "I will go! Send me!" Isaiah 6:8

John was . . . with two of his disciples,
when he saw Jesus walking by.
"There is the Lamb of God!" he said.
The two disciples heard him say this
and went with Jesus.   John 1:35–37

In his book *Prayer from Where You Are,*
James Carroll cites the large puzzle page
that many Sunday newspapers carry.
A favorite puzzle is the drawing of a scene
like a family picnic.
Under it are the words:
"Can you find the hidden person?"
You look and look and see nothing.
You rotate the paper for a different view.
Still nothing!
Then, suddenly, in a cloud you see an eye.
Then in a tree branch you see a mouth.
Eventually, you see the entire face.
Once you find the person,
that drawing is never the same again.
Life is like that drawing.
There's a person hidden in every part in it,
and that person is Jesus.
Once we find Jesus, life is never the same.

To what extent—and where—have I found
at least a part of Jesus in my own life?

If you want an increase in Jesus,
there must be a decrease in self.   Anonymous

JANUARY 5

Jesus found Philip and said to him,
"Come with me!" . . .
Philip found Nathanael and told him,
"We have found the one whom Moses
wrote about. . . . He is . . . from Nazareth."
"Can anything good come from Nazareth?"
Nathanael asked.   John 1:43, 45–46

Frederick Austerlitz was born in Omaha.
He went to Hollywood with stars in his eyes.
He landed a film test in 1933;
the director's evaluation of his talent read:
"Can't act! Slightly bald! Can dance a little."
A sophisticated pundit might have quipped:
"So what did you expect
from the cornfields of Nebraska!"
For years, the memo of Frederick's test
hung above the fireplace
in his Beverly Hills home.
He was now Fred Astaire, a Hollywood legend.
President Ronald Reagan
eulogized him as the "ultimate dancer . . .
who made things look so easy."

How do I respond to negative remarks about
my background, nationality, or religion?

You may not have been responsible
for your heritage,
but you are responsible
for your future.   Author unknown

CHRISTMAS SEASON _____

Some men who studied the stars
came from the East to Jerusalem and asked,
"Where is the baby born to be the king
of the Jews? We saw his star . . . and
we have come to worship him." Matthew 2:1–2

Apollo 11 splashed down in the Pacific
on July 20, 1969, after putting
the first human on the moon.
Later, the *Apollo 11* crew
of Armstrong, Collins, and Aldrin
went on a 23-nation tour.
Aldrin said of their visit to the Vatican:
"It turned out to be one of the most striking
and stirring moments of the trip when
His Holiness Pope Paul VI, a frail, worn man, . . .
unveiled three magnificent porcelain statues
of the Three Wise Men.
He said that these three men were directed
to the infant Christ by looking at the stars
and that we three also reached
our destination by looking at the stars."

How might the stars
help me reach my destination?

A French atheist told a farmer,
"We'll pull down every church steeple
to destroy your superstitions."
"Perhaps," said the farmer,
"but you can't help leaving us the stars."

SPECIAL NOTE _____

Starting January 7, the Lectionary readings
vary from year to year. To determine
which meditation to use today,

- find the current year,
- read across to the page indicated,
- turn to that page and begin.

This will put you in the correct sequence.
(For example, if the year is 1999, turn to
page 62, "Week after Epiphany: Thursday"
and begin.)

Year	Page
1997	60
1998	61
1999	62
2000	63
2001	166
2002	59
2003	60
2004	61
2005	63
2006	64
2007	166
2008	59
2009	61
2010	62

[Jesus went to the territory
of Zebulun and Naphtali,
fulfilling] what the prophet Isaiah had said,
". . . The people who live in darkness
will see a great light.
On those who live in the dark land of death
the light will shine."
From that time Jesus began to preach
his message:
"Turn away from your sins,
because the Kingdom of heaven
is near!" . . .
The news about him spread. . . .
Large crowds followed him.

Matthew 4:14, 16–17, 24–25

A jogger stood atop some rocks
on the Lake Michigan shoreline in Chicago.
The jogger's body silhouetted dramatically
against the dawning sky.
All of a sudden he cried out
across the water, "For God's sake, Jesus,
why don't you do something
about this crazy world?
What's holding you up?"

How would I answer the jogger?

The world is round,
and the place which seems like the end
may be the beginning.   Ivy Baker Priest

TUESDAY

_____ WEEK AFTER EPIPHANY

[A great crowd had been listening to Jesus
and was hungry. Jesus asked his disciples,]
"How much bread do you have?" . . .
They told him,
"Five loaves and also two fish.". . . .
Then Jesus took the five loaves and the two fish,
looked up to heaven, and gave thanks. . . .
Everyone ate and had enough.　　Mark 6:38, 41–42

Few world leaders ever captured
the imagination of the world
as did Mohandas Gandhi in the early 1900s.
He was the architect of India's independence.
His frail body, his simple white costume,
and his tiny round spectacles made him
the easily identified champion of the poor.
"In India," he once said,
"we have got three million people
having to be satisfied with one meal a day,
and that meal consisting of
unleavened bread (chapati)
containing no fat in it, and a pinch of salt.
You and I . . . must adjust our wants . . .
that they may be nursed, fed, and clothed."

How can one person, like myself,
make a difference in the face of such poverty?

Only by giving my five loaves and two fish
to Jesus can he perform anew the miracle
of feeding the hungry on the hillside.

*Jesus made his disciples get into the boat
and go ahead of him to Bethsaida. . . .
After saying good-bye to the people,
he went away to a hill to pray.*   Mark 6:45–46

One day President Harry Truman
found his wife, Bess, burning old letters
he'd written to her over the years.
"Bess," he said, "you shouldn't do that."
Bess replied, "I've read them several times."
"But think of history," said the president.
"I have," Bess replied. Fortunately,
a number of Truman's letters have survived
to help flesh out our picture of him.
Here is an excerpt from a letter
to Bess dated September 1947:
"I went to church this morning!
Had a hundred thousand words to read
for tomorrow's conference
with the congressional leaders
and reorganization commission—
so decided to let the words
go to hell and I'd go to church."

How important do I think it is
to take time off to pray
in the midst of a busy schedule?

"Boys, if you ever pray, pray for me now."
Harry Truman to reporters after his first full day
as president of the United States

THURSDAY

Jesus unrolled the scroll
and found the place where it is written,
"The Spirit of the Lord is upon me. . . .
He has sent me
to proclaim liberty to the captives and . . .
to set free the oppressed."   Luke 4:17–18

Martin Niemoller was hesitant
to oppose the Nazis.
When he finally decided to do so,
he was sent to a concentration camp.
Later, in a famous statement, he said:
"When Hitler attacked the Jews
I was not a Jew,
therefore, I was not concerned.
And when Hitler attacked the Catholics,
I was not a Catholic,
and therefore, I was not concerned.
And when Hitler attacked the unions
and the industrialists,
I was not a member of the unions
and I was not concerned.
Then, Hitler attacked me and
the Protestant church—and
there was nobody left to be concerned."
Congressional Record (Oct. 14, 1968)

How am I opposing evil wherever I find it?

Positive anything
is better than negative nothing.   Elbert Hubbard

Jesus would go away to lonely places,
where he prayed.   Luke 5:16

When winter comes to the South Pole,
total darkness sets in.
Richard Byrd braved four and a half months
of this darkness gathering weather data—
alone. Why alone? He answers,
"To taste peace, quiet, and solitude. . . .
It was all that simple. . . .
We are caught up in the winds
that blow every which way. . . .
The thinking man is driven to ponder
where he is being blown
and to long desperately for some quiet place
where he can reason undisturbed
and take inventory."   *Alone*
The experience changed Byrd dramatically.
He writes: "I live more simply now
and with more peace."
Jesus spent forty days alone in prayer
at the outset of his ministry.
And during it, he set aside times
when he could be alone to pray undisturbed.

What is one change that I have noticed
in my life since I began to pray regularly?

Half the confusion in the world
comes from not knowing
how little we need.   Richard Byrd

SATURDAY

*[John the Baptist compared his role
to that of a bridegroom's best man,
saying of Jesus,]*
*"He must become more important
while I become less important."*   John 3:30

In Jewish weddings, the best man
supervised the wedding invitations
and orchestrated the wedding celebration.
His final job was to keep vigil
at the bridal chamber until the groom arrived.
Once the groom arrived, his job was over
and he quietly withdrew from the limelight.
This is what John the Baptist did.
He took charge of the "wedding" of Israel
(the bride) to Jesus (the bridegroom).
Jesus also used this "wedding" imagery
to explain why his disciples did not fast.
He said, "As long as the bridegroom
is with them, they will not do that."   Mark 2:19

How gracefully do I step from the limelight
when this is the appropriate or proper
thing to do?

*God in heaven,
let me feel my nothingness,
not in order to despair over it,
but in order to feel the more powerfully
the greatness of your goodness.*
                              Soren Kierkegaard

SPECIAL NOTE _____

Turn to page 166 for the feast
of the Lord's Baptism. Ordinary Time
begins the day following the feast.

LENT

Ministry of Jesus

Jesus' preaching and his miracles
were the trumpets of a new era.
They were the "signs" of a new day.

Jesus healed the blind, but behind
this miracle was a deeper meaning.
It was a "sign" to all people
to open their eyes to his works.

Jesus opened the ears of the deaf.
It, too, was a "sign" to all people
to open their ears to his words.

Jesus forgave sinners. Again, his forgiveness
was a "sign" to all people to turn from sin
and begin living new lives.

Jesus set in motion the "Kingdom of God."
And what was this kingdom?
It was a new era in which
love would replace indifference,
light would replace darkness,
and life would replace death.

But the "Kingdom of Satan" would not yield
to the "Kingdom of God" without a battle.
It is this battle that we focus on during Lent.

Jesus said, "When you go without food,
wash your face and comb your hair,
so that others cannot know
that you are fasting—only your Father,
who is unseen, will know." Matthew 6:17–18

John Eagan writes in his spiritual journal
A Traveller toward the Dawn:
"I sign the Lord's cross
in ashes on the foreheads of hundreds.
'Remember, Dave, you are dust
and to dust you will return.' . . .
Each of you came from the dust of the earth
and move forward to return to that dust. . . .
How strongly it hits me. To dust—all. . . .
We come from the creative hand of God
and move . . . through time
on the way to God.
How fast the years go.
Like the arrow's passage through the air,
like the play on the stage, like the flowers
that push up and bloom and fade. . . .
But you, O God, are from forever to forever,
and we are made for you and for you alone."

What might I do during this holy season
to open my heart more fully to God's grace?

Fast from bitterness; feast on kindness.
Fast from impatience; feast on calmness.
Fast from laziness; feast on diligence.

THURSDAY
ASH WEDNESDAY WEEK _____ LENT

Jesus said, "Will you gain anything
if you win the whole world
but are yourself lost or defeated?" Luke 9:25

Newspaper reporters were interviewing
Eugene O'Neill before the Broadway opening
of his play *The Ice Man Cometh.*
O'Neill responded to one question
with a dramatic burst of emotion, saying:
"If the human race is so damned stupid
that in two thousand years
it hasn't had brains enough
to appreciate that the secret of happiness
is contained in one simple sentence
which you'd think any school kid
could understand and apply, then it's time
we dumped it down the nearest drain
and let the ants have a chance.
That simple sentence . . .
'What shall it profit a man
if he shall gain the whole world
and lose his own soul?' "
Editors, *Great Reading from Life*

How do I account for the inability of the
human race to appreciate Jesus' sentence?

What I have
will belong to another someday.
But what I am
will be mine for all eternity. Anonymous

[One day someone asked Jesus
why his disciples didn't fast.
He replied,] "Do you expect the guests
at a wedding party to be sad as long as
the bridegroom is with them? Of course not!
But the day will come when the bridegroom
will be taken away from them,
and then they will fast." Matthew 9:15

Ancient Jews fasted for several reasons.
For example, they fasted to prepare
for the coming of the Messiah
and God's Kingdom.
This explains Jesus' answer to the question
"Why don't your disciples fast?"
Jesus is saying, "The Messiah
and God's Kingdom have come."
To continue to fast now
would be like continuing to ring a doorbell
after the door has been opened.
But the day will come when Jesus
will be taken away from his disciples.
Then it will be time to fast once more.
This time it will be in preparation
for his second coming.

In what sense is Lent a preparation
for the second coming of Jesus?

All of us must appear before Christ,
to be judged by him. 2 Corinthians 5:10

SATURDAY
ASH WEDNESDAY WEEK _____ LENT

[Some Jewish leaders complained to Jesus
and his disciples, saying,] "Why do you eat
and drink with . . . outcasts?" Luke 5:30

A mother asked her child
what she had learned
in her religious education class that day.
The child replied, "I learned the Our Father:
'Our Father who art in heaven,
how did you know my name?'"
The child's humorous misstatement
touches on a profound mystery:
Our heavenly Father does indeed
know each one of us by name.
It touches on a greater mystery still.
Our heavenly Father not only knows
each one of us by name, but loves us
uniquely and desires our salvation.
It is for this reason that Jesus came
into the world, suffered, died, and rose.

Why do/don't I recognize myself
as someone who needs salvation?

My faith tells me that all of us are sinners,
and each of us has gone in our own way
and fallen short of the glory of God.
Religious faith has permitted me
to believe in my continuing possibility
of becoming a better person every day.
President Bill Clinton

The Spirit led Jesus into the desert
to be tempted by the Devil. After spending
forty days and nights without food,
Jesus was hungry. Then the Devil
came to him and said, "If you are God's Son,
order these stones to turn into bread."
But Jesus answered, "The scripture says . . .
'[You] cannot live on bread alone.' "   Matthew 4:1–4

Howard LaFay says that during Holy Week
in Andalusia (southern Spain), "everyone
appears in their finest, even the poorest
households produce a few bouquets."
He continues, "For most of my life
I shared the stern Anglo-Saxon disapproval
of decking statues with silk and jewels
while people struggled for daily bread.
But after [Holy Week] . . . in Andalusia,
I am no longer sure. For this short,
shining season, God's poor live amid
blossoms and brocade, gold and lace.
For an octave of days they lose themselves
in a vision of glory and redemption.
Against this, what is bread?"
National Geographic (June 1975)

How do I explain LaFay's final sentence?

I feel sorry for the person who has never
gone without a meal to buy a ticket
to a concert.   Albert Wiggam (slightly adapted)

"I tell you, whenever you did this
for one of the least important
of these followers of mine,
you did it for me!" Matthew 25:40

An old man was walking along a beach
after a big storm.
Fifty yards up ahead was a woman.
She was picking up starfish
that had been stranded on the beach
by the storm and throwing them back
into the sea.
When the old man caught up with her,
he asked what she was doing.
She explained that the starfish would die
if not returned to the sea before the sun
began beating down on them.
He replied,
"But the beach goes for miles,
and there are thousands of starfish.
How can your effort, no matter
how noble, make a difference?"
Picking up another starfish, she said,
"It makes a difference to this one!"
And with that, she returned it to the sea.

To what extent do I tend to do nothing
because I can do so very little?

The creation of a thousand forests
is in one acorn. Ralph Waldo Emerson

"Do not bring us to hard testing,
but keep us safe from the Evil One."

Matthew 6:13

It was a cold day, and a little girl
was walking to her grandmother's.
Hearing a rustle, she looked down
and saw a snake shivering in the grass.
"Put me under your warm coat," it said.
The girl hesitated and said,
"How do I know you won't bite me?"
The snake said, "Help me, please,
and I will be your friend forever."
So the girl reached down,
picked up the snake,
and placed it under her warm coat.
Immediately, the snake bit her.
"How could you do that? I trusted you,"
she said to the snake.
"Come, now," said the snake. "You knew
what I was when you picked me up."

How would I advise another to avoid
or to resist a recurring temptation?

Temptation is
the tempter looking through the keyhole
into the room where you are living;
sin is your drawing back the bolt and
making it possible for him to enter.

J. Wilbur Chapman

Jesus said, "This generation . . .
seeks a sign, but no sign will be given it,
except the sign of Jonah. Just as Jonah became
a sign to the Ninevites [confronting them
and calling them to a change of heart],
so will the Son of Man be to this generation."
Luke 11:29–30 (NAB)

The *Dallas Morning News* carried a story
about swimmer Jeff Kostoff.
His records and medals fill a whole page
of Stanford University's swimming guide.
But the guide says nothing
about his best friend, who did for Jeff
what Jonah did for the Ninevites
and Jesus did for the Israelites.
Jeff's friend confronted him about wasting
his talents and his time. Jeff says,
"He convinced me to stop screwing around
and concentrate on swimming."

Who is one person who has been a "sign"
for me—calling me "to a change of heart"
and pointing my life in a new direction?
Have I ever acknowledged this to the person—
or thanked the person for the critical role
he or she has played in my life?

Our chief want in life is somebody
who shall make us do what we can.
Ralph Waldo Emerson

Jesus said, "Would any of you . . . give
your son a stone when he asks for bread?. . .
You know how to give good things
to your children. How much more, then,
will your Father in heaven give good things
to those who ask him!"   Matthew 7:9, 11

Children have a simplicity and innocence
that no good person could ever harm.
Take the third grader who responded to the
question "What is a Grandmother?" this way:
"A grandmother is a lady
who has no children of her own. . . .
Grandmothers don't have to do anything
except to be there. . . .
Grandmothers don't have to be smart,
only answer questions like,
'Why isn't God married?' and
'How come dogs chase cats?'
Everybody should have a grandmother,
especially if they don't have television."
Quoted by Dr. James Dobson

How joyfully would I help such a child?
How much more joyfully
does the loving God want to help me?

Why is it that so many church members
say "Our Father" on Sunday and go around
the rest of the week acting like orphans?
                                        E. C. McKenzie

FRIDAY
WEEK 1 _____ LENT

Jesus said,
"If you are about to offer your gift to God . . .
and . . . you remember that your brother
has something against you . . .
make peace with your brother,
and then come back and offer your gift."

Matthew 5:23–24

Humorist Will Rogers made this passage
a keystone of his life. It wasn't surprising,
therefore, that he made it the focus
of his remarks in church one Sunday
when the minister invited him to say
a few words after the sermon. Rogers said:
"When I die, my epitaph or whatever
you call those signs on gravestones
is going to read, 'I joked about
every prominent man of my time,
but I never met a man I dident [sic] like.'
I am so proud of that I can hardly wait
to die so it can be carved.
And when you come to my grave you will
find me sitting there, proudly reading it."

Paula McSpadden Love, *The Will Rogers Book*

How closely do the acts
I perform on Monday
accord with the faith I profess on Sunday?

When we look for the best in others,
we find the best in ourselves.   Author unknown

Jesus said, "You must be perfect—
just as your Father in heaven is perfect."
Matthew 5:48

Most people would say that if they—
or those they depend on each day—
functioned perfectly
99 percent of the time,
they would be more than satisfied.
Not so! Chaos would reign.
Ninety-nine percent isn't good enough.
Jerry Fritz of the Management Institute
of the Madison School of Business
at the University of Wisconsin says:
"• Some 200,000 people would receive
the wrong drug prescription each year.
• Our drinking water would be unsafe
to drink three and a half days of the year.
• Our homes would be without
electricity seven hours a month.
• 22,000 checks would be deducted
from the wrong bank accounts each year.
• Twelve babies would be given
to the wrong parents each year."

What is one thing I ought to begin to do
right now to serve God more perfectly?

The little things?
The little moments? They aren't little.
Jon Kabah-Zinn

[Peter, James, and John were with Jesus
on a mountain.] As they looked on,
a change came over Jesus:
his face was shining like the sun. . . .
A shining cloud came over them,
and a voice from the cloud said,
"This is my own dear Son, with whom
I am pleased—listen to him!" Matthew 17:2, 5

The Book of Genesis says that when Moses
came down from Mount Sinai after talking
with God, "his face was shining." Exodus 34:30
Somewhat similarly, a ancient letter says
that when Saint Elizabeth of Hungary
came from prayer, people often saw
"her face shining marvelously
and light coming from her eyes
like rays from the sun."
It was this kind of "halo" phenomenon that
the disciples saw in Jesus on the mountain.

How well do I radiate the light of my faith
to those with whom I live and work?

With our own eyes we saw his greatness.
We were there when . . . the voice
came to him from the Supreme Glory,
saying, "This is my own dear Son,
with whom I am pleased!"
We ourselves heard this voice . . .
on the holy mountain. 2 Peter 1:16–18

Jesus said,
"The measure you use for others
is the one that God will use for you."

Luke 6:38

A delegation of German officers
came to Marshall Foch after World War I
to ask for the terms of the armistice.
The French general opened a folder
and began reading.
He had hardly gotten into the terms
when the German leader interrupted:
"There must be some mistake.
These are terms no civilized nation
would impose on another!"
"I am glad to hear you say that," said Foch.
"These are not our terms. They're the terms
imposed by the German commander
on the French city of Lille
when it was forced to surrender."

Reported by Sir Basil Thomson

How understanding, compassionate, and
merciful am I in my dealings with others?

"Do not mistreat foreigners. . . .
Treat them as you would an Israelite,
and love them as you love yourselves.
Remember that you were once foreigners
in the land of Egypt. I am the LORD
your God." Leviticus 19:33–34

80

*[Jesus said, "The scribes and the Pharisees
have succeeded Moses as teachers.]
So you must obey and follow everything
they tell you to do;
do not, however, imitate their actions,
because they don't practice what they preach."*

Matthew 23:3

A newspaper dating from 1862
carried this report about Abraham Lincoln.
When asked for his reaction to the election
of a Democratic governor, Lincoln said:
"Somewhat like that boy in Kentucky,
who stubbed his toe
while running to see his sweetheart.
The boy said he was too big to cry,
and far too badly hurt to laugh."

Frank Leslie's Illustrated Newspaper (Nov. 22, 1862)

We get a similar reaction when we read
how the scribes and the Pharisees
abused their leadership role in Jesus' time.
Unfortunately, such abuses
are still prevalent among leaders today.

What are my thoughts
when I reflect on the abuse of leadership
that is still widespread today?

*When the world seems at its worst,
Christians must be at their best.*

Author unknown

Jesus said, "The Son of man . . . [came]
to give his life to redeem many people."
Matthew 20:28

Little Jason was returning home
later and later each afternoon from school.
His father lectured him on punctuality,
but the talks made no impact on him.
Finally, he told Jason
that the next time he was late,
he could expect bread and water for supper.
Sure enough, the next night Jason was late.
When he sat down to supper, he was stunned.
On his plate was a single slice of bread.
Jason saw that his father meant business.
When the punishment had sunk in fully,
Jason's father gave him his own full plate
and took Jason's single slice of bread.
That was all Jason's father ate that night.
Years later, Jason said that
what his father did at supper that night
taught him in the most eloquent way
what Jesus did for the human race
2,000 years ago.

What did Jesus do for us 2,000 years ago?
What am I doing in return for Jesus today?

He endured
the suffering that should have been ours,
the pain that we should have borne. Isaiah 53:4

[Jesus told a parable
about a rich man who was in Hades
for ignoring the plight of a poor man.
"The poor man was named Lazarus, and he]
used to be brought to the rich man's door,
hoping to eat the bits of food that fell
from the rich man's table." Luke 16:20–21

This parable inspired a stirring homily by
Pope John Paul II at Yankee Stadium in 1979.
He said, "We cannot stand idly by,
enjoying our own riches and freedom,
if in any place the Lazarus of the 20th century
stands at our doors [hungry]. . . . The rich man
and Lazarus are both human beings,
both of them equally created
in the image and likeness of God,
both of them equally redeemed by Christ."

How does the parable of Lazarus
and the rich man act as a mirror to me?
How might I respond
to what I see in the mirror?

The poor
of the United States and of the world
are your brothers and sisters in Christ.
You must never be content
to leave them just the crumbs of the feast.
You must take of your substance, and not
just of your abundance. Yankee Stadium homily

*[Jesus told a story about an owner
who rented out his vineyard to tenants
for a share in the crops. When harvest came,
the tenants refused to give the owner
his share. The owner had no choice
but to oust them and turn his vineyard over
to other tenants.] The chief priests
and the Pharisees . . . knew that Jesus
was talking about them.* Matthew 21:45

Many of Jesus' stories
are called window parables:
they act as windows through which
we can look and glimpse vaguely
what the Kingdom of God is like. For example,
it is like buried treasure (Matthew 13:44)
or like a net cast into the sea (Matthew 13:47).
Other stories that Jesus told are called
mirror parables: they act as mirrors
into which we can look and see ourselves.
That is, Jesus composed them so that people
in his parables mirrored people
in his listening audience.

How are God, Israel, the chief priests
and Pharisees, and Jesus' apostles mirrored
in Jesus' vineyard parable? What is its point?
How might I apply this parable to my life?

*Those who would transform the world
must first transform themselves.* Anonymous

*Jesus said, "A man . . . had two sons.
The younger one [took his inheritance,
left home, spent it, and decided to return].
He was still a long way from home
when the father saw him;
his heart was filled with pity,
and he ran, threw his arms around his son,
and kissed him. . . .
[Meanwhile, the older son learned
of his brother's return and
of his father's preparations for a celebration.
He grew angry and stayed outside; he didn't
think his brother deserved a celebration.
His father came out and begged him
to come inside, saying,] 'We had to celebrate . . .
because your brother . . . was lost, but now
he has been found.' "* Luke 15:11–12, 20, 32

Jesus doesn't say if the older son changed
his mind and came in. This is because Jesus
composed his parable so that it mirrored
the attitude of "the Pharisees
and the teachers of the Law,"
who are angry that Jesus is forgiving sinners
and eating with them (Luke 15:2). Only they
can write the ending to Jesus' parable.

How might this parable apply to my life?

Who forgives most shall be most forgiven.
Josiah Bailey

[A woman came to a well. Jesus said
to her,] "Those who drink this water
will get thirsty again, but those
who drink the water that I will give them
will never be thirsty again. . . ."
"Sir," the woman said,
"give me that water!" John 4:13–15

British theologian Frank Sheed says in
Theology and Sanity that people everywhere
are crying out for hope, purpose, and
meaning in life. They have a spiritual thirst
that needs to be satisfied.
And what does the world do?
It says,
" 'Here is a telephone,' or 'Look, television,'
exactly as one tries to distract a baby
crying out for its mother by offering it candy."
Sheed concludes, "The leaping stream
of invention has served extraordinarily well
to keep us occupied,
to keep us from remembering
that which is troubling us." (slightly adapted)

To what extent do I find myself
trying to satisfy a spiritual thirst
in the depths of my soul
with material food and drink?

There's a hole in every human heart
that only God can fill. Anonymous

[One day Jesus was preaching
in the synagogue
in his hometown of Nazareth.
Sensing opposition to his words,
because he was a neighbor, he said,]
"Prophets are never welcomed
in their hometown." [There upon the people
became angry and violent.]   Luke 4:24

Often it is far harder to stand up
to friends and neighbors than to enemies.
Egypt's Anwar Sadat learned this in 1977.
He angered many of his Muslim friends
and neighbors by speaking out courageously
for peace with Israel. He alienated them
further by going to Israel for this purpose.
In 1978
Sadat paid the price for being a "prophet"
in his "hometown." He was assassinated
by Muslim extremists in a hail of gunfire
as he reviewed a Cairo parade.

What keeps me from standing up to friends
and neighbors when justice or truth
clearly calls for it?

Fight all error,
but do it with good humor,
patience, kindness, and love.
Harshness will damage your own soul
and spoil the best cause.   Saint John of Kanty

*Peter asked Jesus, "How many times
do I have to forgive . . . ? Seven times?" . . .
Jesus said, "Seventy times seven."*

Matthew 18:21–22

William Barclay, the Scottish theologian,
tells the story of Tokichi Ishii,
whose cruelty and brutality was legendary.
When Ishii was awaiting execution,
two religious people tried to talk to him.
He "glowered back at them," like an animal.
They were able to leave a Bible, however.
Later, Ishii began to read it. When he came
to the Crucifixion, he was stunned
by the words, "Father, forgive them,
for they know not what they do." He says,
"I was stabbed to the heart, as if pierced
by a five-inch nail. Shall I call it the love
of Christ? Shall I call it compassion?
I do not know. . . .
I only know that I believed
and the hardness of my heart was changed."
Daily Celebration

How ready am I to forgive "seventy times
seven" times? What do I do if I find it hard?

*We are like beasts when we kill.
We are like human beings
when we judge.
We are like God when we forgive.* Anonymous

WEDNESDAY
WEEK 3 _____ LENT

Jesus said, "Whoever disobeys even
the least important of the commandments
and teaches others to do the same,
will be least in the Kingdom of heaven.
On the other hand, whoever obeys the Law
and teaches others to do the same,
will be great in the Kingdom."   Matthew 5:19

A *Time* magazine article on ethics asked,
"What's wrong? Hypocrisy, betrayal,
and greed unsettle a nation's soul."
Commenting on the article,
Charles Colson raised this vexing question:
If 80 percent of Americans are Christian,
why is there a moral crisis in our nation?
He suggests "the same radical individualism
that is eroding other institutions
is eroding the church." Then he adds:
"Perhaps those who claim to be Christians
are arriving at faith on their own terms
that make no demands
on their moral behavior."
"A Bright Light in a Dark Age," *New Covenant* (Oct. 1988)

What is Colson's point?
How might it relate to Jesus' point
in today's gospel?

Moral education is impossible
apart from the habitual vision of greatness.
           Alfred North Whitehead

*Jesus said, "Anyone who is not for me
is really against me;
anyone who does not help me gather
is really scattering."*   Luke 11:23

British artist William Holman Hunt
created a popular painting in 1854.
It shows Jesus knocking at a door.
On his head is a crown of thorns,
and in his hand is a lantern.
The painting seems to have been inspired
by three Bible passages:
"I stand at the door and knock" (Revelation 3:20);
"Carry your cross, and follow me" (Mark 8:34);
"Whoever follows me will . . .
never walk in darkness" (John 8:12).
What made the painting especially popular
is that the door
at which Jesus stands and knocks
has no outside handle.
It can be opened only from the inside.

What theological point was Hunt making
by omitting the door's outside handle?
How does all this apply to me?

*"Listen! I stand at the door and knock;
if any hear my voice and open the door,
I will come into their house and
eat with them, and they will eat with me."*
Revelation 3:20

FRIDAY
Week 3 _____ Lent

Jesus said, "Love the Lord your God
with all your heart, with all your soul,
with all your mind,
and with all your strength."   Mark 12:30

Charles Colson, former White House aide
to President Nixon,
describes how one Friday morning
he was sitting all alone,
staring out at the ocean.
He was wrestling with a question:
Could he accept Jesus
without reservation as Lord of his life?
Suddenly he uttered from the depths
of his soul: "Lord Jesus, I believe You.
I accept You. Please come into my life.
I commit it to You."
He wrote later:
"With these few words that morning,
while the briny sea churned, came a
sureness of mind . . . strength and serenity,
a wonderful new assurance about life,
a fresh perception of myself and the world
around me. I was coming alive to things
I'd never seen before."   *Born Again*

To what extent have I wrestled with the same
question Colson did? If not, should I?

It is never the wrong time
to do the right thing.   Author unknown

[Jesus told a parable about two people
who went to the Temple.
One prayed in a prideful way;
the other, in a humble way.
Jesus ended his parable, saying,]
"Those who make themselves great
will be humbled, and those who humble
themselves will be made great."   Luke 18:14

There's an old poem that pokes fun at those
who make a big show of what they do.
The poet writes—with tongue in cheek:
"The catfish lays ten thousand eggs.
The lowly hen lays one.
The hen will proudly cackle,
To tell us what she's done.
We scorn the humble catfish,
While the lowly hen we prize;
Which only goes to show you—
It pays to advertise."   Anonymous

Thomas Merton describes prayer as
"an expression of who we are. . . . We are
a living incompleteness. We are a gap,
an emptiness that calls for fulfillment."
How does this fit in with Jesus' parable?
How might I apply it to my own prayer?

"Happy are those who know they are
spiritually poor; the Kingdom of heaven
belongs to them!"   Matthew 5:3

SUNDAY
WEEK 4 _____ LENT

Jesus said,
"While I am in the world,
I am the light for the world." John 9:5

Country music singer Hank Williams
wrote a song called "I Saw the Light."
It's about a person stumbling in the night,
refusing to let the Savior in.
Suddenly a stranger appears; it's Jesus!
The song turns from sadness to joy,
and goes something like this:
"Praise Jesus; I saw the light.
No more stumbling in the night!
No more groping in the dark.
Praise Jesus; I saw the light."
Every one of us
can relate to Hank Williams's song.
We have all foundered in the night,
refusing to let the Savior in.
Then Jesus appeared.
"Praise Jesus; we saw the light."

To what extent
am I still stumbling in the night,
refusing to let the Savior in?

From all that dwell below the skies
Let the Creator's praise arise:
Let the Redeemer's name be sung
Through every land, by every tongue.
Isaac Watts (1715)

Jesus went back to Cana in Galilee,
where he had turned the water into wine.

John 4:46

C. S. Lewis observes
that God created a spindly little green vine.
Then God taught the little vine
to draw water through its tiny roots
and, with the sun's help, turn the water
into juice that will ferment
and take on certain qualities.
Thus every year,
from Noah's time till ours,
God turns water into wine.
Lewis concludes by observing
that the miracle of Cana falls short
of what God intended
if its only effect is to dispose us
to affirm Jesus to be the Son of God.
It will achieve its full effect
only if "whenever we see a vineyard
or drink a glass of wine
we remember that here works he
who sat at the wedding party in Cana."

God in the Dock

What is Lewis's point in the final sentence?

God gives us memory
so that we can have roses in December.

James Matthew Barrie

TUESDAY
WEEK 4 _____ LENT

[Crowds of sick people
used to lie by a certain pool in Jerusalem
to await a "stirring of the waters."
When this happened, they rushed into
the pool, hoping to be healed by God.
One person had been sick for 38 years,
but could never reach the water in time.
One day] Jesus said to him,
"Get up, pick up your mat, and walk."
Immediately the man got well.   John 5:8–9

A man was watching a fly burn itself out
trying to fly through a windowpane.
Across the room
a door stood wide open to the outdoors.
The man wondered why
the fly didn't head for the open door.
Maybe the fly thought it could
break through the window on its own
by simply trying harder.
Suddenly the man realized that trying harder
isn't always the right strategy.

There comes a time in life when we realize
that we need the help of Jesus to do
what we need to do or would like to do.
When did I reach such a point in my life?

When we have traveled all ways,
we shall come to the End of all ways,
who says, "I am the way."   Saint Ambrose

Jesus said,
"I can do nothing on my own authority. . . .
I am not trying to do what I want,
but only what he who sent me wants."

John 5:30

A plaque in London contains these words:
"To the memory
of Charles Gordon
Who at all times and everywhere
gave
His Strength to the Weak
His Substance to the Poor
His Sympathy to the Suffering
His Heart to God."
Whether the plaque's author
was aware of it or not,
he was describing the heart of Jesus.
No finer tribute could be paid to a person.

Can I recall some recent occasion
when I went out of my way to help
someone weaker than myself,
someone poorer than myself,
someone suffering more than myself?

I have always held firmly to the thought
that each of us can do something
to bring to an end
some portion of the world's misery.

Albert Schweitzer

THURSDAY
WEEK 4 _____ LENT

Jesus said,
"If I testify on my own behalf, what I say
is not to be accepted as real proof. . . .
The deeds my Father gave me to do,
these speak on my behalf
and show that the Father has sent me."

John 5:31, 36

A very popular teacher named Aesop
lived 700 years before Jesus.
One reason for his great popularity
was that, like Jesus, he used stories
to get across important points.
For example, one of his stories concerns
a dispute between a lion and a man.
The man insists that humans are stronger.
To prove it, he takes the lion to a park
and shows him a statue of a human
ripping apart the jaws of a lion.
The lion looks at the statue and says,
"That statue proves nothing!
A human made it."

I am not a Christian just because
I say I am. How is this statement
an application of the point
that Jesus and the lion make?

How wonderful it would be if we spent
as much energy living our religion
as we do arguing about it. Anonymous

[Jesus stopped traveling in Judea]
because the Jewish authorities there
were wanting to kill him.   John 7:1

Motoring up the steep road above the dam
at Lake Junaluska in North Carolina,
Alice Weldon Perry saw a sign reading
"Dangerous Intersection Ahead."
Simultaneously
she saw a lighted cross atop the hill.
Suddenly it occurred to her that the words
"Dangerous Intersection" referred
not only to the road but also
to the two intersecting beams of the cross.
It was this "intersection" that started her
thinking about how "dangerous" it is
to follow Jesus.
Putting your hand in the hand of Jesus
and following wherever he leads you
is to put at risk your own personal dreams.
Yet, to take this risk
and enter this "dangerous intersection"
is to embark upon an adventure
that surpasses all dreams.

How willing am I to take the hand of Jesus
and enter the "dangerous intersection"?

Plunge into the deep without fear,
with the gladness of April in your heart.
                                        Rabindranath Tagore

SATURDAY
WEEK 4 _____ LENT

When the guards went back,
the chief priests and Pharisees asked them,
"Why did you not bring him?"
The guards answered, "Nobody has ever talked
the way this man does!" John 7:45–46

Someone composed "A Short Course
in Public Relations." It reads:
"The six most important words:
I admit that I was wrong.
The five most important words:
You did a great job!
The four most important words:
What do you think?
The three most important words:
Could you please . . . ?
The two most important words:
Thank you.
The least most important word: I."
Anonymous

"There are millions of words spinning
through the air. . . . Is there one word
strong enough to get through all the
other words and reach and change me? . . .
Is there one word like that?" Norman Habel

In the beginning the Word already existed;
the Word was with God. . . .
The Word became a human being. . . .
We saw his glory. John 1:1, 14

Jesus said,
"I am the resurrection and the life.
Those who believe in me will live." John 11:25

Robert McAfee Brown was on a troop ship
bringing marines back from Japan.
One day they were studying the raising
of Lazarus. After the session a marine said,
"God seemed to speak to me today."
He went on to explain that while in Japan,
he did something that filled him with guilt.
He'd even considered suicide.
During the session the thought struck him
that since Jesus was a man like him,
Jesus could understood his situation.
And since Jesus was also God,
he could help him
in the most powerful way imaginable.
Jesus could raise him to new life,
as he did Lazarus. In short, the marine
had discovered in a personal way
that Jesus was indeed "the resurrection
and the life"—not only in the life to come
but also in this life right now.

How do I want Jesus to be my resurrection
and my life, in this life right now?

The Easter message means
that God can turn . . . broken reeds
like Simon Peter into rocks. Fulton Sheen

[Jesus said
to the woman taken in adultery,]
"I do not condemn you. . . .
Go, but do not sin again."   John 8:11

Mehmet Ali Agca
was convicted of nearly assassinating
Pope John Paul II on May 13, 1981.
After the Holy Father
had fully recovered from his wounds,
he went to Rome's Rebbibia prison
where the Turk terrorist was being held.
There he spoke 20 minutes with him and
forgave him. When asked by reporters
what they talked about,
the Holy Father said,
"What we talked about
will have to remain a secret. . . .
I spoke to him as a brother
whom I have pardoned
and who has my complete trust."

It's often easier to forgive one person
than it is to forgive a group of persons. Why?

Forgiveness is the most necessary
and proper work of every man;
for, though, when I do not a just thing . . .
another man may do it for me,
yet no man can forgive my enemy
but myself.   Edward Herbert, Lord of Cherbury

Many who heard Jesus say these things
believed in him. John 8:30

Bob Beamon jumped 29 feet 2½ inches
in the 1968 Olympics in Mexico City,
breaking the world record by about two feet.
In 1984 he did a TV commercial
for the Summer Olympics in Los Angeles.
It showed Bob saying,
"Back in the Olympic Games of 1968
I set the world record in the long jump.
At the time, some people said
no one would ever jump that far again.
Well, over the years,
I've enjoyed watching them try,
and I told who might have a chance
of breaking my record. Well, there's
one thing I have to say about that . . ."
Viewers expected something boastful.
Instead, Bob's voice softened and he said
in a truly caring and sincere way,
"I hope you make it, kid." A viewer said,
"Bob won more goodwill by that commercial
than by his record jump."

How truly caring and sincere am I?

You can make more friends in two months
by becoming interested in other people
than you can in two years by trying to get
other people interested in you. Dale Carnegie

WEDNESDAY
WEEK 5 _____ LENT

Jesus said, "If you obey my teaching . . .
you will know the truth,
and the truth will set you free. . . .
I . . . tell you the truth I heard from God,
yet you are trying to kill me." John 8:31–32, 40

In the movie *How Green Was My Valley,*
a disillusioned pastor pours out his heart
to his congregation, saying,
"I thought when I was a young man
that I would conquer the world with truth.
Thought I would lead an army
greater than Alexander ever dreamed of,
not to conquer nations
but to liberate mankind—
but only a few of them heard.
Only a few of them understood."
Jesus poured out his heart
in a similar way near the end
of his ministry on earth.
For many Jews had closed
their eyes to his miracles and
their ears to his message.

How open are my eyes and ears
to Jesus' miracles and his message?
How faithfully do I try to follow Jesus?

Do not have Jesus Christ on your lips
and the world in your heart.
Saint Ignatius of Antioch (first century)

*Jesus said, "Whoever obeys my teaching
will never die."* John 8:51

Someone asked an old chief,
"Why are you always talking about Jesus?"
The chief didn't say anything.
Instead, he collected some dry grass
and twigs and arranged them in a circle.
Next he caught a caterpillar,
feeding on a nearby clump of weeds.
He placed it inside the circle.
Then he took a match and set fire
to the dry grass and the twigs.
As the fire blazed up, the caterpillar
began searching for a way to escape.
At this point the old chief
extended his finger to the caterpillar.
Instantly, it climbed onto it.
The chief said, "That's what Jesus did
for me. I was like the caterpillar—
confused, frightened, and without hope.
Then Jesus rescued me.
How can I not talk about my savior
and praise him for his love and mercy?"

How grateful am I
for what Jesus has done for me,
and how do I show it concretely?

*There is a sense in which no gift is ours
till we have thanked the giver.* E. C. McKenzie

[Jesus said to the people,]
"Even though you do not believe me,
you should at least believe my deeds."

John 10:38

Violinist Fritz Kreisler was in Germany
with an hour to spare before leaving
for a concert in London.
He walked into a nearby music store.
The store owner eyed him suspiciously—
and especially his violin case.
Then the owner disappeared
and returned with two policemen.
They arrested Kreisler, saying,
"You have Fritz Kreisler's violin."
"I am Fritz Kreisler," he said.
"You can't pull that on us!" said the police.
Kreisler thought a moment.
Then he requested permission to play.
Although the police didn't believe
his words, they could not doubt
his beautiful playing.

Jesus tried to lead his hearers
to a similar conclusion—but couldn't.
What lesson might the stories of Jesus
and Kreisler contain for me, personally?

People may doubt what you say,
but they will believe what you do.

Lewis Cass

*[The High Priest Caiaphas said
to a solemn assembly of religious leaders,]
"It is better for you to have one man die
for the people, instead of having
the whole nation destroyed."* John 11:50

Ernest Gordon recalls this true story
from a Japanese prison camp in Thailand.
One day when the shovels were counted
after work, the guard on duty went berserk.
He said one shovel was missing. Screaming
in broken English, he ordered the thief
to step up. When no one did, he cocked
his rifle and threatened to fire on the crowd.
At this point, an Australian came forward.
The Aussie stood silently as the guard
beat him. Finally, the guard struck him
a thunderous blow with his rifle on the head.
The Aussie dropped—clearly dead,
but the guard kept beating him savagely.
Then the work crew carried the shovels
and the dead Aussie back to the guard house.
There the shovels were counted again.
No shovel was missing after all.

What are my thoughts as I imagine myself
to be the Aussie, before stepping forward?

*"The greatest love
you can have for your friends
is to give your life for them."* John 15:13

SUNDAY
PALM SUNDAY _____ LENT

*Then Pilate . . . handed Jesus over
to be crucified.*   Matthew 27:26

The historian Eusebius says
the Roman emperor Constantine told him
this story. While preparing for battle,
a cross appeared in the sky
with these words, "In this sign conquer."
Constantine conquered and was converted.
Later he built a church over the site
where Jesus died and rose.
A sliver of wood
believed to be from Jesus' cross
was enshrined in the church
and is honored each September 14th.
A ninth-century writing says of the cross:
"This is the tree
on which the Lord, like a brave warrior
wounded in hands, feet, and side,
healed the wounds of all.
A tree once caused our death,
but now a tree brings life."
Saint Theodore the Studite

How lovingly and reverently do I regard
the cross, the symbol of Christianity?
How patiently do I carry my cross?

*Carry the cross patiently . . .
and in the end it shall carry you.*
                        Thomas à Kempis

*[A woman poured expensive perfume
on the feet of Jesus. Judas criticized her,
saying that it could have been sold
and the money given to the poor.]
But Jesus said, "Leave her alone! . . .
You will always have poor people with you,
but you will not always have me."*

John 12:7–8

The famous French novelist and dramatist
Tristan Bernard often had money problems.
Still he could never pass up a beggar.
One fellow took advantage of Bernard,
timing his visits outside Bernard's home
to the writer's scheduled coming and going.
Bernard never confronted him.
One day this beggar was stunned
to see Bernard pull from his wallet
a rather large bill.
Giving it to the beaming man,
Bernard said,
"We're going on vacation tomorrow.
Here's a two-month supply in advance.
You've a right to a vacation, too."

How do I feel about the common objection
that many beggars take advantage
of people's generosity?

*Kindness is loving people
more than they deserve.*   Joseph Joubert

TUESDAY
HOLY WEEK _____ LENT

[Jesus sat down at table.
Suddenly he grew deeply troubled,
saying,] "One of you
is going to betray me." John 13:21

An old poem reads:
"I watched them tear a building down;
A gang of men in a busy town.
With a mighty heave and lusty yell,
They swung a beam and a side wall fell.
I said to the foreman,
'Are these men as skilled
As the men you'd here if you had to build?'
He laughed and said, 'No indeed!
Just a common laborer is all I need.
And I can wreck in a day or two
What it took the builder a year to do.'
And I thought to myself as I went my way,
'Just which of these roles
have I tried to play?
Am I a builder who works with care
Measuring life by the rule and square,
Or am I a wrecker as I walk the town
Content with the labor of tearing down?'"
Author unknown

Which am I? Why?

Each must make— / Ere life has flown—
A stumbling block / Or a stepping stone.
R. L. Sharpe

*[While eating the Last Supper,
Jesus said to his disciples,]
"I tell you, one of you will betray me."*
Matthew 26:21

A young woman came to the end of Lent.
Listening to Jesus' words about Judas,
she thought about her lack of observance
that Lent. Somewhat repentantly, she wrote:
"Lord,
I hear Judas betrayed you with a kiss.
It hurts when friends turn against you.
Sorry I wasn't there to stick up for you.
Lord,
I hear your friends fled at your arrest.
That's when you needed them most.
Sorry I wasn't there to stand by you.
Lord,
I hear you fell carrying the cross.
It must have been heavy.
Sorry I wasn't there to give you a hand.
Lord,
if I had just had more time this Lent,
I could have shown you
how much I love you.
Sorry I was so busy—doing trifling things."

How do I feel about my Lenten observance?

*Life can be understood backward,
but it must be lived forward.* E. C. McKenzie

[After the feet washing, Jesus told Peter,]
"You do not understand now
what I am doing,
but you will understand later." John 13:7

"Up in a quaint old attic,
as the raindrops pattered down,
I sat paging through an old schoolbook—
dusty, tattered, and brown.
I came upon a page that was folded down.
Across it was written in childish hand:
'Teacher says to leave for now,
'tis hard to understand.'
I unfolded the page and read.
Then I nodded my head and said,
'Teacher was right—now I understand.'
There are lots of pages in the book of life
that are hard to understand.
All we can do is fold them down and write:
'Teacher says to leave for now,
'tis hard to understand.'
Then someday—maybe only in heaven—
we will unfold the pages again,
read them and say, 'Teacher was right—
now I understand.' "
Old poem by an unknown author, reconstructed from memory

What is one thing I find hard to understand?

Trust in the LORD with all your heart.
Proverbs 3:5

Pilate handed Jesus over to them
to be crucified. . . . After the soldiers
had crucified Jesus, they took his clothes
and divided them into four parts,
one part for each soldier. John 19:16, 23

A doctor in a town in Paraguay
was an outspoken critic
of the human rights abuses
of the government.
One day the local police apprehended
his teenage son and tortured him to death.
Rather than dress his son for the funeral,
the father displayed his naked, scarred body
on the blood-soaked mattress on which
he had been tortured to death.
It was a powerful, courageous statement.
It put injustice on grotesque display
and dramatized in a modern way
what happened on Good Friday.
The crucified body of the Son of God
was displayed on the cross
to dramatize the grotesque evil of sin.

What have I done for Jesus in the past?
What am I doing for Jesus in the present?
What should I do for Jesus in the future?

To repent is to alter one's way of looking
at life; it is to take God's point of view,
instead of my own. Anonymous

SATURDAY
HOLY WEEK _____ LENT

Jesus has been raised, just as he said.
Matthew 28:6

Jane was being received into the Church
at the Easter Vigil service, but she wasn't
sure her deceased father would approve.
At the service, each candidate was given a card
with the poem "I Carry a Cross in My Pocket."
When Jane saw it, she began to cry.
Later she said that just before he died,
her father took the same poem from his wallet
and gave it to her as a memento.
She said that when the priest gave it to her,
it was as if her father were reaching down
from heaven, touching her, and saying,
"Jane, I approve."

Why might beautiful things like this happen
to some people and not to others?

I carry a cross in my pocket. . . .
It is not for identification. . . .
It's simply an understanding
Between my Savior and me. . . .
It reminds me to be thankful
For my blessings day by day
And strive to serve him better
In all that I do and say. . . .
Reminding no one but me
That Jesus Christ is Lord of my life
If only I'll let him be. Author unknown

EASTER

Resurrection of Jesus

Three days after Jesus' crucifixion,
his distraught, defeated disciples were
amazingly and inexplicably transformed.
They set out ecstatically and courageously,
shouting to all the world,
"Jesus is risen! Jesus is risen!"

Had they been deluded or dishonest
about their claim,
certainly one or more of the eleven
would have confessed this
under the pressure of death. But none did!

Their witness never wavered.
Rather, they experienced an amazing power
that even enabled them to work miracles!
The lives and message of these men
changed the course of human history.

No reasonable explanation
has ever been given to account for
their transformed lives,
except their own:
they had seen Jesus alive.

Robert L. Cleath, *Hope in the Midst of Horror*

Early on Sunday morning . . .
Mary Magdalene went to the tomb
and saw that the stone
had been taken away from the entrance.
She went running to Simon Peter and [John]. . . .
[They ran to the tomb, saw that it was empty,]
and believed.   John 20:1–2, 8

Years ago a man was looking at a painting
of the Crucifixion in a shop window.
Suddenly a little boy appeared and said,
"That's Jesus on the cross, sir.
They nailed him there.
That lady there is his mother.
She's looking at what they did.
When Jesus died, sir, they buried him
over there by the edge of the picture."
The boy's faith
moved the man so much he couldn't speak.
He patted the boy's shoulder and walked on.
Suddenly the boy appeared again.
"I forgot to tell you, sir. It's okay! It's okay!
Because Jesus rose!"

How can I make Jesus' death and rising
as alive for me as it was for the boy?

Universe / and every universe beyond,
spin and blaze, / whirl and dance,
leap and laugh / as never before. . . .
Christ has smashed death.   Norman Habel

MONDAY
WEEK 1 _____ EASTER

[When the women learned Jesus had risen, they] ran to tell his disciples.   Matthew 28:8

In his story *St. Francis,* Nikos Kazantzakis
has the mystic say to a novice:
"Each year at Easter, I used to watch
Christ's Resurrection. All the faithful
would gather around His tomb and weep,
weep inconsolably, beating on the ground
to make it open. And behold!
In the midst of the lamentations
the tombstone crumbled . . . and Christ
sprang from the earth and ascended
to heaven, smiling at us and
waving a white banner.
There was only one year I did not see Him
resurrected. That year a theologian
of consequence . . . mounted the pulpit . . .
and began to elucidate on the Resurrection
for hours on end. He explained and explained
until our heads began to swim;
and that year the tombstone did not crumble,
and, I swear to you,
no one saw the Resurrection."

How do I interpret Saint Francis's words?
What message might they hold for me?

*The Gospels do not explain Easter;
Easter explains the Gospels.*
         J. S. Whale (slightly adapted)

[Jesus said to Mary Magdalene,
"Go to my disciples]
and tell them that I am returning to . . .
my God and their God."
So Mary Magdalene . . .
related to them what he had told her.

John 20:17–18

Caryll Houselander writes:
"I was in an underground train,
a crowded train in which
all sorts of people jostled together . . .
going home at the end of the day.
Quite suddenly I saw in my mind,
but as vividly as a wonderful picture,
Christ in them all . . . living in them . . .
rejoicing in them, sorrowing in them. . . .
I came out into the street
and walked a long time in the crowds.
It was the same thing here,
on every side, in every passerby—Christ."
A Rocking-horse Catholic

How do I experience the risen Jesus
present in our world—
filling it and everyone
with his truth and his power?

Jesus' power working in us is able to do
so much more than we can ever ask for,
or even think of. Ephesians 3:20

[When the two disciples reached Emmaus,
they said to Jesus, whom they still
did not recognize,] "Stay with us. . . ."
So he went in to stay with them. . . .
[And] they recognized the Lord
when he broke the bread.   Luke 24:29, 35

After meditating on the Emmaus event,
someone wrote:
"Lord Jesus, look with love on those of us
who have left you behind
in some distant, unmarked tomb.
Seek us out as you did the two disciples
on the road to Emmaus.
Walk along beside us and explain
the Scriptures to us, as you did to them.
Fan to flame the dying embers of our faith
and make our hearts burn again
within us. Come into our house
and sit at table with us.
Take into your hands our humble bread.
Bless it and fill it with your risen presence.
Then break it and release the blindness
of our eyes that we may recognize you
in all your Easter glory."

What is significant about the fact
that the disciples recognized the risen Jesus
in the breaking of the bread?

"Do this in memory of me."   Luke 22:19

Jesus said to them, "This is what is written:
the Messiah must suffer and must rise
from death three days later." Luke 24:46

One August afternoon, in a preseason game,
Darryl Stingley of the New England Patriots
was viciously hit by safety Jack Tatum
of the Oakland Raiders.
He was left paralyzed from the chest down.
Today Darryl can use only one hand
and is confined to a wheelchair.
But he insists that in some ways
his life is better now than before.
"I had tunnel vision in my playing days,"
he said. "All I wanted was to be
the best athlete I could,
and a lot of things were overlooked.
Now I've come back to them.
This is a rebirth for me.
Not only physically but spiritually. . . .
I really have a lot more meaning and purpose
to live for now than ever before."

What is the nearest thing to Stingley's
death-rising experience I've had in my life?

To be controlled by human nature
results in death; to be controlled
by the Spirit results in life and peace. . . .
If we share Christ's suffering,
we will also share his glory. Romans 8:6, 17

FRIDAY
WEEK 1 _____ EASTER

[The disciples fished all night and
caught nothing. As they neared shore,
Jesus saw them and said, "Recast your net."
They did] and could not pull it back in,
because they had caught so many fish.

John 21:6

The career of novelist A. J. Cronin
almost ended before it began.
Halfway into his first book, *Hatter's Castle*
(now translated into 19 languages),
he became discouraged and tossed it
into the wastebasket.
Then he went outside into the rain
and walked down a lonely rural road.
He came upon an old farmer working alone
in the rain, ditching a huge field.
The sight of the farmer—not discourage
by the size of the field or the rain—
inspired him to go back and try again.
Years later he credited his brilliant career
to the farmer's silent inspiration.

One could say that Jesus spoke to Cronin
through that farmer, saying,
"Recast your net and try again."
Can I recall Jesus ever speaking to me
through the silent witness of someone?

Lighthouses blow no horns; they only shine.

Dwight L. Moody

[Jesus told his disciples,]
"Go throughout the whole world and
preach the gospel to all people."   Mark 16:15

Leopold Pfefferberg,
a Polish Jew who survived the Holocaust,
promised Oskar Schindler, a Catholic,
that he'd tell the world how Schindler risked
his life over and over during World War II
to save hundreds of Jews.
Leopold moved to the United States,
opened a luggage shop in California,
and told Oskar's story
to every "movie type" he met.
Finally, in 1980, Thomas Keneally heard
the story while waiting for his credit card
to clear in the luggage shop. Two years later,
Keneally's book, *Schindler's List,*
made publishing history.

It took 45 years to find the "right person"
who would tell Schindler's story
to the world overnight.
In a similar way, Jesus commands us
to persevere in preaching the Gospel,
with a view to finding the "right person"
who will tell it to the world overnight.
How am I carrying out Jesus' command?

It takes twenty years
to make an overnight success.   Eddie Cantor

These [books] have been written
in order that you may believe
that Jesus is the Messiah, the Son of God,
and that through your faith in him
you may have life. John 20:31

Captain Gilbert Greene, an early friend
of Abraham Lincoln, has preserved for us
several stories that illustrate
Lincoln's great love for the Bible. He says:
"There was a copy of the New Testament
with a flexible cover which lay on his table.
It was worn almost through
with the rail-splitter's fingers.
He once recited to me Christ's Sermon
on the Mount without making a mistake.
He said to me more than once
that he considered Paul's sermon
on Mars Hill [Acts 17:22–34] the ablest
and most eloquent literary production
ever spoken by mortal lips,
or recorded by human pen."
Frederick Iglehart, *The Speaking Oak*

Have I ever experimented with reading
the Bible passages in this book? For example,
have I tried reading them out loud,
or pausing after reading to savor them?

Lay hold of the Bible until the Bible
lays hold of you. William H. Houghton

[Jesus said to Nicodemus,]
"No one can enter the Kingdom of God
without being born of water and the Spirit.
A person is born physically
of human parents,
but is born spiritually
of the Spirit." John 3:5–6

There's a moving scene in *The Green Years*
where Charles Coburn toasts his
great-grandson on his "spiritual" birthday
into manhood. Coburn says:
"I'm an old man. My life is almost over.
Here, with the sunset in my face,
it thrills me to see these young people
marching on. Let us drink to youth. . . .
To Robert, who will this day,
unstained by the evils of the world,
look to the future. Today I stood
at Robert's side as he embraced the faith.
Almighty, I stand by his side
as he enters manhood."

How supportive and affirming am I
of the young people around me
as they set out on their spiritual journey?

Baptism signifies that the old Adam in us
is to be drowned . . .
and that the new person
should daily come forth. Martin Luther

As Moses lifted up
the bronze snake on a pole in the desert,
in the same way
the Son of Man must be lifted up,
so that everyone who believes in him
may have eternal life.   John 3:14–15

On March 6, 1987, Andrew Parker
was aboard the British ferry that capsized
off the Belgium coast, killing 134 people.
After the ferry keeled over,
Parker stretched his six-foot-three body
across a deep water-filled gap between
two sections of the ferry.
His wife, daughter, and 18 passengers—
unable to leap across the gap—
used Andrew's body as a human bridge
to reach safety. Prime Minister Thatcher
called Parker's deed the most unselfish act
of bravery during the disaster.
Someone compared the image of Parker
making himself a "bridge" between
the two sections of the boat to save people
to Jesus making himself a "bridge" between
heaven and earth to save the human race.

What keeps me from a deeper faith in Jesus?

In nothing do we more nearly approach
the gods than in doing good to other people.
                                      Cicero

God loved the world so much
that he gave his only Son,
so that everyone who believes in him
may not die but have eternal life.

John 3:16

A unknown poet was groping for words
to express the feelings of the heart—
that death is not an end,
but a spectacular birth into eternal life.
The poet wrote:
"Do not stand at my grave and weep
I am not there, I do not sleep
I am a thousand winds that blow
I am a diamond glint of snow
I am the sunlight on ripened grain
I am the autumn rain
When you awake in the morning hush
I am the swift uplifting rush
of birds circling in flight
I am the stars that shine at night
So do not stand at my grave and cry
I am not there. I didn't die."

How do I feel about
the poet's choice of images
to express the poet's belief
in eternal life?

Christ changed the dark door of death
into a shining gate of life. Anonymous

THURSDAY
WEEK 2 _____ EASTER

*Jesus said, "Whoever believes in the Son
has eternal life."*   John 3:36

Britain's Captain Robert Scott and
four companions reached the South Pole
on January 18, 1912, only to learn
that Norwegian Roald Admunsen had arrived
34 days earlier to gain the title
"Discoverer of the South Pole."
Tragedy struck on their way home.
All five froze to death.
In the final moments of life, Edward Wilson,
the team physician, wrote this to his wife:
"All the things I had hoped
to do with you after this Expedition
are as nothing now, but there are greater
things for us to do in the world to come.
I feel so happy now in having got the time
to write to you. . . . Your little testament
and prayerbook will be in my hand
or in my vest pocket when the end comes."

How deep is my faith in Jesus
and his promise of eternal life
to those who believe in him?

*If I find in myself a desire that
no experience in this world can satisfy,
the most probable explanation is
that I was made for another world.*
                                          C. S. Lewis

*[One day Jesus was watching his disciples
return empty-handed from fishing. He said,]
"Throw your net out on the right side
of the boat." [They did and caught so many fish
they] could not pull it back in.*   John 21:6

Liz bought a potted gardenia.
She took good care of it, but it didn't bloom.
Disappointed, she set it on the back porch.
In the days ahead, everything went wrong:
her child got sick, a debt came due,
she had a misunderstanding with a friend.
One morning Liz became very depressed.
She decided to go to the laundry;
at least she could wash clothes.
As she stepped onto the back porch,
she noticed a lovely fragrance.
Turning, she saw the gardenia had bloomed.
Now Liz realized why it hadn't bloom before.
It was missing something important—
"the sun." Later at the laundry, it hit Liz.
What was true of the gardenia
was true of her life, also;
it was missing something—"the Son."

The woman's "gardenia" experience
and the disciples' "fishing" experience
invite me to ask: If something seems to be
missing from my life, could it be "the Son"?

"You can do nothing without me."   John 15:5

SATURDAY
WEEK 2 _____ EASTER

[The disciples were crossing the lake
when a storm blew up.
They] had rowed about three or four miles
when they saw Jesus walking on the water,
coming near the boat,
and they were terrified.
"Don't be afraid," Jesus told them,
"it is I!" John 6:19-20

A duck hunter bought a retriever.
He was amazed when he saw the dog
retrieve a duck by simply
running across the water of the lake.
Thirty minutes later,
his hunting partner joined him—
just as another duck flew over the lake.
The hunter fired, the duck fell,
the dog ran across the water and retrieved it.
This happened several more times,
but the hunting partner made no comment.
Finally, the hunter said to his partner,
"Did you notice anything about that dog?"
"I certainly did," said his partner.
"He can't swim."

When it comes to the amazing things
that Jesus did, how are many people
like the hunter's partner in the story?

We see things not as they are,
but as we are. H. M. Tomlinson

*[Two broken disciples were returning
to Emmaus, unaware that Jesus had risen.
Suddenly he came alongside them,
but they didn't recognize him.
After listening to their sad story,
Jesus said,] "How foolish you are,
how slow you are to believe everything
the prophets said! Was is not necessary
for the Messiah to suffer these things
and then to enter his glory?"* Luke 24:25–26

Noreen Towers had worked hard among
the poor, but with no evident results.
One night she went to bed, planning to quit.
The next morning, shortly after she awoke,
something happened.
It was as if Jesus himself said to her,
"Can you not trust my plan for you?"
She writes: "Then I realized
that I did not have to see the plan;
I only had to trust him. I arose from my bed
a different person." Noreen had gone to bed
"a broken, defeated person" and arose
"a person with unshakable hope and faith."
International Christian Digest

When was I closest to being "a broken,
defeated person"? What kept me going?

*How else but through a broken heart
May the Lord Christ enter in?* Oscar Wilde

MONDAY
WEEK 3 _____ EASTER

Jesus said, "Do not work for food that spoils;
instead, word for the food
that lasts for eternal life."   John 6:27

Some senior citizens
were sharing school memories
that were still fresh in their minds
after 60 years.
One such memory was an example
their teacher had used to give them an idea
of how long "eternity" or "eternal life" was.
She said,
"Imagine a metal ball a mile in diameter.
Every hundred years an eagle flies past it,
brushing it ever so slightly with its wing.
After a million years,
the friction of the eagle's wing produces
a microscopic scuff on the ball's surface.
When the metal ball disappears as a result
of these scuffs, 'eternity' is just starting."
It is this mind-boggling eternity of joy
that God has prepared for us.

Why am I so foolish, at times,
to risk an eternal life of joy in heaven
for a fleeting hour of pleasure on earth?

"What no one ever saw or heard,
what no one ever thought could happen,
is the very thing God prepared
for those who love him."   1 Corinthians 2:9

"I am the bread of life," Jesus told them.
"Those who come to me
will never be hungry." John 6:35

Father David Shilder celebrates daily Mass
in prison. He says, "And I mean celebrate!
If people on the other side of the fence
sang and responded to prayers as well
as inmates do, the roof would blow off and
the walls would burst in the parish church."
A favorite story Father likes to tell
concerns a prisoner who told him,
"When you are not here, Father,
I sit on my bunk, repeat to myself
the words of Consecration, eat a cracker,
and take a sip of water. . . .
You don't know how much it means to me
to have God in my life after all these years
of not knowing God's love."
Father readily admits that not all inmates
take Mass that seriously. "But," he adds,
"how many people in the average parish
outside take Mass that seriously?"
The Catholic Digest (Aug. 1993)

How seriously do I take Mass? What might
I do to make it more meaningful?

If God were to appear to starving people,
he would not dare appear in any other form
than food. Mohandas Gandhi

WEDNESDAY
WEEK 3 _____ EASTER

Jesus said, "Those who believe in me
will never be thirsty. . . .
Everyone whom my Father gives me
will come to me. . . .
And I will raise them
to life on the last day." John 6:35, 37, 40

Thomas Merton accepted Jesus at 23,
became a *New York Times* reporter at 24,
and decided to become a priest at 26.
His decision came at Saint Xavier Church
in New York as he knelt before
the Blessed Sacrament. He writes:
"I fixed my eyes on . . . the white Host.
And then it suddenly became clear to me
that my whole life was at a crisis. . . .
'Do you really want me to be a priest?
If you do, say so. . . .'
The hymn was ending. . . .
I looked straight at the Host, and I knew now,
Who it was that I was looking at,
and I said, 'Yes, I want to be a priest,
with all my heart.'" *The Seven Storey Mountain*

What was one of the most important decisions
I ever made concerning how
I felt I was being called to follow Jesus?

"What my Father wants is that all
who see the Son and believe in him
should have eternal life." John 6:40

[When Jesus said he was the bread
from heaven, people started grumbling,
because they knew his father and mother.
Jesus said,] "The bread that I will give you
is my flesh, which I give
so that the world may live." John 6:51

Elizabeth Ann Seton
was the first native-born American saint.
Her husband died,
leaving her with five children.
Later she visited Italy and
was deeply moved by the profound faith
of the people concerning the Mass. She wrote:
"How happy we would be if we believed
what these dear souls believe,
that they possess God in the Sacrament and
that He remains in their churches and
is carried to them when they are sick. . . .
The other day . . . I fell on my knees
without thinking when the Blessed Sacrament
passed by [being carried to the sick]. I cried . . .
to God to bless me if He was there."
Shortly afterward, she was blessed with faith.

What do I believe Jesus meant when he said,
"The bread that I will give you is my flesh"?

The effect of our sharing in the body and
blood of Christ is to change us
into what we receive. Saint Leo the Great

[Jesus said to the people,] "The bread that
I will give you is my flesh. . . ." This started
an angry argument. . . . "How can this man
give us his flesh to eat?" . . . Jesus said . . .
"Those who eat my flesh and drink my blood
have eternal life." John 6:51–54

Charles de Foucald was born into wealth
in France in 1858. During his youth
he lived only for himself and pleasure.
He wrote: "I was so completely selfish . . .
so completely irreligious,
and utterly given over to wickedness,
that I was only a step away from insanity."
In this state of mind, he began entering
the Church of Saint Augustine in Paris.
There he would repeat over and over,
"My God, if you exist,
let me come to know you."
One day at the elevation of the sacred Host
at Mass, the gift of faith entered his heart.
"In a single moment," he said, "my heart
was touched and I believed." The result?
Charles was utterly and totally transformed.

Why do/don't I believe that Jesus is present
in the Blessed Sacrament as food and drink?

O Jesus present in the Blessed Sacrament
in our churches . . . help us to seek You
and find You. Charles de Foucald

[Jesus told the people,] "I am the living bread
that came down from heaven. If you eat
this bread, you will live forever." . . .
Many of his followers heard this and said,
"This teaching is too hard." . . .
[They] would not go with him any more.

John 6:51, 60, 66

Blaise Pascal, a mathematical genius,
lived in 17th-century France. By the age of 18
he had built several computing machines,
pioneers of our computers.
Pascal was not only highly intelligent
but also deeply religious.
Concerning faith doubts, he once said:
"If you want to strengthen your faith,
do not augment your arguments
but prune your passions." In other words,
the more faithfully we live the Gospel,
the more deeply it can take root in us.

Faith is also like the sun. Sometimes
it shines so brightly I could never question it.
At other times it goes behind a cloud
and vanishes completely. In the words
of today's gospel, it becomes unreasonable and
"too hard." What do I do when this happens?

Two harmful excesses are to be avoided:
excluding reason, and
admitting nothing but reason.　Blaise Pascal

Jesus said,
"I am the gate for the sheep. . . .
I have come in order that
you might have life—
life in all its fullness."   John 10:7, 10

In his book *The Holy Land,* John Kelman
tells a story that puts flesh and blood on
Jesus' words, "I am the gate for the sheep."
He writes:
"A shepherd near Hebron, when asked
why the sheep pen there had no gate,
answered quite simply, 'I am the gate.'
He meant that at night
when the sheep gathered within the
circular stone wall of the enclosure,
he lay down in its open entrance to sleep,
so that no sheep might stray
from its shelter without wakening him,
and no ravenous beast might enter
but across his body."

How does the Hebron shepherd's response
help me better appreciate Jesus' love for me?

Every time I read the things that Jesus said . . .
I am more and more convinced
of the necessity of following him. . . .
In him we are able to see God and
to understand God's feelings toward us.
                          Charles Schulz, creator of *Peanuts*

Jesus said,
"There are other sheep which belong to me
that are not in this sheep pen.
I must bring them, too; they will listen
to my voice, and they will become one flock
with one shepherd." John 10:16

"I have walked by the [O'Hare Airport] chapel
on numerous occasions and there will be
a Muslim on the prayer rug in front, praying,
a Catholic on a kneeler, praying, and a Jew
on the side in prayer, all exactly
at the same time and in the same place.
It's beautiful that we can all be here together
praying to God in different languages,
and with different prayers,
and in different postures, but all with the
same basic kind of faith, love, and respect."
John Jamnicky, *Christian Science Monitor* (Dec. 2, 1992)

What would I say to Jesus
about the state of religion
and the need for its values in our age?

The great paradox of our age is this:
In the interest of tolerance, we are aggressively
seeking to scrub religious values, and even
reminders of our religious heritage out of our
public life. Yet it is that religious heritage that
is essential for the recovery of our character.
Charles Colson, Special Counsel to President Nixon

TUESDAY
WEEK 4 _____ EASTER

"My sheep listen to my voice;
I know them, and they follow me.
I give them eternal life,
and they shall never die."   John 10:27–28

In ancient England, dinner guests
used to entertain other guests after meals.
At one dinner an actor was present
and did a fabulous rendition of Psalm 23,
"The Lord is my shepherd."
Everyone stood and applauded.
Then a guest noticed the old aunt of the host
dozing in the back of the room.
She was deaf and had missed
almost all of the entertainment.
The guest shouted,
"Auntie, come up and do something."
Everyone applauded.
Then she recited the same psalm.
When she finished, there wasn't a dry eye
in the room. Later, the guest asked the actor,
"Your rendition was fabulous.
So why were we so moved by the aunt?"
He replied, "Simple—I know the psalm,
but old auntie knows the shepherd."

How well do I know the shepherd?

In prayer it is better to have a heart
without words than words
without a heart.   John Bunyan

Jesus said in a loud voice,
"Whoever believes in me believes
not only in me but also in him who sent me.
Whoever sees me sees also him who sent me.
I have come into the world as light,
so that everyone who believes in me
should not remain in the darkness."

John 12:44–46

"Our deepest fear
is not that we are inadequate.
Our deepest fear
is that we are powerful beyond measure.
It is our light, not our darkness,
that most frightens us. . . .
We were born to make manifest
the glory of God that is within us.
It's not just in some of us; it is in everyone.
And when we let our own light shine,
we subconsciously give other people
permission to do the same.
As we are liberated from our own fear,
our presence automatically liberates others."

Marianne Williamson, *A Return to Love*

Why should my deepest fear be my light,
not my darkness?

There is no saint without a past—
and no sinner without a future.

Anonymous

Jesus said,
"Whoever receives anyone I send
receives me also;
and whoever receives me
receives him who sent me."   John 13:20

Ensworth Reisner remembers a minister
who had very little money.
He was just scraping by.
One day a destitute family came to him.
The minister was moved to pity
and gave them
all the money he had on hand.
Then, as they left, he said,
"Thank you for the privilege
of letting me help you."
Reisner says, "Those remarkable words
taught me an important lesson.
When people give you the opportunity
to help them, they give you the opportunity
to be like God.
And for that we should give them thanks."

What keeps me from having the same attitude
that Ensworth Reisner has?

God has given us two hands—
one to receive with
and the other to give with.
We are not made cisterns for hoarding;
we are channels made for sharing.   Billy Graham

"Do not be worried and upset,"
Jesus told them. . . . "There are many rooms
in my Father's house, and I am going
to prepare a place for you." John 14:1–2

A dying woman who lived
15 miles out in the country sent for Lincoln
to draw up her will.
When she had signed it, she asked him
to read a few passages from the Bible.
Joshua Speed, who was with Lincoln,
said he began by reciting from memory
Psalm 23 ("The Lord is my shepherd").
Then he recited John 14, where Jesus says,
"I go to prepare a place for you." He closed
by reciting "Rock of Ages, Cleft for Me."
Minutes later, the woman died peacefully.
Speed said, "As we rode home in the buggy,
I expressed surprise
that he should have acted as pastor
as well as attorney so perfectly,
and he replied: 'God and eternity
were very near to me today.'"

Emanuel Hertz, ed., *Lincoln Talks: A Biography in Anecdote*

What moves me most about this story?

A Christian should aspire
to do the will of God:
nothing more, nothing less, nothing else.

Author unknown

*Philip said to Jesus, "Lord, show us
the Father. . . ." Jesus answered,
"For a long time I have been with you all;
yet you do not know me."* John 14:8–9

A pastor began his sermon by holding up
a large piece of white cardboard.
Then he drew a large dot on it
and asked, "What do you see?"
"A dot," the congregation chorused back.
"What else do you see?" the pastor asked.
A long pause followed.
Then the congregation chorused,
"Nothing else!"
The pastor replied, "You're overlooking
the most important thing of all!"
Again there was a long silence.
Suddenly, in the midst of it, a little girl
called out, "We're overlooking the piece
of white cardboard." "Right," said the pastor.

How does the pastor's brief exercise
illustrate the point that Jesus makes
with Philip in today's gospel?
In other words, why did Philip fail to see
the face of God in Jesus?

*Jesus prayed, "Father, Lord of heaven
and earth! . . . You have shown
to the unlearned what you have hidden
from the wise and learned."* Luke 10:21

*[Jesus said to his disciples,] "I am going
to prepare a place for you."* John 14:2

Grubs worms at the bottom of a pond
couldn't understand why those
who climbed up the stems of the water lilies
never returned to tell them what they found.
They agreed that the next one to climb up
should return to tell them what it found.
One day the leader of the grubs decided
to climb up the stem.
When he reached the top, he was astounded.
Everything was fantastically beautiful.
Even more astounding
is what then happened to him.
He changed into a gorgeous dragonfly.
As he circled the pond,
peering down at his friends under the water,
he couldn't figure out how to return to them.
Then he realized that even if he did get back,
his friends would never recognize him.

How is this story like one of Jesus' parables?
What might it be saying to me, personally?

*From the voiceless lips
of the unreplying dead there comes no word.
But in the night of Death,
Hope sees a star, and listening Love
can hear the rustle of a wing.*

Robert Green Ingersoll

*Jesus said, "My Father will love those
who love me; I too will love them
and reveal myself to them."* John 14:21

Walter Pidgeon plays a minister
in the movie *How Green Was My Valley*.
In one scene he tells his flock that love—
not fear—should motivate their presence
at Sunday worship.
He challenges them, saying:
"Why do you come here? . . .
I know why you've come. I've seen it
in your faces Sunday after Sunday.
Fear has brought you here. . . .
Fear of divine . . . fire from the skies.
The vengeance of the Lord. . . .
But you have forgotten
the love of Jesus. . . .
Death, fear, flames, horror. . . .
Hold your meeting then, but know that,
if you do this in the name of God
and in the house of God,
you blaspheme against Him and His word."

How aware am I of the incredible truth
that Jesus loves me more than I love myself?
What can I do to deepen my awareness?

*Those who worship merely from fear
would worship the devil too, if he appear.*
Proverb

[Referring to his death,
Jesus said to his disciples,]
"Peace is what I leave with you;
it is my own peace that I give you." John 14:27

The day after comedian Jack Benny died,
the local florist delivered to his widow,
Mary, a single long-stemmed red rose.
It contained no card or identification.
When another rose arrived the next day,
Mary called the florist.
She was informed that Jack had said
that if anything ever happened to him,
the florist was to send a long-stemmed red rose
to her every day for the rest of her life.
Later, Mary learned that Jack
had even arranged for it in his will.
This same kind of tender love led Jesus
to leave us a similar gift: his "own peace."
Every day at every Mass,
right after the recitation of the Lord's Prayer,
the presider reminds us of the precious gift.
He says in Jesus' name,
"I leave you peace, my peace I give you."

One of the greatest gifts I can give others
is to share with them Christ's gift of peace.
How can I best do this?

Lord, make me an instrument of your peace.
Saint Francis of Assisi

WEDNESDAY
WEEK 5 _____ EASTER

Jesus said,
"A branch cannot bear fruit by itself;
it can do so only if it remains in the vine.
In the same way you cannot bear fruit
unless you remain in me." John 15:4

A popular tradition concerns a Greek slave
named Aesop. Like Jesus, he used stories
to teach people, especially small children.
One of his stories is about a man
who had several sons
who were always fighting among themselves.
One day he called them together
and set in front of them
a bundle of small branches.
Then he invited each son to try to break
the bundle in half. Of course, no son could.
Then the father untied the bundle and gave
the branches—one by one—
to the sons to break. They did so with ease.
The father then made his point:
"My sons, if you remain united,
you will be able to withstand any enemy.
If you do not remain united,
any enemy will be able to defeat you."

How does the story of the branches relate
to Jesus' story of the vine and the branches?

If one part of the body suffers, all the other
parts suffer with it. 1 Corinthians 12:26

*Jesus said. "If you obey my commands,
you will remain in my love."*   John 15:10

Law is sometimes referred to
as love's *prod* and love's *compass*.
It serves as love's *prod*
by spurring us into action when we are slow
to respond to "love's call."
For example, as Mother's Day
reminds and spurs us
to make a "loving response" to "love's call,"
so laws do the same thing.
In a similar way,
law also serves as a *compass* to love.
It does this because we aren't always
as open to the Spirit as we should be.
So we don't always hear clearly
what "loving response" the Spirit is
inviting us to make in a given situation.
When this happens,
law acts as a *compass,* guiding us
to the kind of response "love's call"
invites us to make in a given situation.

If it is true that we can't legislate love,
then why pass laws relating to love?

*Law cannot make a man love me,
but it can keep him from lynching me,
and that's pretty important.*
                              Martin Luther King Jr.

FRIDAY
WEEK 5 _____ EASTER

Jesus said, "The greatest love
you can have for your friends
is to give your life for them." John 15:13

Each year Frank Gajouniczek
visits Auschwitz to lay a wreath on the bunker
where a priest named Maximillian Kolbe
died in his stead. It happened like this.
A prisoner escaped from the Nazi camp.
The next morning the camp commander
forced all the other prisoners to stand
all day in the blazing hot sun.
At 6 P.M.,
after many had fainted and were beaten,
he picked ten men at random
to die because of the escapee.
One was Gajouniczek. An eyewitness says:
"He screamed that he wanted to live to see
his wife and children. . . .
Then suddenly Father Kolbe . . .
stepped forward . . . to take the man's place.
In camps like Auschwitz it was unheard of
that somebody would die for another.
It restored our faith in the human race."

What was one of the most generous acts
that I freely chose to do in my life?

The best use of life
is to spend it for something
that outlasts life. William James

"Remember what I told you:
'Slaves are not greater than their master.'
If people persecuted me,
they will persecute you too. . . .
They will do all this to you
because you are mine."   John 15:20–21

Charles Colson,
Special Counsel to President Nixon,
was implicated in Watergate and imprisoned.
In prison he underwent a deep conversion.
Shortly after Colson's conversion
became public, William Buckley Jr. wrote:
"I am interested in the leers that greet
the news of Charles Colson's conversion. . . .
Some treat the whole thing as a huge joke,
as if W. C. Fields had come out
for the Temperance Union. . . . To say that you
have discovered Christ, in our secular society,
is to say something that causes people
to wince with embarrassment. . . .
For Colson to say that he has found Christ
is like Coca-Cola announcing
it has discovered Pepsi."
Chicago Daily News (June 27, 1974)

How comfortable am I in my commitment
to Christ? How open am I about it? Why?

Witness is like perfume. If it's really good,
you won't have to advertise it.   Anonymous

[Jesus said to his disciples,]
"When I go, you will not be left all alone;
I will come back to you. . . .
When that day comes, you will know that
I am in my Father and that you are in me,
just as I am in you."   John 14:18, 20

An eight-year-old named Danny
explained his "theology" of God as follows:
"One of God's main jobs is making people.
He makes these to put in place of the ones
that die so there will be enough people
to take care of things here on earth. . . .
Atheists are people who don't believe in God.
I don't think there are any in Chula Vista.
At least there aren't any who come
to our church. . . .
If you don't believe in God, you will be lonely,
because your parents can't go with you
everywhere, like to camp; but God can.
It's good to know he's around
when you're scared of the dark or
when you are thrown in the deep water
by the big kids."

Why is it that kids often grasp some great truth
of the faith so simply and correctly?

God is for us—that is good.
God is with us—that is better.
God is in us—that is best!   Author unknown

[Jesus promised his disciples,]
"I will send the Holy Spirit to you. . . .
And you, too, will speak about me."
John 15:26–27

In a scene in the film *Network,*
Peter Finch explains his "calling"
to speak the truth to his TV audience:
"The voice said to me,
'I want you to tell the people the truth,
not an easy thing to do, because
the people don't want to know the truth.'
And I said, 'You're kidding.
What the hell should I know about truth?'
But the voice said to me,
'Don't worry about the truth.
I will put the words in your mouth.'
And I said,
'What is this, the burning bush? . . .
I'm not Moses.'"
Possibly Jesus' disciples felt the same way
when Jesus promised to send the Spirit
to help them preach the "good news"
of God's Kingdom to the entire world.

Where and how do I encounter
the Holy Spirit working in my life
or elsewhere in today's world?

O Holy Spirit, Paraclete, perfect in us
the work begun by Jesus.   Pope John XXIII

*Jesus said, "It is better for you that I go away,
because if I do not go, the Helper [Holy Spirit]
will not come to you."* John 16:7

During the religious oppression in China
in the 1950s, a small child named Mei
was in prison with her Christian mother.
The child had a remarkable faith
and believed that the Spirit comes
to all Christians much as the Bible says:
"Peter and John
placed their hands on [the believers],
and they received the Holy Spirit." Acts 8:17
And so she requested
and received the Holy Spirit in this way.
Meanwhile, unsuspecting Chinese guards
let Mei run freely throughout the prison.
When Christians outside the prison found
a way to smuggle Communion to prisoners,
it was Mei who gave it to them—
even those in solitary confinement.
She said, "I'm not afraid; the Spirit
is within me." From a report by F. Steels

How do I experience the Spirit's presence
in my everyday life?

*The Spirit produces love, joy, peace,
patience, kindness, goodness,
faithfulness, humility, and self-control.*
Galatians 5:22–23

[Before ascending, Jesus told his disciples,]
"I have much more to tell you, but now
it would be too much for you to bear.
When, however, the Spirit comes,
who reveals the truth about God,
he will lead you into all the truth."

John 16:12–13

Lincoln had bad news for his Cabinet.
He introduced it by telling this story.
A worker came to a farmer with the news,
"One of your team of oxen dropped dead."
The farmer stood silently for a moment.
Then before he could say anything,
the worker said, "The other oxen died too."
When the farmer regained his composure,
he said, "Why didn't you tell me right away
that both of my oxen were dead?"
The worker said, "I didn't want to tell you
too much at one time. I was afraid
it might be too much for you to bear."

Jesus' words and Lincoln's story invite me
to reflect that some things can't be rushed,
the aging of wine, for instance.
What message might this hold for me
right now in my own life?

Everything that happens in this world
happens at the time God chooses.

Ecclesiastes 3:1

THURSDAY
WEEK 6 _____ EASTER

Jesus said,
"In a little while you will not see me
any more, and then a little while later
you will see me." John 16:16

A seven-year-old was eating her cereal
as her dad rushed by.
She grabbed his arm, gave him a kiss,
and said, "You didn't say "Good morning!"
He apologized, gave her a hug, and said,
"Sorry, dear, I've was preoccupied,
thinking about my problems at work."
She said, "Did you say your prayers
this morning, Daddy?" "No," he confessed.
"Come," she said.
"This will take us only one minute."
She took him by the hand, closed her eyes,
and said in a soft voice: "Jesus said,
'Don't be afraid. I am with you always.' "
Then she added,
"Just think about that, Daddy,
and you'll feel much better."

Think about that episode for a minute.
What might it be saying to you?

DISCIPLE   *Where must the seed be sown*
               to bring the most fruit
               when it is grown?
MASTER   *Plant it in the heart of a child.*
                             Author unknown

Jesus said, "I will see you again, and
your hearts will be filled with gladness,
the kind of gladness that no one
can take away from you."   John 16:22

The 50-year-old film *It's a Wonderful Life*
grew out of a parable on a Christmas card.
It's about a man
who thought his life was a total failure.
One day an angel appeared and showed him
how his life impacted the lives of hundreds
of people. The man was stunned
and filled with gladness at what he saw.
In the 1990s, computers colored
the 50-year-old black-and-white film,
erased the static from its soundtrack,
and transformed it into an even greater film.

It's a Wonderful life is a kind of parable
of my own life. Jesus has called me
to work for the spread of God's Kingdom.
And he has promised that when he returns,
he will fill me with gladness and transform me
beyond anything I ever dreamed possible.
How well am I living out my calling?

If seeds in the black earth
can turn into such beautiful roses,
what might the heart of man become
in its long journey to the stars?
                    G. K. Chesterton

SATURDAY
WEEK 6 _____ EASTER

[Jesus said, "When I ascend to heaven,]
the Father will give you whatever you
ask of him in my name." John 16:23

A child wrote
his description of Jesus for his teacher:
"Jesus is God's Son.
He used to do all the hard work,
like walking on water and doing miracles,
and trying to teach people—
who didn't want to learn. . . .
They finally got tired
of him preaching and crucified him.
But he was good and kind like his Father
and he told his Father . . . to forgive them. . . .
His Dad (God) . . . told him he didn't have
to go out on the road any more.
And now Jesus helps his Dad by listening
to prayers and seeing which ones
are important for God to take care of
and which ones he can take care of himself."

Why is it that kids
often grasp the great truths of faith
so simply and correctly?
How confidently do I pray to Jesus,
risen and reigning in glory in heaven?

Jesus impacted the lives
of his followers more powerfully
after his death than before it. Anonymous

Jesus said, "Eternal life means to know you,
the only true God, and to know
Jesus Christ, whom you sent." John 17:3

Keith Miller's job took him regularly across
a long stretch of Texas desert. He writes:
"I came to love the silence, the stillness,
and the vastness very much. I became
fascinated by the changes in the desert.
The white, hot noonday blast with the
heat waves rising . . . visibly off the highway
. . . would change into an amazing coolness.
The magnificent sunsets hinted
at something wonderful and very real
beyond the horizon. . . .
I began to sense something
of the majesty of God in the world.
There awoke in me a realization
that I must somehow learn more about God
and find out about Jesus Christ. . . .
This restlessness grew until one night
at home in the middle of the night
I woke Mary Allen and said,
'Honey, I've got to go back to school
to find out about God.' "
A Taste of New Wine

How eager am I to find out more
about God and Jesus Christ? Why?

Jesus said, "Who do you say I am?" Luke 9:20

Jesus said,
"The world will make you suffer.
But be brave!
I have defeated the world!" John 16:33

Hysteria over the bombing of Pearl Harbor
in 1941 led the United States to imprison
100,000 citizens of Japanese descent.
A third-generation citizen, Carole,
was born in one of these prison camps.
In time she married Jim, also a prisoner.
They had a girl whose feet twisted inward.
Hard work corrected the defect so that
by age six the girl was walking properly.
To strengthen and develop the girl's legs,
Carole enrolled her in an ice-skating class.
This meant they both had to rise
at 4 A.M. daily to get to the rink and do
the lessons and the workouts before school.
The girl not only developed strong legs
but also developed into a good figure skater.
In 1992 Carole and Jim Yamaguchi watched
their daughter Kristi win the gold medal
in figure skating at the Winter Olympics
in Albertville, Canada.

What lessons might I draw from the story
of Carole, Jim, and Kristi Yamaguchi?

Do not let evil defeat you; instead,
conquer evil with good. Romans 12:21

*[Jesus said to his Father,] "I have finished
the work you gave me to do."* John 17:4

Leonardo da Vinci painted his famous
Last Supper on a dry plaster wall.
Shortly after he finished it, the plaster
got water-soaked and was badly damaged.
In 1943 a bomb destroyed the roof
of the building, leaving the painting
exposed to the elements for three years.
Since 1979 an art restorer, Mrs. Brambilla,
has been cleaning the painting and
trying to restore it to its original surface.
She spends her days peering through a huge
magnifying glass and applying solvents
to paint scales the size of a grain of rice.
In 16 years she has inched her way across
70 percent of the 15-by-28-foot painting.
The price to her health has been enormous.
Her eyesight is permanently altered,
and a chronic pain pulses through her neck
and shoulders. But, like Jesus, she perseveres
in the work she feels she's been called to do:
preserving a masterpiece, which was
the culmination of all of Leonardo's talent.

How persevering am I in living my faith?

*Just over the hill is a beautiful valley,
but you must climb the hill to see it.*
E. C. McKenzie

[Jesus prayed to the Father
for his disciples, saying,]
"I sent them into the world. . . .
And for their sake I dedicate myself to you,
in order that they, too,
may be truly dedicated to you." John 17:18–19

Sister Francesca told this story.
The father of one of her fifth graders died.
The class attended his funeral.
Their devotion at the Mass was great.
A week later,
a man came into the parish rectory
and inquired about instructions.
When asked what sparked him
to take this big step, he explained
that he had attended the funeral Mass
and was deeply moved
by what he saw and heard,
especially the devotion of the children.

The best way to help others
dedicate themselves to Jesus and his work
is to so dedicate ourselves more fully.
How well am I doing this?
How might I improve my dedication?

People don't really pay much attention
to what we say about our religion,
because they'd rather watch
what we do about it. E. C. McKenzie

Jesus said,
"I pray not only for my disciples,
but also for those who believe in me
because of their message.
I pray that they may all be one."

John 17:20–21

"I pray because I am a Christian,
and to do what a Christian must do,
I need strength.
I pray because there is much confusion
in my life,
and to do what is right I need light.
I pray because I have doubts,
and to keep growing in my faith
I need help.
I pray because I must make decisions,
but the choices are not always clear,
so I need guidance.
I pray because most of what I have
has been given to me,
and I ought to give thanks.
I pray because Jesus prayed,
and if he considered it important,
so should I." M. L.

Which of the above do I relate to most?

Prayer enlarges the heart
until it is capable of containing
God's gift of himself. Mother Teresa

After they had eaten, Jesus said to Simon . . .
"Do you love me . . . ?" "Yes, Lord,"
he answered, "you know that I love you."

John 21:15

Erma Bombeck had fantasized
that her 25th wedding anniversary
would take place under a big white tent
with hundreds of guests milling around
and with an orchestra playing "our song."
It turned out quite differently.
Her kids simply threw a few hamburgers
on a grill, scarfed them down, and split—
leaving her and her husband to clean up.
After everything was put away,
her husband came over and said solemnly,
"Close your eyes." She did.
When she opened them, he held in his hand
a jar of cauliflower, packed in pickle juice.
"I hid this from the kids," he said,
"because I know how much you like
cauliflower packed in pickle juice."
Erma ended with this beautiful remark,
"Maybe love is that simple."

What did Erma mean?
Can I recall a similar incident in my life?

Chains do not hold a marriage together.
It is threads, hundreds of tiny threads,
which sew people together. Simone Signoret

There are many other things that Jesus did.
If they were all written down one by one,
I suppose that the whole world
could not hold the books.   John 21:25

Neil Postman has done a count of the space
given over to communication today.
It includes "260,000 billboards;
11,520 newspapers; 11,556 periodicals . . .
more than 500 million radios;
more than 100 million computers.
Ninety-eight percent of American homes
have a television set. . . .
There are 40,000 book titles
published every year . . .
and every day in America
41 million photographs are taken."
Technopoly: The Surrender of Culture to Technology

"Television is an invention
whereby you can be entertained
in your living room by people
you wouldn't have in your house."
David Frost

How do I decide which things
I will watch and read, and which I will not?

The Lord's Prayer contains 56 words;
the Gettysburg Address, 256 words;
the Ten Commandments, 297 words;
the Declaration of Independence, 300 words.

SUNDAY

Jesus said,
"Receive the Holy Spirit."   John 20:22

Jesus likened the Spirit to water.   John 7:38
"Water descends from heaven as rain.
It is always the same, but it produces
different effects in different things:
one in the palm tree, another in the vine. . . .
It adapts to each creature."   Saint Cyril
It is the same with the Spirit. Paul writes:
"No one can confess 'Jesus is Lord,'
without being guided by the Holy Spirit.
There are different kinds of spiritual gifts,
but the same Spirit gives them.
There are different ways of serving,
but the same Lord is served. . . .
The Spirit's presence is shown
in some way in each person
for the good of all."   1 Corinthians 12:3–5, 7

How does the Holy Spirit impact me?

The Spirit gives me
* *new eyes to see the face of Jesus*
in all who stand in need,
* *new ears to hear the voice of Jesus*
in all who cry to heaven for justice,
* *a new tongue to tell the message of Jesus*
to all who have never heard it,
* *a new heart to share the love of Jesus*
with all who have never experienced it.

THE LORD'S BAPTISM

[One day Jesus came to John for baptism.
John said,]
"I ought to be baptized by you. . . ."
Jesus said, "Let it be so for now."

Matthew 3:14–15

John had told people to be baptized
as a sign that they intended
to turn from sin and return to God.
This raises a question: If Jesus was sinless,
why did he ask to be baptized by John?
By becoming one of us, Jesus became
a member of our sinful human family.
He would not separate himself from it—
even its sinfulness.
In this, he teaches us an important lesson.
We cannot separate ourselves
from our sinful human family either,
especially its "family" sins:
disregard for the poor,
disrespect for all forms of human life,
discrimination against human differences.

How do these "family" sins affect me?
Do they tend to depress or challenge me?
Jesus died for our "family" sins;
what ought I to do about them?

The only thing needed for evil to triumph
in today's world is for good people
to do nothing. Edmund Burke (slightly adapted)

SPECIAL NOTE _____

On the day following the Lord's Baptism,
the Lectionary readings vary
from year to year. To determine the
meditation to use today,

- locate the current year,
- read across to the week and page,
- turn to them and begin.

This will put you in the correct sequence
for the rest of the year. (For example, if the
year is 1999, begin with Week 8, page 219.)

Year	Week	Page
1997	7	212
1998	9	226
1999	8	219
2000	10	233
2001	9	226
2002	7	212
2003	10	233
2004	9	226
2005	7	212
2006	9	226
2007	8	219
2008	6	205
2009	9	226
2010	8	219

ORDINARY TIME

Following of Jesus

The same Jesus
who walked in people's midst
in gospel times
continues to walk in people's midst today.

The Jesus
who called Simon and Andrew
on the seashore
is the same Jesus who calls us today.

The invitation
that Jesus extended to them
is the same invitation he extends to us:
"Come follow me!"

And just as their response
to this invitation
changed their lives forever,
so our response to it
will change our lives forever.

This is the great mystery
of our Christian faith that we ponder
during the season of Ordinary Time.

ORDINARY TIME _____

As Jesus walked along the shore
of Lake Galilee, he saw two fishermen,
Simon and his brother Andrew,
catching fish with a net.
Jesus said to them, "Come with me,
and I will teach you to catch people."
At once they left their nets
and went with him.   Mark 1:16–18

General Dwight Eisenhower was commander
of the U.S. forces in Europe
during World War II.
He used to illustrate the art of leadership
by taking a string about 12 inches long
and placing it on a table.
Then he'd say to officers around him,
"Pull or draw the string, and it will follow you
in any direction that you pull or draw it.
But, push or shove the string, and it will
snarl up and go in different directions.
It's the same with people. Draw or pull them
and they'll go in the direction
that you go, but push or shove them
and they'll go in a different direction."

What kind of leader am I around friends?
With my family? On the job?

A leader is someone
who knows the way, goes the way,
and shows the way.   Author unknown

TUESDAY
WEEK 1 _____ ORDINARY TIME

A man with an evil spirit . . . screamed
[at Jesus], . . . "I know who you are—
you are God's holy messenger!"
Jesus ordered the spirit,
"Be quiet, and come out of the man!"
[The spirit obeyed.]   Mark 1:23–25

An old Jewish legend describes a visit
of the Roman emperor to Rabbi Joshua.
The emperor was demanding to see
the "Holy One, the Most High of Israel."
Rabbi Joshua shook his head: "Impossible!"
The emperor said, "No excuses!"
The rabbi escorted the emperor outside.
As they stood in the bright sunlight,
the rabbi squinted and said to the emperor,
"Gaze on the face of the sun for a minute."
The emperor replied, "Impossible!"
Rabbi Joshua replied, "If it is impossible
for you to gaze on the face of the sun—
the lowly servant of the Holy One—
by what logic do you expect to gaze
on the face of the Holy One?"

Why would the evil spirit
"see" the real Jesus
when many people could not?
What keeps me from seeing Jesus better?

True spiritual vision is the ability
to see the invisible.

Long before daylight, Jesus got up and . . .
went out of town to a lonely place,
where he prayed. Mark 1:35

Musician André Kostelanetz once visited
the French artist Henri Matisse.
When Kostelanetz got to Matisse's home,
his nerves were tattered and he was tired.
Matisse noticed this and said, "My friend,
you must find the artichokes in your life."
With that, he took Kostelanetz
to his garden.
When he reached the patch of artichokes,
Matisse stopped. He told Kostelanetz that
every morning after he's worked a while,
he comes to this patch of artichokes
to pause, be still, and drink in the colors.
Matisse added, "No one is allowed
to disturb me from this ritual. . . .
It gives me fresh inspiration,
necessary relaxation,
and a new perspective toward my work."

Why would/wouldn't I classify Matisse's
ritual as prayer? What is the closest thing
to a "patch of artichokes" in my life?

Certain thoughts are prayers.
There are moments when,
whatever the attitude of the body,
the soul is on its knees. Victor Hugo

THURSDAY
WEEK 1 _____ ORDINARY TIME

A man suffering from a dreaded
skin disease came to Jesus. . . .
Jesus was filled with pity,
and reached out and touched him. . . .
At once the disease left.   Mark 1:40–42

Doctors removed a malignant tumor
from the small intestines
of eleven-year-old Ian O'Gorman.
"Besides the surgery," said Ian,
"I had tubes up my nose
and I had butterflies in my stomach."
To keep the cancer from returning,
doctors put him on chemotherapy.
When he lost all of his hair
and became totally bald,
thirteen of his fifth-grade classmates
didn't want him to feel different,
so they got their parents' permission
to shave their heads.
Jim Alter, their teacher, was so inspired
that he, too, shaved his head.

How sensitive am I
to the needs of those who are hurting?
How compassionate?

You may call God love;
you may call God goodness.
But the best name for God is compassion.
                                        Meister Eckhart

*[Some people brought a paralytic to Jesus
to be healed.] Seeing how much faith
they had, Jesus said to the paralyzed man,
"My son, your sins are forgiven."
[At once the man was healed.]*   Mark 2:5

Harold Hughes described himself as
"a drunk, a liar, and a cheat."
He was so convinced he'd never change
that he decided to end it all.
At the last moment, however,
he remembered enough from the Bible
to realize that to take one's life is wrong.
So he knelt down sobbing and explained
to God why he was going to end it all.
Suddenly, something happened
that he never experienced before in his life.
He wrote later:
"God was reaching down and touching me.
Like a stricken child lost in a storm,
I suddenly stumbled into the warm hands
of my Father. Joy filled me, so intense
it seemed to burst my breast."
Ten years later, Harold Hughes
was elected governor of Iowa.

When did I, perhaps,
feel God "touching me"?

*Jesus said, "Happy are those who mourn;
God will comfort them!"*   Matthew 5:4

SATURDAY
WEEK 1 _____ ORDINARY TIME

Jesus saw a tax collector,
Levi son of Alphaeus, sitting in his office.
Jesus said to him, "Follow me."
Levi got up and followed him.   Mark 2:14

Presidential aide Charles Colson
was imprisoned in the Watergate scandal.
Out of his prison experience
grew his present ministry to prisoners.
In *Born Again,*
he tells how it all took shape in his mind.
One day he thought to himself:
"Just as God felt it necessary
to become man to help His children,
could it be that I had become a prisoner
to better understand [prison life]? . . .
Could I ever understand the horrors
of prison life by visiting a prison? . . .
Of course not. . . . For the rest of my life
I would know and feel what it is like
to be imprisoned, the steady,
gradual corrosion of a man's soul. . . .
Out of these startling thoughts
came the beginning of a revelation—
that I was being given a prison ministry."

How do I experience Jesus calling me
to follow him more closely?

Since you have accepted Christ Jesus . . .
build your lives on him.   Colossians 2:6–7

*John [the Baptist] saw Jesus coming . . .
and said, "There is the Lamb of God,
who takes away the sin of the world!
This is the one I was talking about."*
John 1:29–30

Describing his life in postwar Germany,
Bruce Larson says, "I felt
that I was swimming in a sea of garbage.
Worse yet, the garbage was inside me."
Then one night Bruce was standing guard
in a bombed-out building in Stuttgart.
As he lifted his eyes skyward,
he could see millions of stars
shining through the charred rafters
of the wrecked building.
With all the faith he could muster,
he prayed, "Lord, if you are really there,
and if you really care, take over my life."
That night
Bruce Larson met Jesus Christ
and understood for the very first time
what John the Baptist meant when he said,
"There is the Lamb of God,
who takes away the sin of the world!"

What moment in my life comes closest
to paralleling this moment in Larson's life?

*"To understand,
you must turn from evil."* Job 28:28

[When asked why his disciples didn't fast,
Jesus said,] "Do you expect the guests
at a wedding party to go without food?
Of course not! As long as the bridegroom
is with them, they will not do that.
But the day will come when
the bridegroom will be taken from them,
and then they will fast." Mark 2:19–20

Mohandas Gandhi used fasting
as a tactic in his nonviolent opposition
to the British.
He also fasted for the "moral lapses"
of his followers and
as a "prayer" or "prelude to prayer,"
saying, "All fasting, if it is a spiritual act,
is an intense prayer or a preparation for it.
It is a yearning of the soul
to merge in the divine essence. . . .
How far I am in tune with the Infinite,
I do not know. But I do know that the fast
has made the passion for such a state
intenser than ever."

Did I ever fast for a period of time?
What motivated my fasting?
How did it impact my life and thinking?

Whoever fasts but does not other good
saves his bread but goes to Hell.
                              Italian proverb

*[Some Pharisees rebuked Jesus for letting
his hungry disciples strip wheat grains
from stalks on the Sabbath and eat them.
Jesus defended their action, saying,]*
*"The Sabbath was made
for the good of human beings;
they were not made
for the Sabbath."*   Mark 2:27

An Eastern holy man was just concluding
his morning prayers outside a hillside cave.
His body was dirty; his hair, uncombed—
not because he was lazy or crude,
but because he was poor and, at this time
of the year, the only stream within miles
contained barely enough water for drinking.
Two tourists walked by. Seeing the man—
and unaware that he understood their
language—they said, "Look at that old fellow.
His body is absolutely filthy!"
The holy man looked up and smiled,
"But, pray God, my heart is clean!"

The critical attitudes of the tourists
and of the Pharisees invite me to ask,
How critical or self-righteous do I tend to be?

*Criticism is like dynamite.
It has its place,
but it should be handled only by experts.*
                                    E. C. McKenzie

WEDNESDAY
WEEK 2 _____ ORDINARY TIME

Some people . . . watched Jesus closely
to see whether he would [heal]
on the Sabbath. . . . Jesus was angry . . .
but at the same time he felt sorry for them,
because they were so stubborn and wrong.

Mark 3:2, 5

Columnist Cheryl Lavin startled
her *Dallas Morning News* readers
after the 1992 Academy Awards.
She bluntly criticized the stars who wore
red ribbons "to raise AIDS awareness."
Her point? AIDS awareness
is plenty high among people today.
What is needed is AIDS action.
"Pinning a red ribbon to your tux
or five-figured gown," she wrote,
"trivializes a deadly disease. . . .
Think of the truly meaningful things
all those stars . . . could have done.
But they didn't. They put on a ribbon."

How might we compare
the Sabbath observance of some people
in Jesus' time
to the "red ribbon" observance of the stars
in our time?

Perfection of means and confusion of goals
seem—in my opinion—
to characterize our age. Albert Einstein

The sick kept pushing their way to Jesus
in order to touch him.   Mark 3:10

Alexis Carrel was a Nobel prize winner
and an unbelieving French surgeon.
Then he saw a girl healed before his eyes
at the shrine of Lourdes in France.
He was stunned, unable to think.
Later, he and two other doctors examined
the girl and agreed she was totally healed.
But he still had "intellectual doubts."
That night he went for a long walk
to think things out.
Later, he wrote (in the third person)
in his book *The Voyage to Lourdes:*
"Back in the hotel . . . he took the big
green notebook from his bag and sat down
to write. . . . It was now three o'clock. . . .
A new coolness penetrated the open window.
He felt the serenity of nature enter his soul.
All intellectual doubts vanished."
Carrel went on to become a deeply
committed Christian the rest of his life.

Why do/don't I find it hard to accept
Jesus' invitation to believe with all my heart?

A miracle . . . strengthens faith.
But faith in God is less apt to proceed
from miracles than miracles
from faith in God.   Frederick Buechner

FRIDAY
WEEK 2 _____ ORDINARY TIME

[Jesus chose twelve men,]
whom he named apostles.   Mark 3:14

Concerning the twelve-person system,
the British essayist G. K. Chesterton said,
"Whenever our civilization
wants a library to be catalogued,
or a solar system to be discovered,
or any other trifle of this kind,
it uses its specialists.
But when it wishes anything done
which is really serious,
it collects twelve ordinary men
standing around." Jesus did exactly this.
He chose "twelve ordinary men
standing around" to carry out
the most important undertaking
in the history of the world.

What key point is Chesterton making?
Why would Jesus pick ordinary men
rather than seasoned religious leaders?

[It seems clear that Jesus fixed
the number of men at twelve]
to symbolize the people of Israel
with its traditional twelve tribes.
In a bold figure they were represented
as "sitting on the twelve thrones
as judges of the twelve tribes." Luke 22:30
C. H. Dodd, *The Founder of Christianity*

Jesus and his disciples had no time to eat.
When his family heard about it,
they set out to take charge of him,
because people were saying,
"He's gone mad!" Mark 3:20–21

Jacob Braude quotes an item from
a Boston newspaper dating from the 1880s.
It concerns a man named Joshua Coppersmith,
who was arrested in New York for trying
to raise money for a device he says
will be able to transmit a human voice
over wire. The newspaper says:
"He calls the instrument a 'telephone'
which is obviously intended
to imitate the word 'telegraph'
and win the confidence of those who know
the success of the latter instrument.
Well-informed people know that
it is impossible to transmit the human voice
over wires. . . . The authorities who
apprehended this criminal
are to be congratulated." *Speakers Encyclopedia*

How "down" am I on things I am not
"up" on? How do I react to unfair criticism?

The biggest man with the biggest ideas
can be shot down by the smallest men
with the smallest minds.
Think big anyway! Theodore Roethke

SUNDAY
WEEK 3 _____ ORDINARY TIME

Jesus began to preach his message:
"Turn away from your sins, because
the Kingdom of heaven is near!" Matthew 4:17

An inmate on a Kentucky death row wrote:
"Father, I come to you a bent and
broken man, and humble myself before you,
with no strength left to stand.
I come to you from prison,
from a place that's called death row,
and ask you to take pity, Lord,
on this convict's wretched soul. . . .
Replace this hate with blessed love
and dry these tear-stained eyes;
have mercy on this awful man;
please hear his mournful cries.
I'm sorry for all the grief
I've caused you and everyone;
forgive me, Lord,
for letting down your only Son. . . .
So wash me, Lord, with your loving blood
that was spilled so long ago,
and welcome me unto thy bosom and
comfort this poor lost soul." Jack Joe Holland

What are my feelings
when I pray Jack Joe's prayer aloud
in a subdued voice?

Through sin do we reach the light.
Elbert Hubbard

[Some religious leaders accused Jesus
of receiving his power to expel demons from
the "chief of the demons." Jesus asked,]
"How can Satan drive out Satan?"   Mark 3:23

The gospels mention Satan
some 30 times. Many of these references
come from the mouth of Jesus himself.
John Knox Jessup admits
that few people today take the Devil seriously.
He adds, however, that among these few
are some of Christianity's finest minds.
And they have a simple explanation for
the Devil's demise from our consciousness.
The Devil himself planned it that way.
Jessup cautions those who feel the Devil
is an affront to the intellect, saying,
"Although the Devil offends reason,
it is not therefore unreasonable
to recognize his existence.
He simply dwells
in a different dimension of reality."

How do I explain Jessup's caution
to those who consider the Devil
an affront to the human intellect?

Be alert, be on watch! Your enemy, the Devil,
roams around like a roaring lion,
looking for someone to devour. Be firm
in your faith and resist him.   1 Peter 5:8–9

A crowd was sitting around Jesus,
and they said to him,
"Look, your mother and your brothers
and sisters are outside, and they want you."
Jesus answered . . . "Whoever does
what God wants is my brother, my sister,
my mother."   Mark 3:32–33, 35

Three golden-agers—
Peter, Paul, and Annie—
were seated together on a park bench,
"philosophizing" about life's treasures.
Peter volunteered that *fame* and *fortune*
are great treasures, but they are fleeting.
Paul observed that *family* (mother,
father, brothers, sisters) and *friends*
are greater treasures,
but they can accompany us only to the grave.
Annie noted that the greatest treasure
is a loving heart, filled with deeds
performed in harmony with God's will.
This treasure accompanies us
across the narrow bridge of death
into the great beyond of eternity.

Which of these treasures am I pursuing
with the greatest energy and commitment?

If you cannot find happiness along the way,
don't assume you will find it
at the end of the road.   Author unknown

"A man . . . went out to sow grain.
As he scattered the seed in the field,
some of it fell along the path,
and the birds came and ate it up. . . .
But some seeds fell in good soil . . .
and bore grain."   Mark 4:3–4, 8

Sow seed that will yield a joyful harvest.
First, sow three rows of pea seed:
>   Patience
>   Perseverance
>   Prayerfulness

Second, plant three rows of squash seed:
>   Squash anger.
>   Squash criticism.
>   Squash gossip.

Third, plant three rows of lettuce seed:
>   Let us be unselfish.
>   Let us be forgiving.
>   Let us be loving.

Finally, you've got to sow turnip seed!
>   Turn up with a ready hand.
>   Turn up with a gentle smile.
>   Turn up with a listening heart.

Pick a vegetable from each row
that you need to eat more of
for better health.

Who has health has hope;
who has hope has everything.   Arab proverb

THURSDAY
WEEK 3 _____ ORDINARY TIME

Jesus said, "In the measure you give
you shall receive, and more besides.
To those who have, more will be given;
from those who have not,
what little they have will be taken away."

Mark 4:24–25 (NAB, 1970)

A golden chariot halted beside a beggar.
The king emerged, held out his hand,
and said, "What do you have to give me?"
Anger rose in the beggar's heart,
for he thought the king was mocking him.
But then he saw the king was very serious.
So he opened his beggar's pouch
and gave the king his tiniest kernel of corn.
That night, when the beggar dumped
the corn out, he discovered that
the tiniest kernel had changed into gold.
The beggar wept and wept,
for he was both sad and glad:
sad that he'd not given the king more,
glad that he'd at least given him something.
And so, as a result of that experience,
the beggar learned a great secret.

What great secret did the beggar learn?

No matter how poor I am,
I have something to share.
If I share it, I become rich beyond belief.
If I refuse, I grow even poorer.   Anonymous

Jesus preached his message . . .
using many . . . parables.   Mark 4:33

One day a fish came upon divers
photographing the dark depths of the ocean.
He swam off to warn the fish elders
about the weird invaders from outerwater.
But the elders ridiculed him, saying,
"There's no life in outerwater—
too much oxygen and far too little water.
Besides, the bright sun would kill all life."
Someone used this "modern parable"
to illustrate how hard it is
to explain to people anything
that is beyond their everyday experience.
Jesus had a similar problem when he tried
to explain God's Kingdom to people.
It was too far beyond their experience.
And so he turned to parables.

Why were parables useful
in helping people grasp truths
beyond their experience?
What is one such truth I find hard to grasp?

Parables are
earthly stories with heavenly meanings.
They build a bridge from the known
to the unknown. They stretch the mind
to embrace spiritual realities
beyond our ordinary, earthly experience.

188

SATURDAY
WEEK 3 _____ ORDINARY TIME

[Jesus and his disciples were at sea.]
Suddenly a strong wind blew up,
and the waves began to spill over
into the boat. . . .
Jesus was in the back . . . sleeping. . . .
The disciples woke him up and said,
"Teacher . . . we are about to die."
Jesus stood up and commanded the wind,
"Be quiet!" and he said to the waves,
"Be still!" The wind died down,
and there was a great calm. Mark 4:37–39

"Lord of the wind and waves,
calm our storm when we are afraid.
Lord of the loaves and fishes,
be our food when we are hungry.
Lord of the lambs and flocks,
seek us out when we are lost.
Lord of signs and wonders,
show yourself when we have doubts.
Lord of the blind and lame,
take our hand when we falter.
Lord of the fields and flowers,
care for us when others don't.
Lord of all that lives, be our God.
We are your people." M. L.

How confidently and prayerfully
do I turn to Jesus in time of need?

They stand best who kneel most. E. C. McKenzie

*Jesus said, "Happy are those
who know they are spiritually poor;
the Kingdom of heaven belongs to them!"*
                                                    Matthew 5:3

At age 40, Lee Atwater was known
for his savvy, vitality, and charisma.
As President Bush's campaign manager
he had a bright future ahead of him.
Then his health suddenly went bad.
The problem turned out to be a brain tumor
that would take his life quickly.
During his illness, he observed
that something was not right
both with our society and himself.
Then he noted: "My illness helped me
to see that what was missing in society
is what is missing in me—
a little heart, a lot of brotherhood."
He concluded, "We must . . . speak
to this spiritual vacuum
at the heart of American society."

What can just one person do
when it comes to speaking
to the spiritual vacuum
in American society?

*Who loseth wealth loseth much . . .
but who loseth the spirit loseth all.*
                    Elbert Hubbard (slightly adapted)

MONDAY
WEEK 4 _____ ORDINARY TIME

[Jesus took pity on a possessed man and]
asked him, "What is your name!"
The man answered, "My name is 'Mob'—
there are so many of us!" . . .
[Shortly,] the evil spirits went out of the man.
Mark 5:9, 13

Christopher Marlowe
was a 16th-century British writer.
Among his works is a play entitled
The Tragic History of Doctor Faustus.
Faustus is a brilliant man
who grows tired of his boring existence.
He decides to sell his soul to the Devil
for the right to command the evil spirits
of the other world.
His close friends are shocked and urge him
to repent and seek God's mercy.
He ignores their pleas.
For 24 years Dr. Faustus enjoys
the status and the power given him
by the Devil. Finally, the last day
of Faustus's life on earth arrives.
When the clock strikes midnight,
Dr. Faustus cries, "O, spare me, Lucifer!"

What are my thoughts as I imagine myself
to be Dr. Faustus a minute before midnight?

"Will you gain anything if you win
the whole world but are yourself lost?" Luke 9:25

[Jairus asked Jesus to come to his house,
where his daughter had just died.
Jesus took with him Peter, James, and John.
They] went into the room where the child
was lying. . . . [Jesus] said to her,
"Talitha, koum," which means, "Little girl,
I tell you to get up!" She got up at once.

Mark 5:40–42

Jesus frequently went to homes.
Besides going to the home of Jairus,
he also went to the homes of the following:
the young newlyweds in Cana (John 2:2),
Peter in Capernaum (Mark 1:29),
Simon the Pharisee in Capernaum (Luke 7:36),
Zacchaeus in Jericho (Luke 19:5),
Mary and Martha in Bethany (John 12:2),
the two disciples in Emmaus (Luke 24:29).
And each time Jesus visited a home,
he left behind a blessing.

When did Jesus last visit my home?
What blessing did he, perhaps, leave behind?

Lord, visit our home and bless it.
Bless its roof, that it may protect us
from winter cold and summer heat.
Bless its doors, that they may remain open
to friend and foe alike.
Bless its rooms, that they may be places
where peace and love reside.   Anonymous

Special Note _____

Starting with Wednesday of the fourth week of Ordinary Time, the Lectionary readings vary from year to year, depending on when Ash Wednesday (start of Lent) falls in that year.

The following table shows the date on which Ash Wednesday falls in the years ahead. Locate the current year and, on the date indicated, turn to page 67 (Ash Wednesday) and begin there.

1997	February 12
1998	February 25
1999	February 17
2000	March 8
2001	February 28
2002	February 13
2003	March 5
2004	February 25
2005	February 9
2006	March 1
2007	February 21
2008	February 6
2009	February 25
2010	February 17

ORDINARY TIME _____ WEEK 4

[Some people from Jesus' hometown
rejected him, saying,]
"Isn't he the carpenter,
the son of Mary?" . . .
Jesus was not able to perform
any miracles there . . .
because the people did not have faith.

Mark 6:3, 5–6

A speaker was lecturing on Scripture.
Afterward, a woman gave him this note:
"On the 12th anniversary
of my daughter's emotional illness,
I asked Jesus to heal her,
as he did the woman in the gospel
who had a hemorrhage for 12 years. . . .
I simply told Jesus that
I believed he could heal our daughter, and
that I had enough faith for both of us. . . .
The next day we noticed
the first signs pointing to a recovery.
That was six years ago.
Today she is a healthy young woman.
Even more beautifully,
Jesus is using her to help others."

How deep is my faith in Jesus right now?
What is one way that I might deepen it?

Give me faith, Lord,
and let me help others find it.   Leo Tolstoy

[Jesus sent his disciples out
to preach and to heal.]
So they went out and preached that
people should turn away from their sins.
They drove out many demons,
and rubbed olive oil on many sick people
and healed them.   Mark 6:12–13

A Vietnam soldier was badly wounded
by a mortar shell. Later, he described
what then happened: "Our chaplain
bent over me and began to pray.
After I saw him . . . I started to go out—
I figured for the last time. . . .
Then a split second before I went out,
I felt oil on my forehead.
And something happened
which I will never forget—
something which I have never experienced
before in my life! . . . I just burst with joy. . . .
I was on Cloud 9. I felt free of body and mind."
Letter to Ralph Talkin, S.J.

This description of the sacrament
of the Anointing of the Sick affirms
that Jesus still heals people today
through anointing with oil.
Why are some people healed and others not?

When we do what we can, God will do
what we can't do.   Anonymous

[John the Baptist was jailed
for protesting Herod's wrongful marriage.
He kept saying,] "It isn't right."   Mark 6:18

The classic film *On the Waterfront*
deals with the sinful practices
of hiring bosses on New York loading docks.
In one scene Father Barry lectures the
longshoremen for cooperating with them:
"Some people think the crucifixion
took place on Calvary. They better wise up.
Taking Joey Doyle's life to stop him
from testifying is a crucifixion. . . .
Whoever sits around and lets it happen—
keeps silent about something he knows
has happened—shares the guilt. . . .
When the hiring boss blows his whistle,
Jesus stands alongside you in the shape-up.
He sees you get picked
and some of you get passed over.
He sees the family man worried
about getting . . . [rent and food money]
for the wife and kids.
He sees you selling your souls for a day's pay."

What is one evil I deplore
in today's world? What is one thing
I might do to combat or oppose it?

Those who stand for nothing
fall for everything.   Alexander Hamilton

SATURDAY
WEEK 4 _____ ORDINARY TIME

"Let us go off by ourselves
to some place where we will be alone
and you can rest a while."   Mark 6:31

Rabbi David Wolpe tells the story
of a rabbi's child
who used to stray off into the forest.
At first his father let him stray.
But when it got to be a regular routine,
the father grew concerned.
What was his child doing there?
Besides, the forest was dangerous.
One day he asked the child,
"Why do you go into the forest each day?"
The child said, "I go to find God."
The father responded,
"That's a wonderful thing to do, my child.
And I'm pleased you search for God.
But, my child, you should realize
that God is the same everywhere."
The child answered,
"I know that, Father;
but I am not the same everywhere."

What is the child's point?
Where do I find God most easily?

At cool of day, with God I walk
My garden's grateful shade;
I hear God's voice among the trees
And I am not afraid.   Anonymous

Ordinary Time _____ Week 5

Jesus said,
"Your light must shine before people,
so that they will . . . praise your Father."
                                    Matthew 5:16

Many rural villages in India
are totally without electricity.
People use tiny oil lamps, much like those
used in Jesus' time, to light their homes.
The temple in one of these rural villages
has a large frame hanging from its ceiling.
Cut into the frame are a hundred slots
into which tiny oil lamps can be placed.
When the people go to the temple after dark,
they carry their oil lamps from their homes
to guide them through the darkness.
Upon arriving in the temple,
they place their lamp in one of the slots
in the frame.
By the time the last villager arrives,
the darkness of the temple has been
transformed into a glorious sea of light.

What important spiritual point
does this story illustrate?
What might it be saying
to me about my own life—right now?

Every believer in this world
must become a spark of light.
                        Pope John XXIII

MONDAY
WEEK 5 _____ ORDINARY TIME

*People would take their sick
to the marketplaces and beg Jesus to let
the sick at least touch the edge of his cloak.
And all who touched it were made well.*
Mark 6:56

England was involved in the Crimean War
in Russia from 1845 to 1856. The wounded
lay side by side in makeshift hospitals
that were terribly overcrowded and filthy.
The wind blew the stench from open sewers,
making breathing difficult. Rats ran wild.
Into this incredible, hopeless situation
came Florence Nightingale
and 38 nurses she had trained in England.
Sometimes she spent 20 straight hours
on her feet, directing sanitation efforts
and bandaging the wounded.
The bedridden soldiers worshiped her
and would "kiss her shadow
as it fell across their pillows."

If the sick and the needy are to experience
Jesus' healing presence today,
it must be through loving, caring people.
How ready am I to be the healing presence
of Jesus in today's world?

*Blessed is the influence
of one true, loving human soul on another.*
George Eliot

*Some Pharisees and teachers of the Law . . .
asked Jesus, "Why is it that your disciples
do not follow the teaching handed down
by our ancestors . . . ?" Jesus answered them,
"How right Isaiah was when he prophesied
about you! . . . You have a clever way
of rejecting God's law in order to uphold
your own teaching."* Mark 7:1, 5–6, 9

In one *Peanuts* cartoon, Charlie Brown
is shooting arrows at a wooden fence.
After each arrow leaves Charlie's bow
and sticks into the fence, Charlie runs up
and draws a target around it, so that the arrow
is always in the center of the bull's-eye.
Lucy enters, sees what Charlie is doing,
and says, "You're doing it all backwards.
You're supposed to draw the target first.
Then shoot the arrow at it." Charlie says,
"I know what you're supposed to do,
but when you do it my way you never miss."

When it comes to following Jesus' teaching,
do I tend to do it "my way"?
Do I tend to do things "backwards"?
Do I pick out the teachings I like,
follow them, and ignore the rest?

*We cannot break God's laws—
but we can break ourselves against them.*
A. Maude Royden

WEDNESDAY
WEEK 5 _____ ORDINARY TIME

Jesus said,
"Nothing that goes into you from the outside
can really make you unclean. . . .
It is what comes out of you
that makes you unclean." Mark 7:18, 20

Dennis Byrd broke his neck
in a Pro football game against Kansas City.
It left him paralyzed and demoralized.
Then a miracle happened.
Within ten months he was walking again.
Dennis admits he prayed for a miracle.
But it was not that he'd walk again.
It was that he would be a complete person,
whether he walked again or not.
Now Dennis is praying for another miracle—
that people in his situation will draw hope
and strength from his faith in God.
That leads us to Jesus' point in today's gospel.
The things that make us unclean or destroy us
do not come from without, but from within.
As *food* from *without* can't make us unclean,
neither can *fate* from *without* defeat us.
Defeat and uncleanness are "inside jobs."

What "inside job" threatens to destroy me
or make me unclean—right now in my life?

Unless there is within us
that which is above us, we shall soon yield
to that which is about us. Peter Forsyth

*[A non-Jewish woman begged Jesus to drive
a demon out of her daughter. Jesus replied,]
"Let us first feed the children [of Israel]. . . ."
"Sir," she answered, "even the dogs
under the table eat the children's leftovers!"
So Jesus said to her, "Because of that answer . . .
you will find that the demon
has gone out of your daughter!"* Mark 7:27–29

During the 1930s depression, transients
showed up daily at our home for food.
My mother never turned them away.
At times, however, she did explain
that she had eight mouths to feed
and very little food to go around.
(Sometimes, when transients saw the food
she gave them, they left it,
and the family dog got it.) This brings us
to today's gospel. Jesus makes it clear
that his first mission is to Jews.
They were prepared by the Scriptures
to understand it. (Later, others will be sent
to evangelize the non-Jewish world.)
Like my mother (whose first mission was
to her family), Jesus shared his mission
with those who had faith and special needs.

With whom do I share Jesus' message? How?

*We must preach to the poor with our hands
before we preach with our lips.* Saint Peter Claver

FRIDAY
WEEK 5 _____ ORDINARY TIME

Some people brought Jesus a man
who was deaf and could hardly speak. . . .
Jesus . . . said to the man,
"Ephphatha," *which means,* "Open up!"
At once the man was able to hear . . .
and he began to talk without any trouble.

Mark 7:32, 34–35

Helen Keller was blind, deaf, and dumb.
In *The Story of My Life* she tells how
Miss Fuller taught her to talk:
"She passed my hand lightly over her face,
and let me feel the position of her tongue
and lips when she made a sound. . . .
I labored night and day. . . .
My work was practice, practice, practice. . . .
I used to repeat ecstatically,
'I am not dumb now.' . . .
My mother pressed me close. . . .
Mildred seized my free hand and kissed it
and danced, and my father expressed
his pride and affection in a big silence."

Do I have some kind of inability
to "speak" or "hear"
that I would like Jesus
to heal in me? What is it?

The chief exercise of prayer is to speak
to God and to hear God speak to you
in the depths of your heart. Saint Francis de Sales

*Jesus ordered the crowd to sit down
on the ground. Then he took the seven loaves
[and] gave thanks to God. . . . Everyone ate
and had enough—there were about four
thousand people.*   Mark 8:6, 8

Walter Petrvage grew up in a small town
in Pennsylvania. Among his fond memories
is his father's deep compassion.
For example, on the night of the senior prom
he took his father's car without permission.
In his rush to get away without detection,
he left the driver's door slightly open
to check clearance
as he backed out of the narrow garage.
It hit the garage, springing the hinges.
He lay awake most of the night worrying.
When he came downstairs about noon,
his dad said, "I took the Chevy to the body shop.
They'll have it fixed tomorrow.
We can decide who'll pay for it then."
He paused and then said,
"Did you have a good time at the prom?"
Catholic Digest (June 1996)

How compassionate am I—as Jesus was
to the crowd and the father to his son?

*My father didn't tell me how to live;
he lived, and let me watch him do it.*
Clarence Budington Kelland

SUNDAY
WEEK 6 _____ ORDINARY TIME

Jesus said,
"Make peace with your brother."　　Matthew 5:24

Michael Landon got the inspiration
for his 1980s TV series, *Highway to Heaven,*
while driving down a Los Angeles freeway.
Traffic was horrendous. Horns were blaring.
Tempers were flaring, and many people
were shouting from their car windows.
Landon shook his head and asked himself,
"Why is there so much anger everywhere?"
His mind went back to his childhood,
and he reflected on the anger that often
raged between his mother and his father.
Suddenly an idea flashed across his mind:
Why not produce a TV series dedicated
to the idea that kindness, not anger,
is the key to solving life's problems?
In other words,
the series would dramatize
Jesus' point in his Sermon on the Mount:
Loving concern for one another
is what the Kingdom of heaven is all about.

What are some concrete ways
by which my life can become more loving?

Let me be a little kinder,
Let me be a little blinder
To the faults of those around me.
　　　　　　　　　　　Edgar Guest

*Some Pharisees . . . asked Jesus to perform
a miracle to show that God approved of him.*
Mark 8:11

"Here is a young man who . . . worked
in a carpenter shop until he was thirty. . . .
He never owned a home. He never had
a family. He never went to college. . . .
He had no credentials but himself.
While he was still a young man
the tide of public opinion turned against him.
His friends ran away. . . . He was nailed
to a cross between two thieves. . . .
When he was dead, he was laid in
a borrowed grave. . . . Nineteen centuries
have come and gone, and today he is . . .
the leader of the column of progress.
I am far within the mark when I say that
all the armies that ever marched,
and all the kings who ever reigned,
put together, have not affected the life
of man upon this earth
as has that One Solitary Life." Author unknown

In what sense is the life of Jesus
a greater sign of God's approval
than any one miracle
could ever have been?

*He shows you stars
you never saw before.* Alfred Lord Tennyson

TUESDAY
WEEK 6 _____ ORDINARY TIME

[Jesus warned his disciples,]
"Be on your guard
against the yeast of the Pharisees
and the yeast of Herod." Mark 8:15

A young singer was having a dinner date
with a charming young man.
Of course, she was eager to make
the best possible impression on him.
So she talked about her career:
how it got started, the rave reviews
the critics were giving her,
and her anticipation of a gold record
for her latest recording.
After dominating the conversation
for most of the meal, she paused,
smiled, and said,
"Enough about me! Let's talk about *you!*
What did *you* think of my latest recording?"

People who talk about things
they can't afford tend to omit from the list
such things as self-centeredness, pride,
and insensitivity toward others.
Which of these three
do I need to work on more resolutely?

Pride has a way
of concealing my faults from myself,
and revealing them to everyone else—
especially my loved ones. Author unknown

*[Jesus placed his hands on a blind man
and asked,] "Can you see anything?"* . . .
*Jesus again placed his hands
on the man's eyes.
This time . . . he saw everything clearly.*
Mark 8:23, 25

In his book *The Christian Vision,*
John Powell tells of meeting a young man
who grew up unable to see objects
that were more than a few feet
from his eyes.
His parents were poor and uneducated
and did not seek help for him.
When he was 18, the young man
went to an eye doctor for the first time.
After fitting the young man with lenses,
the doctor told him to look out the window.
"Wow!" the young man exclaimed.
"This is incredible, absolutely incredible.
I can't believe how beautiful everything is!"

Helen Keller, who was blind, said,
"The greatest calamity . . .
is to have sight and fail to see."
Do I have a "blindness"
from which I need Jesus to heal me?
What is it?

The real voyage of discovery consists . . .
in seeing with new eyes. Marcel Proust

THURSDAY
WEEK 6 _____ ORDINARY TIME

Jesus and his disciples went away
to the villages near Caesarea Philippi. . . .
Then Jesus began to teach his disciples:
"The Son of Man must suffer much and be
rejected by the elders, the chief priests,
and the teachers of the Law.
He will be put to death,
but three days later he will rise to life."

Mark 18:27, 31

There's an old poem
that goes something like this:
"I put a nail in my wallet
for nobody but me to see–
as a personal reminder
that the Son of God died for me.
Each time I reach in my pocket,
pull out and open my wallet,
the nail is there reminding me
of the price Jesus paid for me.
And so the nail in my wallet
reminds me in a loving way
to strive to serve Jesus better
in all I do and all I say."

What did I do for Jesus yesterday?
What might I do for him today?

Today's opportunities
erase yesterday's failures.

Gene Brown

Jesus said, "Do you gain anything
if you win the whole world
but lose your life?"   Mark 8:36

Jon Robin Baitz wrote a three-act play
called *Three Hotels*.
Each act takes place at a different hotel
and a different time. The first act
introduces us to a business executive,
Kenneth, who gained a fortune
selling baby food to African women.
He knows the food is bad for the babies,
but he closes his eyes to this fact.
The second act introduces us to his wife.
She is embittered and destroyed
by what her unscrupulous spouse is doing.
The final act takes place years later.
Kenneth sits all alone,
overwhelmed by the evil he now realizes
he has wrought on so many people.
He has lost everything: his marriage,
his job, his self-respect, his very soul.

Is there anything in my life
that even remotely threatens to do to me
what the business executive's pride
and greed did to him?

This is the test. . . . How much
is there left in you after you have lost
everything outside of yourself?   Author unknown

Jesus took with him Peter, James, and John,
and led them up a high mountain. . . .
As they looked on, a change came over Jesus,
and his clothes became shining white. . . .
Then a cloud appeared and covered them
with its shadow, and a voice came
from the cloud,
"This is my own dear Son—listen to him!"

Mark 9:2–3, 7

Albert Schweitzer wrote:
"Jesus comes to us as One unknown,
without a name, as of old, by the lakeside. . . .
He speaks to us the same word:
'Follow thou me!' and sets us to the tasks
which he has to fulfill in our time. . . .
And to those who obey him,
whether they be wise or simple,
he will reveal himself in the toils,
the conflicts, the sufferings which they
shall pass through in his fellowship,
and . . . they shall learn
in their own experience who he is."

What task has Jesus set to me to fulfill?

One day he will come.
Once in the stillness . . . you will know
[who he is] . . . not from a book
or the word of someone else,
but through him.   Romano Guardini

Jesus said, "Love your enemies."   Matthew 5:44

The Italian team of Monti and Siorpraes
was heavily favored to win
the Olympic bobsled event in 1964
in Innsbruck, Austria.
They had great first and second runs, but the
little-regarded British team of Nash and Dixon
had a sensational and better first run.
Their axle broke, however,
just before their scheduled second run.
They were crushed.
Monti amazed everyone by removing the bolt
from the Italian sled and giving it
to the British team so they could finish.
Nash and Dixon went on to win the gold
in a tremendous upset victory, while Monti
and Siorpraes settled for the bronze.
In a bit of poetic beauty, four years later,
Monti led the Italian two- and four-man sleds
to victory in 1968.

The sportsmanship of the Italians in 1964
is a beautiful image of the kind of love
Jesus invites us to show our enemies
in daily life. How well am I showing it?

For when the One Great Scorer comes
To write against your name,
He marks—not that you won or lost—
But how you played the game.   Grantland Rice

MONDAY
WEEK 7 _____ ORDINARY TIME

[A man begged Jesus to heal his son,
saying,] "Help us, if you possibly can!"
"Yes," said Jesus, "if you yourself can!
Everything is possible
for the person who has faith." Mark 9:22–23

A snorting bull
was charging a fleeing man in an open field.
The man's only possible escape was a tree.
But the tree's lowest branch
was almost twelve feet off the ground.
It was absolutely impossible for the man
to leap up and grab the branch.
But the man realized
that he had no other option open to him
but to try.
So he ran with the speed of the wind
and made a tremendous leap.
He missed the branch on his way up
but managed to catch it on his way down.

How do I see the words of Jesus
about faith and the story
about the bull and the man
relating to my situation in life right now?

Only when we learn to see
the invisible
will we learn to do
the impossible.
       Frank Gaines (slightly adapted)

Jesus sat down, called the twelve disciples,
and said to them,
"Whoever wants to be first
must . . . be the servant of all."   Mark 9:35

Twice a year geese migrate
in a beautiful V formation, as a flock.
Philip Yancey explains:
"That's the secret of their strength. . . .
Cooperating as a flock,
geese can fly at 71 percent longer range. . . .
The lead goose cuts a swath through the
air resistance, which creates a helping uplift
for the two birds behind him.
In turn, their beating makes it easier
on the birds behind them. . . .
Each bird takes his turn as the leader.
The tired ones fan out to the edges of the V
for a breather, and the rested ones
surge forward to the point of the V
to drive the flock onward."   *Campus Life* magazine
Yancey says that if a goose becomes sick
and needs to rest, another goose will
stay with it until it can continue again.

How ready am I to place myself
at the service of all, especially the needy?

O God, help us to be masters of ourselves
that we may be servants of others.

                              Sir Alec Paterson

WEDNESDAY
WEEK 7 _____ ORDINARY TIME

[When John tried to stop a man
from driving out demons in Jesus' name,
Jesus said,] "Do not try to stop him . . . because
no one who performs a miracle in my name
will be able soon afterward to say evil things
about me. For whoever is not against us
is for us." Mark 9:39–40

A *Peanuts* cartoon shows Snoopy studying
Charlie Brown and thinking: "Poor Charlie!
He's always worried about whether people
like him. I don't have that problem.
I know exactly whether people like me or not:
they either pat me on the head or kick me."
It was like that with Jesus.
There was no in-between.
You were for him or against him.

Why was there no in-between with Jesus?

[A man] who said the sort of things Jesus said . . .
would either be a lunatic or the Devil. . . .
You must make your choice.
Either this man was, and is, the Son of God
or else a madman or something worse.
You can . . . kill him as a demon,
or you can fall at his feet and call him
Lord and God. But let us not come with any
patronizing nonsense about his being
a great human teacher. He has not left that
open to us. He did not intend to. C. S. Lewis

*Jesus said, "If anyone should cause
one of these little ones to lose faith in me,
[woe to that person]."*   Mark 9:42

A skinny boy with a shoeshine kit
stood at the edge of a sidewalk cafe.
A woman felt a surge of admiration for him
for trying to be a man and earn a living.
Just then a man charged out of the cafe,
grabbed the boy, and threw him
like a bag of garbage into the street.
The boy held tightly to his kit
to keep its contents from flying all over.
The woman's heart went out to the boy.
Why did the man treat the boy so brutally?
The boy hadn't picked anybody's pocket.
He hadn't stolen anyone's purse.
He hadn't tried to sell drugs.
As the boy limped off, ashamed
and humiliated, the woman wondered:
"How will this cruel experience
affect the boy's attitude
toward work and people?
Will it snuff out the tiny spark of initiative
and hope that once flickered in his heart?

What might Jesus say to the boy? The man?

*Have a heart that never hardens,
and a temper that never tires,
and a touch that never hurts.*   Charles Dickens

FRIDAY
WEEK 7 _____ ORDINARY TIME

Jesus said, "At the time of creation,
'God made them male and female,'
as the scripture says. 'And for this reason
a man will leave his father and mother
and unite with his wife,
and the two will become one.'
So they are no longer two, but one."

Mark 10:6–8

An old poem by an unknown poet
asks the question, What is love?
The poet responds by listing six answers.
They go something like this.
"Love is:
silence—when words would hurt,
patience—when another's curt,
deafness—when another's mad,
gentleness—when another's sad,
promptness—when a need is seen,
courage—when life is mean."

Of the poet's examples of love,
at which do I score highest? Lowest? Why?
What is one concrete thing I might do
to make my love more like Jesus' love?

What does love look like?
It has feet to go to the poor and needy.
It has eyes to see misery and want.
It has ears to hear sighs and sorrows.

Saint Augustine

Some people brought children to Jesus
for him to place his hands on them,
but the disciples scolded the people.
When Jesus noticed this,
he was angry and said to his disciples,
"Let the children come to me,
and do not stop them." Mark 10:13–14

Thomas Merton writes in his biography,
The Seven Storey Mountain:
"It was Sunday. . . .
The sound of church bells
came across the bright fields. . . .
Suddenly, all the birds began to sing
in the trees above my head,
and the sound of the birds singing
and the church bells ringing
lifted my heart with joy.
I cried out to my father: 'Father,
all the birds are in their church.'
And then I said:
'Why don't we go to church?'
My father looked up and said:
'We will . . . some other Sunday.' "

How do I help
to bring children to Jesus?

Treat a child
as though he already is the person
he's capable of becoming. Haim Ginott

[Jesus taught us to trust in God, saying,]
"Look at the birds: they do not plant seeds,
gather a harvest and put it in barns;
yet your Father in heaven takes care of them!
Aren't you worth more than birds?"

Matthew 6:26

When Hitler took power,
the Jews became fair game.
Paul Waldemann writes: "My cousin Hans,
through a friend in Zurich,
obtained a visa to Switzerland.
Lucky Hans! . . . The days dragged on—
days of gloom and hopelessness.
One afternoon I looked out the window
and saw some sparrows hopping around,
looking for a few morsels of food.
For a fleeting moment, I envied
those little birds. How carefree they were!
How easily they could fly across borders. . . .
A question came to my mind:
Does God care for the sparrows? . . .
And if he takes care of them—
perhaps he will help me, too!
For the first time I felt a glimmer of hope,
and my heart felt a little lighter."
Richer Than a Millionaire

What keeps me from trusting God totally?

Trust to the known God the unknown future.

Jesus said, "It is much harder for
a rich person to enter the Kingdom of God
than for a camel to go through
the eye of a needle."   Mark 10:25

Fishing boats made Monterey, California,
a "pelicans' paradise."
Fishermen cleaned their fish
and threw the entrails to the waiting birds.
It was all play and no worry for pelicans.
The good life was theirs to milk and enjoy.
Then something terrible happened.
Entrails became commercially valuable.
Overnight, the pelicans lost their "good life."
Worse yet, the "good life" had made them
so content and soft that they lost not only
the art of survival but also
the discipline for survival. The result?
Vast segments of the pelican population
grew weak and died of starvation.

How might the pelican story serve
as a commentary on Jesus' words
about the difficulty of the rich
to enter God's Kingdom?

Who never ate bread in sorrow,
Who never spent the darksome hours
Weeping and watching for the morrow
He knows you not, you heavenly Powers.
Johann Wolfgang von Goethe

TUESDAY
WEEK 8 _____ ORDINARY TIME

*Jesus said, "Many who are now first
will be last."* Mark 10:31

Henry VIII
is one of Shakespeare's best-known plays.
In the play, an ambitious Cardinal Woolsey
is questing for wealth and greatness.
His patron is the powerful Henry VIII
of England, whom he serves zealously.
Then a reversal of fortunes takes place.
Henry is angered when he learns
that Woolsey doesn't see eye to eye with him
on his decision to divorce the queen
and marry a lady-in-waiting, rather than seek
an alliance with France through marriage.
Henry is also angered when he learns
of the wealth Woolsey has amassed.
And so the king strips him of everything.
At this point a chastened Woolsey
confides to his only friend, Cromwell:
"Had I served my God with half the zeal
I served my king, he would not . . .
have left me naked to my enemies."

How zealous is my service of God
compared to my service of worldly things?

*Jesus said, "No servant
can be the slave of two masters. . . .
You cannot serve both God and money."*
Luke 16:13

*[The mother of John and James asked Jesus
to let her sons sit at his right and his left
when he became king.]*
*When the other ten disciples heard about it,
they became angry with James and John.*

Mark 10:41

To: Jesus of Nazareth
From: Jerusalem Business Consultants, Inc.:
We have reviewed the resumés
of your candidates for managerial posts.
We recommend you continue your search.
Peter is too emotional and prone
to faulty snap judgments.   Luke 22:33
James and John lack a team spirit and are
prone to be hotheads.   Matthew 20:20–21, Luke 9:54
Thomas will miss meetings and is a skeptic.
Simon is a left-wing political zealot
who would fight constantly with Matthew,
an establishment tax collector
currently under investigation by our bureau.
The only candidate you should retain
is the highly motivated and competitive
Judas Iscariot.   (Inspired by similar accounts)

What do I think Jesus was looking for most
in those he chose to be his twelve apostles?

*[God said,] "I do not judge as people judge.
They look at the outward appearance,
but I look at the heart."*   1 Samuel 16:7

A blind beggar named Bartimaeus . . .
began to shout, "Jesus! Son of David!
Have mercy on me!"
Many people scolded him
and told him to be quiet.
But he shouted even more loudly. . . .
Jesus stopped and said, "Call him." . . .
"Teacher," the blind man answered,
"I want to see again." "Go," answered Jesus,
"your faith has made you well."
At once he was able to see.   Mark 10:46–49, 51–52

The rabbi of Wikowo said to his son,
"Give an offering to that blind beggar."
The boy did so, but he did not tip his hat,
a custom used to show respect.
The rabbi questioned his son,
"Why did thee fail to tip thy hat in respect?"
The boy said,
"Because he's blind, Father, and cannot see."
The rabbi responded,
"Maybe he's an impostor and can see.
In any event, go back and tip thy hat."
Adapted from a story by Moshe Hakotum

If I were the rabbi's son,
how would I interpret my father's action?
What application might it have for me today?

Wherever you see another, there I am.
       Rabbinical saying concerning God

Jesus said, "Have faith in God . . .
and you will be given
whatever you ask for." Mark 11:22, 24

James Murdoch spent three weeks
in the White House as the guest
of President Abraham Lincoln.
One night, before the Battle of Bull Run,
Murdoch couldn't sleep.
Suddenly he heard moaning.
He went to see what it was. He writes:
"I saw the President
kneeling beside an open window.
His back was toward me. . . .
Then he cried out
in tones so pleading and sorrowful:
'O thou God that heard Solomon
on the night when he prayed for wisdom,
hear me; I cannot lead this people,
I cannot guide the affairs of this nation
without thy help.
I am poor, and weak, and sinful.
O God! . . . hear me and save this nation.'"
Emanuel Hertz, ed., *Lincoln Talks: A Biography in Anecdote*

Can I recall a time when I prayed from
the depths of my being, as Lincoln did here?

Prayer is an expression of who we are. . . .
We are a living incompleteness . . .
that calls for fulfillment. Thomas Merton

[Jesus asked some Jewish leaders
where John's right to baptize came from.
They caucused and said,]
"If we answer, 'From God,' he will say,
'Why, then, did you not believe John?'
But if we say, 'From human beings . . .'
[John's followers will be angry with us,"
so they said,] "We don't know."

Mark 11:31–33

"You've got to have the goods, my boy,
If you would finish strong;
A bluff may work a little while,
But not for very long;
A line of talk all by itself
Will seldom see you thru;
You've got to have the goods, my boy,
And nothing else will do.
The fight is pretty stiff, my boy,
I'd call it rather tough,
And all along the routes are wrecks
Of those who tried to bluff—
They could not back their lines of talk,
To meet the final test.
You've got to have the goods, my boy,
And that's no idle jest."   Author unknown

How "up front" am I in my dealings?

The hardest thing to hide
is something that is not there.   Eric Hoffer

*Jesus said, "Not everyone who calls me
'Lord, Lord' will enter the Kingdom of heaven,
but only those who do what my Father
in heaven wants them to do."* Matthew 7:21

Saint Ignatius of Loyola founded the Jesuits,
who run nearly 30 universities and
50 high schools in the United States alone.
Ignatius was born in Spain
just before the discovery of America.
Orphaned at age 16,
he eventually entered the military.
During a battle, a cannonball shattered
his right leg and changed his life forever.
Perhaps he is best known for his book
The Spiritual Exercises of Saint Ignatius.
A memorable prayer from the book reads:
"Take, Lord, and receive
all my liberty, my memory,
my understanding, and my entire will—
all that I have and call my own.
You have given it all to me.
To you, Lord, I return it.
Everything is yours, to do with what you will.
Give me only your love and your grace.
That is enough for me."

Why do I find this prayer hard to pray?

*[Jesus prayed to his Father,] "Not my will . . .
but your will be done."* Luke 22:42

MONDAY
WEEK 9 _____ ORDINARY TIME

Jesus said,
"Surely you have read this scripture?
'The stone which the builders
rejected as worthless turned out to be
the most important of all.' " Mark 12:10

Zane Grey, famous author of Western novels,
practiced dentistry in New York
before becoming a full-time writer.
One of his earliest literary attempts
was called *Riders of the Purple Sage.*
After reviewing it, a New York publisher
called it junk and told him to quit writing
and stick with filling teeth. Grey took it
to another publisher, who bought it
and parlayed it into a million copies.
In similar scenarios, Louisa May Alcott,
celebrated author of *Little Women,*
led an early life of dire poverty.
Actress Lucille Ball was paralyzed
in a car accident
and never expected to walk again.

What is one obstacle I have had to battle
in my life? With what results?

For every hill I've had to climb . . .
For all the blood and sweat and grime . . .
My heart sings but a grateful song—
These were things that made me strong.
                                    Anonymous

[Some Pharisees tried to trap Jesus
by asking him if it was lawful to pay taxes
to the emperor. Jesus foiled their plot.
Asking them for a Roman coin, he said,]
"Whose face and name are these?"
"The Emperor's," they answered. . . .
Jesus said, "Well, then, pay to the Emperor
what belongs to the Emperor,
and pay to God what belongs to God."

Mark 12:16–17

Tip O'Neill served 34 years in Congress.
On the wall of his office
hung these words from the last speech
that Hubert Humphrey
(Vice President under Johnson) ever gave:
        "The moral test of government
                is how it treats
                those who are
        in the dawn of life, the children;
                those who are
        in the twilight of life, the aged;
                and those who are
                in the shadows of life,
        the sick, the needy, and the handicapped."

How do I evaluate our government
by this test? How do I evaluate myself?

From now on, any definition of a successful
life must include serving others. George Bush

228

WEDNESDAY
WEEK 9 _____ ORDINARY TIME

Some Sadducees, who say that people
will not rise from death, came to Jesus
[and made fun of his teaching
about a life after this life]. . . .
Jesus answered them,
"How wrong you are! . . . Haven't you
ever read in the Book of Moses . . . ?
There it is written that God said to Moses,
'I am the God of Abraham, the God of Isaac,
and the God of Jacob.'
He is the God of the living, not of the dead.
You are completely wrong!"   Mark 12:18, 24, 26–27

After reflecting on Jesus' teaching
about our resurrection to a new life,
William Jennings Bryan said:
"If the invisible germ of life in the grain
of wheat can pass unimpaired
through three thousand resurrections,
I shall not doubt that my soul has power
to clothe itself with a body
suited to its new existence when
this earthly frame has crumbled into dust."

Apart from Jesus' teaching, what are
some reasons why it is appropriate
that there be a life after this one?

We are not completely born
until we are dead.
  Benjamin Franklin (slightly adapted)

THURSDAY
ORDINARY TIME _____ WEEK 9

Jesus said,
" 'Love the Lord your God
with all your heart,
with all your soul, and
with all your mind.' "   Mark 12:30

Fifteen-year-old Therese Martin
entered the Carmelite convent in France.
From the day she entered,
she dreamed of doing "great" things for God.
The years passed without her dream
being even remotely realized.
Naturally, she was disappointed.
Then one day she was reading Saint Paul,
where he says the "best" way to holiness
is not doing "great" things for God,
but "loving" things.   1 Corinthians 12:31–13:13
After reading this, she wrote in her journal:
"O Jesus . . . at last I have found my calling:
my calling is to love."

This episode in the life
of Saint Therese of Lisieux
invites me to ask,
What are some of the loving things
that I have done for God in the past week?
In the past twenty-four hours?

We cannot do great things,
only small things with great love.
                          Mother Teresa

FRIDAY
WEEK 9 _____ ORDINARY TIME

Jesus said,
"The Holy Spirit inspired David to say:
'The Lord said to my Lord:
Sit here at my right side. . . .'
[After saying this, Jesus asked,
"If David called the Messiah] 'Lord' . . .
how can the Messiah
be David's descendant?"   Mark 12:36–37

Jesus does not imply
that the Messiah isn't David's descendant.
Rather, he affirms that
the Messiah transcends human descent.
The Greek word for "Lord"
that Jesus uses is *kurios.*
Greeks reserved it for *God.*
In other words,
Jesus affirms that the Messiah is both
the "Son of Man" and the "Son of God."
He is both
David's descendant and David's Lord.

What convinces me most that Jesus
is both "Son of Man" and "Son of God"?

What greater grace
could God have made to dawn on us
than to make his only Son
become son of man,
so that a son of man might in turn
become son of God?   Saint Augustine

[Seeing a poor widow drop into the Temple
treasury a few small coins, Jesus said,
"She gave more] than all the others. . . .
She gave all she had to live on."   Mark 12:43–44

Eric Zorn, a *Chicago Tribune* columnist,
couldn't believe what he saw.
Dennis Dunn, dressed in a blue sport coat
and holding a coffee can, was begging
money from winos on Chicago's West Side.
Dunn explained that he was working
for Making Choices, a prison ministry
that provides guidance and social support
for youth released from a detention center.
To get to meetings, the youth have to cross
gang boundaries. The ministry needed a van
to pick them up. Most of the funds
came from suburbanites,
but Dunn thought people in the area
wanted to feel a part of the ministry.
"A waitress at Edna's Soul Food Restaurant . . .
emptied her tip apron. . . . A guy with his bottle
in a bag tossed in a pair of dimes."
Dunn said, "No matter what you've heard . . .
these neighborhoods are filled with people
who care." Even the winos. Unbelievable.

What two things in this story spoke to me?

As the purse is emptied the heart is filled.
                                      Victor Hugo

*[Some Pharisees criticized Jesus for eating
with outcasts. Jesus responded,]*
*"People who are well do not need a doctor,
but only those who are sick. Go and
find out what is meant by the scripture . . .
'It is kindness that I want,
not animal sacrifices.' "*   Matthew 9:12–13

McCall's magazine asked Eleanor Roosevelt,
wife of President Franklin D. Roosevelt,
about her philosophy of life. She responded:
"I have a few ideas
that I think are useful to me.
One is that you do whatever comes your way
as well as you can, and another is that you
think as little as possible of yourself and
as much as possible about other people. . . .
The third is that you get joy
out of giving to others and should put
a good deal of thought into the happiness
that you are able to give."

Is my attitude toward people
closer to that of Jesus, the Pharisees,
or Eleanor Roosevelt?

*Treat people as if they were
what they ought to be,
and you will help them to become
what they are capable of being.*
        Johann Wolfgang von Goethe

*Jesus said, "Happy are those
who work for peace; God will call them
his children!"* Matthew 5:9

A few months after the Gulf War,
a *New York Times* story reported that
General Norman Schwarzkopf's video
Desert Storm was such a hit
that a publishing company bid $5 million
for the right to publish his memoirs.
The same edition of the *Times*
reported on the poverty in postwar Iraq.
An accompanying photograph
showed a child in a blanket,
limbs withered and body emaciated.
The child was one of countless infants
brought to hospitals by Iraqi mothers
who could not afford the $50 for a can
(three-day supply) of baby formula.

Petrarch listed the five great enemies
of peace as avarice, ambition,
envy, anger, and pride.
Which of these do I, perhaps,
need to keep a special personal check on?

*A day will come when a canon
will be exhibited in museums,
just as instruments of torture are now,
and people will be astonished that
such a thing could have existed.* Victor Hugo

TUESDAY
WEEK 10 _____ ORDINARY TIME

Jesus said,
"Your light must shine before people,
so that they will see the good things you do
and praise your Father in heaven."

Matthew 5:16

Mohandas Gandhi won independence
for India with his enlightened strategy
of nonviolent, passive resistance.
Gandhi also worked tirelessly to bring
the light of hope to India's untouchables,
the downtrodden people of Hindu society.
One day he was boarding a moving train.
One of his shoes slipped off and fell
on the track. To the amazement of those
around him, he quickly removed
the other shoe and threw it back
along the track, close to the other one.
When asked why he did this, he said,
"The poor man who finds the shoe
lying along the track will now have a pair."
Gandhi's whole life was one of letting
the light of his great soul shine on others.

To what extent do I let the light of my soul
shine forth into the world, especially
to light the way for those in darkness?

Holy men and women serve this world
by reflecting in it the light of another.

John W. Donohue

Jesus said, "Whoever obeys the Law
and teaches others to do the same,
will be great in the Kingdom of heaven."
Matthew 5:19

Author Jerome Weidman attended
a public school on New York's East Side.
He had a third grade math teacher
named Mrs. O'Neill. One day when she was
grading test papers, she noticed that
12 students had given the same odd wrong
answer to a question. The next day she asked
the 12 students to stay after the dismissal
bell. Then without accusing any of them,
she wrote 18 words on the chalkboard:
"The measure of our real character
is what we would do
if we would never be found out."
She then added the name of the person
who said them: Thomas Babington Macaulay.
Weidman said later: "I don't know about
the other 11 students. Speaking for only one
of the dozen with whom I am on intimate
terms, I can say this: it was the most
important single lesson of my life."

Can I recall an important lesson
that someone taught me in my youth?

Don't compromise yourself.
You are all you've got. Janis Joplin

THURSDAY
WEEK 10 _____ ORDINARY TIME

Jesus said, "You have heard . . .
'Do not commit murder. . . .' I tell you:
if you are angry with your brother
you will be brought to trial. . . .
So if you are about to offer your gift to God
at the altar and there you remember that
your brother has something against you,
leave your gift there in front of the altar,
go at once and make peace
with your brother, and then come back
and offer your gift to God."   Matthew 5:21–24

In *War As I Knew It,* General Patton writes:
"The first Sunday I spent in Normandy . . .
I went to a Catholic Field Mass
where all of us were armed.
As we knelt in the mud in a slight drizzle,
we could . . . hear the roar of the guns,
and the whole sky was filled with airplanes
on their missions of destruction . . .
quite at variance with the teachings
of the religion we were practicing."

How might Jesus respond
to Patton's point?

Never think that war,
no matter how necessary,
nor how justified, is not a crime.
Ask the infantry and ask the dead.
Ernest Hemingway

Jesus said, "If your right eye
causes you to sin . . . throw it away!
It is much better for you to lose a part
of your body than to have your whole body
thrown into hell." Matthew 5:29

A young couple got a delightful surprise
in the mail: two theater tickets
to a popular musical on Sunday night.
A note in the envelope was signed,
"Guess who? You'll find out Sunday night."
So the couple prepared for a fun night,
expecting some friend
to join them at the theater
and take them to dinner afterward.
They enjoyed the show immensely,
but their "secret donor" didn't show.
When they got home, they were shocked.
Their wedding gifts and apartment were rifled.
A note read, "Now you know who!"

Jesus had in mind people like that thief
when he said if your eye—or whatever—
tempts you to sin (e.g., steal), it is better
to throw it away than for your entire body
to be lost for all eternity.
How do I handle temptations to sin?

Jesus can help those who are tempted,
because he himself was tempted
and suffered. Hebrews 2:18

SATURDAY
WEEK 10 _____ ORDINARY TIME

[Speaking of oaths, Jesus said,]
"Just say 'Yes' or 'No'—
anything else you say
comes from the Evil One."   Matthew 5:37

A mother tells this story.
Her friend Kay was a stickler for demanding
that her children tell the truth.
One day when Kay was busy, the phone rang.
Kay's little daughter answered and yelled,
"Mommy! It's for you. It's that lady
who talks a lot." Kay yelled back,
"I'm too busy to talk to her right now.
Tell her I just stepped out."
Suddenly Kay realized what she was doing.
She apologized repentantly to her daughter
and took the call.

Early on in history,
"oath taking" became necessary
because of the sinfulness
of the human race.
In today's gospel reading, Jesus tells
the people to cultivate a truthfulness
that makes "oath taking" unnecessary.
How faithful am I to this teaching of Jesus?

The liar's punishment
is not in the least that he is not believed,
but that he cannot believe anyone else.
                              George Bernard Shaw

*Jesus said, "Pray to the owner of the harvest
that he will send out workers
to gather in his harvest."* Matthew 9:38

In Alan Paton's *Cry, the Beloved Country,*
someone thanks a preacher for his kindness
and says, "You are a good man."
The preacher says, "No,
I'm just a weak, sinful man, but the Lord
has laid his hand on me, and that is all."
Commenting on the preacher's response,
Father John Eagan, S.J., writes
in *A Traveller Toward the Dawn,*
"To me that says it all.
The Lord has laid his hands on me,
and that is all.
When I was a freshman at Campion . . .
in the first closed retreat of my life,
unexpectedly God broke through to me
personally and touched my life deeply.
I can remember the day clearly
and . . . I thank God for his gift.
I'll never understand it."

Have I ever felt the hand of God laid on me?
What do I understand by the expression
"the hand of God laid on me"?

*Why not let Jesus take over my life?
He can do more with it than I can.*
Anonymous

MONDAY
WEEK 11 _____ ORDINARY TIME

Jesus said,
"You have heard that it was said,
'An eye for an eye,
and a tooth for a tooth.'
But now I tell you: do not take revenge
on someone who wrongs you." Matthew 5:38–39

Frank Harris III
wrote in the *Chicago Tribune:*
"As America's darker citizens,
we have plenty of 'opportunities' to hate.
Hate is, after all, one of the few things
that African-Americans have had
more 'opportunity' to experience
than our white countrymen."
Then Harris
turned an important corner, saying:
"Hate is blinding, not visionary.
Hate is draining, not fulfilling.
Hate is destructive, not constructive. . . .
Hate is wasted passion
that can deny us the vision and strength
to construct a positive plan
toward achieving . . . full equality.
That is why we must not hate."

How do I deal constructively
with my feelings of hate?

Hate is like burning down your house
to get rid of a rat. Harry Emerson Fosdick

Jesus said, "You have heard that it was said,
'Love your friends, hate your enemies.'
But now I tell you: love your enemies."

Matthew 5:43–44

Abraham Lincoln succeeded Buchanan
as president in 1861.
Ed Stanton, a member of Buchanan's cabinet,
disdained Lincoln. He ridiculed him publicly,
calling him the "original gorilla."
A year into the presidency,
Lincoln had to replace his Secretary of War.
He chose Stanton, explaining,
"I know the terrible things he said about me.
But he's the best man for the job."
Shortly after Lee surrendered to Grant,
Lincoln was assassinated.
One of the first public officials to reach
Lincoln's side was Stanton.
When Lincoln breathed his last,
Stanton said with heartfelt sincerity,
"There lies the world's greatest ruler.
Now he belongs to the ages."

How do I respond to ridicule?
What keeps me from responding
as Lincoln did?

Without love and compassion for others,
our own apparent love for Christ is fiction.

Thomas Merton

WEDNESDAY
WEEK 11 _____ ORDINARY TIME

*Jesus said, "When you help a needy person,
do it in such a way that even your closest friend
will not know about it."* Matthew 6:3

The *New York Times* ran this amazing story.
Tammie Murphy, donations clerk
at St. Jude's Children's Research Hospital
in Memphis,
gets about 700 donation envelopes daily.
One day she opened a plain envelope with
no return address. Inside was a McDonald's
Monopoly Sweepstakes card.
It showed a $1 million "Instant Winner."
The hospital called McDonald's.
Officials came with a representative
of the Arthur Andersen accounting firm.
After checking the card with
a jeweler's eyepiece, he declared it a winner.
McDonald's and St. Jude officials agreed
to respect the donor's apparent desire
to remain anonymous.
They made no effort to find out who it was.
Later, the *Reader's Digest* ran the story
in the magazine's feature "Heroes for Today."

When was the last time I gave generously—
and anonymously—to a good cause?

*It is possible to give without loving,
but it is impossible to love without giving.*
Richard Brounstein

Jesus said,
"This, then, is how you should pray:
'Our Father in heaven.' "   Matthew 6:9

In his book *God Calling*, A. J. Russell
has God ask the reader this question:
"Have you ever thought what it means
to be able to summon at will
the God of the World?"
God goes on to say
that even important people
cannot visit a head of state
with such freedom of access.
They must make an appointment
well in advance. Then God says:
"But to My subjects I have given the right
to enter My Presence when they will.
Nay more, they can summon Me
to bedside, to workshop—and I am there.
Could Divine Love do more?"

How deeply do I appreciate being able
to summon God to my side, wherever I am,
at any time of the day or night
without having to make an appointment?

Before the judgment seat
one the most embarrassing things
that we will have to answer for
will be our lack of prayer—
one of God's greatest gifts to us.   Anonymous

FRIDAY
Week 11 _____ Ordinary Time

Jesus said, "The eyes are like a lamp
for the body. If your eyes are sound,
your whole body will be full of light;
but if your eyes are no good,
your body will be in darkness.
So if the light in you is darkness,
how terribly dark it will be!"   Matthew 6:22–23

Gladys Campbell keeps a copy of Sallman's
Portrait of Christ in her bedroom.
It's next to her dressing table. She explains,
"Each morning when I put on my contact
lenses, I look over at the face of Jesus.
If it is fuzzy and blurred,
I know my contact lenses are in wrong.
But if Jesus' face is clear and distinct,
I know they're in right."

It would be great if each day we could
put on spiritual contact lenses
that would allow us to see the face of Jesus
more clearly and distinctly. When Jesus' face
becomes blurred in my spiritual vision,
how do I go about making it clear again?

The holiest men and women still need Christ
as their Prophet, as "the light of the world."
For he does not give them light
but from moment to moment;
the instant he withdraws, all is darkness.
                              John Wesley

Jesus said, "Look at the birds:
they do not plant seeds,
gather a harvest and put it in barns;
yet your Father in heaven
takes care of them!
Aren't you worth much more than birds?"

Matthew 6:26

The Manx shearwater, a small bird,
makes its home in tiny holes in a cliff
on an island off the coast of Wales.
A researcher caught a shearwater,
put a band on its leg,
and had it flown 3,000 miles to Boston.
There his colleague released it.
Twelve and a half days later,
the bird showed up
at the same tiny hole
from which it had been taken.
Scientists still can't figure out
how these birds have acquired
such a remarkable power of navigation.

What message might the shearwater hold
for me personally? Why?

We pledge allegiance to the planet
and all the people on it;
to the sea and to all that swims within it;
to the sky and all that soars across it.

Anonymous

SUNDAY
WEEK 12 _____ ORDINARY TIME

*Jesus said, "Those who declare publicly
that they belong to me, I will do the same
for them before my Father in heaven.
But those who reject me publicly,
I will reject before my Father in heaven."*
                                    Matthew 10:32–33

Tip O'Neill was a member of
the House of Representatives for 34 years.
In the memoirs of his political life,
Tip says that he'll never forget
a day in Missouri in 1960
when he was with Jack Kennedy
in a campaign parade. He writes:
"Somebody mentioned that
in the neighborhood
we were driving through
there was a good deal of concern
over the Catholic issue.
Then we passed a Catholic school,
with all the nuns standing outside,
holding their Kennedy signs.
'Stop the car,' said Jack. He got out
and shook hands with all the sisters,
and I loved him for it."

How ready am I to do what I think is right,
even if it means risking my popularity?

*Who sells principles for popularity
is soon bankrupt.*   E. C. McKenzie (slightly adapted)

Ordinary Time _____

Jesus said, "God will judge you
in the same way you judge others,
and he will apply to you the same rules
you apply to others." Matthew 7:2

A woman played back her answering
machine. One call was from a teacher
who requested her to call concerning
her son's irresponsible behavior.
The teacher left no number
so that the woman couldn't let her know
that she had misdialed the call.
A day later another misdialed call
informed "Bob" of a schedule change
in an important business meeting.
Again no number was left. The woman
wondered what impact these two mistakes
would have on the people involved.
Would the teacher erroneously judge
that the mother didn't care enough
to return the call?
Would Bob's boss draw the conclusion
that Bob was irresponsible?

How prone am I
to jump to conclusions and, perhaps,
make judgments
that could cause grave harm to others?

A person's judgment is no better
than his information. Anonymous

TUESDAY
Week 12 _____ Ordinary Time

Jesus said, "God will judge you
in the same way you judge others. . . .
How dare you say . . .
'Please, let me take that speck
out of your eye,' when you have a log
in your own eye?"   Matthew 7:2, 4

"My son took a 'vacation' from Mass.
One day I asked him when he planned
to return. Without hesitation he said,
'When you quit smoking.'
I was shocked, but recovered enough
to reply, 'Will you give me a month
to work at it?' He graciously agreed.
I quit just before Christmas.
But my motherly instinct told me
not to push him on keeping his end
of the bargain. So I didn't 'bug' him.
Yet I wondered if he had kept it.
Last Sunday he told me a story.
I said, 'Where'd you read that?'
He said, 'Father told it at Mass today.'
I was so proud of him,
I could hardly hold back the tears."
Mother to the author

Am I as critical with myself as I am
with others, especially loved ones?

If we tap the best in ourselves,
we will bring out the best in others.

Jesus said, "Any tree
that does not bear good fruit
is cut down and thrown in the fire."

Matthew 7:19

At one point in the movie story *The Alamo,*
"showdown time" comes and
the defenders have to vote their consciences.
John Wayne stands up and says:
"Now I might sound like a Bible-beater
yelling up a revival
at a river-crossing camp-meeting,
but that don't change the truth none.
There's right and there's wrong.
You gotta do one or the other.
You do the one and you're living.
You do the other,
and you may be walking around
but you're dead as a beaver hat."

Can I recall a time in my life
when "showdown time" came
and I had to choose
between the hard right and the easy wrong?

Who can separate his faith from his actions,
or his belief from his occupation?
Who can spread his hours before him, saying:
"This is for God and this for myself. . . ."
He who wears his morality but as
his best garment were better naked.   Kahlil Gibran

THURSDAY
WEEK 12 _____ ORDINARY TIME

*Jesus said, "Not everyone who calls me
'Lord, Lord' will enter the Kingdom
of heaven, but only those who do
what my Father . . . wants them to do."*

Matthew 7:21

In *American Way* magazine a cartoon
by W. B. Park shows a man in his fifties
dressed in a baseball suit and hat.
He is seated in an easy chair.
Resting against one side of the chair
are a baseball bat and glove.
On the other side of the chair is a table
with a telephone on it.
Across from the man sits his wife.
She wears a patient but frustrated look.
The caption reads:
"I don't want to step on your dream, Walter,
but if they haven't called after thirty years,
perhaps it's time to go on to something else."
That cartoon makes a good point.
There's a time to dream,
but there's also a time to face up to reality
and assume responsibility for your life.

In what area of my life might I be failing
to assume the kind of responsibility
that I know God wants me to assume?

*You can't steal second base
and keep your foot on first.* Frederick R. Wilcox

[A leper approached Jesus, saying,] "Sir,
if you want to, you can make me clean."
Jesus reached out and touched him.
"I do want to," he answered. "Be clean!"
At once the man was healed.   Matthew 8:2–3

Evidence is mounting
to show that when hands are placed
on sick people with a desire to heal them,
their recovery rate improves.
One explanation for this amazing fact is
that the loving touch of loving people
releases within a sick person
an energy that promotes healing.
If this explanation is correct, and
if Jesus is God, and if God is love—
infinite love—then the touch of Jesus
could not help but release in a person
an enormous healing energy.
It would have been a "miracle"
if the people he touched
had *not* been healed.

How easily do I reach out in a loving way
to pat the head of a sick person,
to wipe the tears of a child,
to show affection for a family member?

[God said,] "My saving power
will rise on you like the sun and
bring healing like the sun's rays.   Malachi 4:2

SATURDAY
WEEK 12 _____ ORDINARY TIME

[When Jesus offered to go to the home
of a Roman officer to heal his servant,
the officer said,] "Just give the order,
and my servant will get well. . . ."
When Jesus heard this, he was surprised
and said to the people following him,
"I tell you, I have never found anyone
in Israel with faith like this." Matthew 8:8, 10

Alexander the Great headed up
the largest empire ever ruled by one man.
According to an ancient story,
he became gravely ill one day and called
a doctor who had attended him for years.
Just before the doctor arrived,
Alexander was handed a note
warning him that the doctor
had been bribed to poison him.
When the doctor arrived, he poured out
a liquid for Alexander to drink.
After drinking it,
Alexander gave the note to the doctor.
It was an incredible gesture of faith.

Jesus' words and Alexander's faith
invite me to inventory my faith—
not in a mere man, but in God's own Son.
How can I strengthen it?

It is love that makes faith, not faith love.
John Henry Newman

Jesus said, "You can be sure that
whoever gives even a drink of cold water
to one of the least of these my followers
because he is my follower,
will certainly receive a reward."   Matthew 10:42

A brutal scene in Victor Hugo's novel
Notre Dame of Paris shows Quasi Modo,
the hunchback, chained to a wheel
and being scourged before a huge mob.
As blood flows from his wounds,
he calls out pathetically for water.
The mob responds by jeering him and pelting
him with stones. Suddenly, a little girl
with a gourd of water in her hand
pushes through the crowd
and gives him a drink.
The girl's loving action makes him do
what his torturers could not do.
A tear rolls down his cheek.

What do I imagine went on in the minds
of Quasi Modo and the mob as they watched
the little girl's compassionate act?

Yours are the only hands
with which God can do his work. . . .
Yours are the only eyes
through which God's compassion
can shine upon a troubled world.
Saint Teresa of Avila

MONDAY
WEEK 13 _____ ORDINARY TIME

[A man wanted to follow Jesus, but delayed,
saying,] "First let me go back and bury
my father." "Follow me," Jesus answered,
"and let the dead bury their own dead."

Matthew 8:21–22

A decision to leave all and follow Jesus is
the most important one we will ever make.
It means leaving family and friends
and following wherever Jesus leads us.
Making such a decision can create a crisis.
Doubts can arise: Is it the right choice?
Maybe I should delay making it for a while.
Such temptations to "second guess"
or delay are not unusual.
In *Reveille for Radicals,* Saul Alinsky notes
that the Chinese word for "crisis" is written
with two symbols. The first is the symbol
for "danger"; the second, for "opportunity."
A "crisis" is a "dangerous opportunity."
It's a time for decisiveness, not dallying.
It's a time for looking forward, not backward.

What decision about Jesus should I ponder?

[Before making a decision]
recall the face of the poorest,
most helpless person you have ever seen,
and ask yourself
if the step you contemplate will be
of any use to that person.   Mohandas Gandhi

Jesus got into a boat,
and his disciples went with him.
Suddenly a fierce storm hit the lake,
and the boat was in danger of sinking.
But Jesus was asleep.
The disciples went to him and woke him up.
"Save us, Lord!" they said.
"We are about to die!"   Matthew 8:23–25

At about two o'clock in the afternoon
of March 7, 1915, the *Lusitania* was sunk
by a German submarine off the Irish coast.
Nearly 1,200 people died. A year later,
a British sailor saw a corked bottle
bobbing up and down in the North Atlantic.
It contained a message from the *Lusitania,*
written just before it sank.
The message read:
"Still on deck with a few people.
The last boats have left.
We are sinking fast.
The orchestra is still playing bravely.
Some men near me are praying with a priest.
The end is near. Maybe this note . . ."
At that point the note stopped.

What aspect of this story struck me most?
What message might it hold for me?

Death is not a period,
but a comma in the story of life.   E. C. McKenzie

WEDNESDAY
WEEK 13 _____ ORDINARY TIME

[Jesus expelled demons from two men.
The demons entered some pigs,
causing them to leap into the sea.
Disturbed by these events, the people]
begged Jesus to leave their territory.

Matthew 8:34

Early Christmas Eve 1986,
Apollo 8 began its flight around the moon.
On the third orbit
Colonel Frank Borman radioed
this Christmas prayer back to earth:
"Give us, O God, the vision
that we can see love in the world
in spite of human failure.
Give us the faith to trust Thy goodness
in spite of our ignorance and weakness.
Give us the knowledge
that we may continue to pray
with understanding hearts,
and show us what each one of us can do
to set forward the coming
of the day of universal peace. Amen."

In spite of disappointments—
like the one in today's gospel—
Jesus never lost the spirit expressed
in Borman's prayer. How about me?

Keep a green tree in your heart and perhaps
the singing birds will come.   Chinese proverb

[One day Jesus told a paralyzed man,]
"Your sins are forgiven." Then some
teachers of the Law said to themselves,
"This man is speaking blasphemy!"
Jesus perceived what they were thinking,
and so he said, "Why are you thinking
such evil things?"   Matthew 9:2–4

President Truman prayed this prayer
regularly throughout his entire life:
"O Almighty and Everlasting God,
Creator of Heaven, Earth, and the Universe.
Help me to be, to think, to act what is right,
because it is right; make me truthful,
honest, and honorable in all things;
make me intellectually honest,
for the sake of right and honor
and without thought of reward to me.
Give me the ability to be charitable,
forgiving, and patient with my fellowmen—
help me to understand their motives
and their shortcomings—even as Thou
understandest mine! Amen, Amen, Amen."

What is one prayer I pray regularly?

He prayeth best who loveth best
All things both great and small;
For the dear Lord, who loveth us,
He made and loveth all.

            Samuel Taylor Coleridge

FRIDAY
WEEK 13 _____ ORDINARY TIME

[Some Pharisees criticized Jesus
for eating with sinners. Jesus replied,]
"I have not come to call respectable people,
but outcasts." Matthew 9:13

Presidential aide Charles Colson
was sent to prison for his role
in the Watergate scandal.
Speaking to 900 prisoners in Atlanta,
Colson said bluntly,
"Jesus Christ came into this world
for the poor, the sick, the hungry,
the homeless, the imprisoned.
He is the Prophet of the loser.
And all of us assembled here are losers.
I am a loser just like every one of you.
The miracle is that God's message
is specifically for those of us
who have failed." Charles Colson, *Life Sentence*
Once out of prison,
Colson set up the Prison Fellowship Program,
which involves 1,200 volunteers
and reaches into 500 prisons.

Which of the following groups
do I help most and least and why:
the poor, the sick, the hungry,
the homeless, the imprisoned?

I am truly poor, not when I have nothing,
but when I do nothing. Anonymous

Jesus said, "No one patches up an old coat
with a piece of new cloth,
for the new patch will shrink and make
an even bigger hole in the coat." Matthew 9:16

A cowhand rode into a Western town.
After six drinks in a saloon, he went to
the local cinema to see *The Perils of Pauline.*
Just as he walked in, the movie villain
was pursuing the lovely, sweet Pauline.
The cowhand drew his gun
and emptied it into the villain on the screen.
The only thing he accomplished, however,
was to riddle the screen with holes.
Someone said later, "The cowhand's heart
was in the right place, but his strategy was
all wrong. If he wanted to stop the villain,
he should have shot the projector—
the source of the problem—not its shadow.

How flawed is my strategy for trying
to turn my life over to Jesus?
Am I, perhaps, focusing on the shadow,
not the source?

Starr Daily (a reformed criminal)
is the best living proof I've ever seen
that "a new creation in Jesus Christ"
is not just the old man patched up,
but an altogether new person
living in the same body. Peter Marshall

SUNDAY
WEEK 14 _____ ORDINARY TIME

Jesus said, "Learn from me,
because I am gentle and humble in spirit."
Matthew 11:29

One day the Welsh monk Saint Malo
decided to spend the day working outside.
Early on he began to perspire,
so he took off his coat and laid it aside.
At the end of the day,
when he went back to pick it up,
he discovered that a mother wren
had built a nest inside it.
The saint's gentleness
and his legendary respect for nature
left him no alternative but to leave his coat
in the field and not disturb the nest.
Some say the story is a pious legend.
Be that as it may,
it does have a modern parallel.
Some time ago, the newspapers reported
how a participant in a golf tournament
"let go his chance of winning,
because he would not play his ball
out of a thrush's nest."

These stories invite me to inventory
my gentleness and my respect for nature.

You can tell all you need to know
about a nation by the way it treats
animals and beaches. Frank Deford

[A woman said,] "If only I touch his cloak,
I will get well." Jesus turned around
and saw her, and said, "Courage, my daughter!
Your faith has made you well."
At that very moment
the woman became well.   Matthew 9:21–22

In *Miracles Do Happen,* Sister Briege McKenna
describes a healing service in Hawaii.
One of those present
was a Mormon girl with deformed hands.
At one point in the service, the priest
took the monstrance (housing the sacred host)
and blessed the people. The Mormon girl
did not fully understand Catholic teaching
on the Eucharist, but she knew
that her Catholic friend who brought her
believed Jesus was truly present in it.
So she looked at the sacred host and
asked Jesus to lessen the pain in her hands.
At that moment
she felt something enter her body.
It left her hands totally healed.

How deep is my faith in the Eucharist?
What is the purpose of miracles?

For those who believe in God,
no explanation is needed;
for those who do not believe in God,
no explanation is possible.   Author unknown

[Jesus went from town to town teaching.]
As he saw the crowds,
his heart was filled with pity . . .
because they were . . .
like sheep without a shepherd.
So he said to his disciples, "The harvest
is large, but there are few workers
to gather it in."   Matthew 9:36–37

Sherry Lansing is the most powerful woman
in the movie industry. She is chairwoman
of Paramount Pictures and has worked
on such classic films as *Chariots of Fire,*
The China Syndrome, and *Fatal Attraction.*
Sherry credits her mother for her success.
After Sherry's dad died of a heart attack,
her mother took over the family business.
Sherry still remembers an office manager
saying to her mother, "But you can't do this.
You know nothing about the business."
Her mother said, "I can do it! Teach me."

People in Jesus' time—and people today—
hunger for Jesus' message of hope,
but there are few willing to teach them.
How do I explain the unwillingness of people
to teach others about this message?
How willing am I?

Jesus said,
"Listen, then, if you have ears!"   Mark 4:23

These are the names of the twelve apostles:
first, Simon (called Peter) and his brother
Andrew; James and his brother John,
the sons of Zebedee; Philip and Bartholomew;
Thomas and Matthew, the tax collector;
James son of Alphaeus, and Thaddaeus;
Simon the Patriot, and Judas Iscariot,
who betrayed Jesus. Matthew 10:2–4

The "call of Jesus"
resulted in a dramatic "career change"
for the twelve apostles. For example,
Matthew went from collecting taxes
to preaching the word of God.
This "career change" made him famous.
Many people since his time
have also become famous
as a result of a "career change."
Marilyn Monroe began work in a factory.
Dancer Josephine Baker began as a maid.
President Gerald Ford was a male model.
Comedian Bob Hope was a boxer.
Singer Perry Como was a barber.
TV's Johnny Carson was a magician.
Comedienne Carol Burnett was an usherette.

What was my first job or "profession"?
What "second profession" have I considered?

If at first you don't succeed,
you are running about average. M. H. Alderson

THURSDAY
WEEK 14 _____ ORDINARY TIME

Jesus said,
"You have received without paying,
so give without being paid." Matthew 10:8

In his book *What Is a Jew?*
Morris Kertzer says every Hebrew child
learns the story of Honi the traveler.
One day Honi met an old man
planting tiny fruit trees. He asked him,
"When will the trees bear fruit?"
The old man replied,
"Probably years after I am dead."
Honi said, "Why plant them, then,
if you'll never eat their fruit?"
The old man replied,
"I didn't find the world without trees
when I was born, so I plant them
for others, as they did for me."

If someone asked four of my friends to list
my virtues, why would/wouldn't they list
a "sense of service" as one of them?

I realize how much
my own inner and outer life
is built upon the labors of others,
both living and dead,
and how earnestly I must exert myself
in order to give in return
as much as I have received.
Albert Einstein (slightly adapted)

[Jesus told his apostles,] "I am sending
you out like sheep to a pack of wolves.
You must be as cautious as snakes
and as gentle as doves. . . .
Everyone will hate you because of me.
But whoever holds out to the end
will be saved."   Matthew 10:16, 22

Voltaire was a French philosopher and wit.
Often in trouble with authorities,
he was exiled to England in the early 1700s.
At that time anti-French feelings ran high.
One day Voltaire was surrounded
by an angry mob in London.
The people began shouting,
"Hang him! Hang the Frenchman!"
Pleading for silence, Voltaire cried out,
convincingly, "Men of England!
You wish to kill me because I am French.
Has not the good God punished me enough
by not letting me be born an Englishman?"
This delightful appeal tickled the mob
so much that they cheered Voltaire and
escorted him safely back to his dwelling.

How well do I keep my cool and respond
diplomatically when people say things
that make me fighting mad?

Every survival kit
should include a sense of humor.   F. C. McKenzie

SATURDAY
WEEK 14 _____ ORDINARY TIME

Jesus said,
"What I am telling you in the dark
you must repeat in broad daylight,
and what you have heard in private
you must announce from the housetops."

Matthew 10:27

A church property lay at a busy crossing.
Hardly five minutes passed
without drivers sitting in idling cars,
waiting for the light to turn green.
One day a parishioner got an idea
not only for lessening their boredom
but also for spreading the Gospel.
A sign was built to provide
both entertainment and "food for thought."
Each week a thought appears on it,
such as: "Your seat in eternity:
Will it be smoking or nonsmoking."

Anonymous

"If God loved us as much as we love God,
where would we all be?"   Anonymous

"Feeding the hungry is greater work
than raising the dead."   John Chrysostom

Can I think of a way we might preach
God's word more creatively? How?

Discovery consists in seeing what
everyone has seen and thinking what
nobody has thought.   Albert Szent-Gyorgyi

[Jesus said, "A farmer planted seed.
Some fell on the path and birds ate it.
Some fell on rocky soil, grew quickly,
but died when the sun baked the soil.]
Some of the seed fell among thorn bushes,
which grew up and choked the plants.
But some seeds fell in good soil." Matthew 13:7–8

A teacher explained that the seed
stood for God's word; the seedbeds,
for the four kinds of hearts
into which God's word can fall.
Then she asked the students to write down
(1) what seedbed their own heart is like,
(2) why it is like this, and
(3) how they might change their situation.
One boy wrote:
"My heart is most like the thorn bushes.
I hear God's word in church,
but I forget it as soon as I return home.
This is because my father is mentally sick,
which puts my family on edge. I don't know
what I can do to change my situation."

How would I respond to the boy?
What seedbed is my heart most like?
Why? How might I improve my situation?

[The Lord told Paul in prayer,] "My grace
is all you need, for my power is greatest
when you are weak." 2 Corinthians 12:9

MONDAY
WEEK 15 _____ ORDINARY TIME

Jesus said,
"Those who try to gain their own life
will lose it; but those who lose their life
for my sake will gain it." Matthew 10:39

The film *Mass Appeal* centers around
Father Tim Farley, pastor of Saint Francis.
His life is comfortable, his manner tactful,
and his sermons are cushioned
so as not to disturb his parishioners.
Then the roof falls in.
A seminarian named Mark Dodson
is assigned to Saint Francis.
He is just the opposite of Father Tim.
His blunt idealism rankles parishioners;
but his honesty and sincerity touch
a deep chord in Father Tim, who
protects him and works hard to help him.
One day Mark asks Father Tim
why he's doing this for him.
Father Tim replies, "Because you're a lunatic.
The Church needs lunatics,
and you are one of those priceless lunatics
that come along every so often
and make the Church alive."

How do I interpret Father Tim's point?

The more the world is at its worst,
the more we need the Church at its best.
Anonymous

*[Many people failed to repent their sins
and reform. Jesus warned them, saying,]
"Did you want to lift yourself up to heaven?
You will be thrown down to hell!"*

Matthew 11:23

Alexander Pope was a giant
in the literary world
of 18th-century England.
His *An Essay on Man* ponders
human nature and its role in our universe.
He concludes that we humans are
a strange mix of power and weakness,
and a baffling blend of knowledge and error.
Our predominant driving forces
are self-love and reason.
Self-love greatly determines what we do,
and reason restrains our impulses.
In an oft-quoted passage in his essay,
Pope sums us up in these poetic terms:
"Created half to rise, and half to fall;
Great lord of all things, yet a prey to all;
Sole judge of truth, in endless error hurled;
The glory, jest, and riddle of the world!"

How does Pope's conclusion about humans
support my need for Jesus and his mission?

*Character cannot be purchased, inherited,
rented, or imported from afar.
It must be homegrown.*   E. C. McKenzie

WEDNESDAY
WEEK 15 _____ ORDINARY TIME

[Jesus prayed,] "I thank you because you have shown to the unlearned what you have hidden from the wise." Matthew 11:25

An old rabbi went on a long journey,
taking with him three things:
a rooster to wake him early each day,
a donkey to carry him during the day,
a Bible to read each night.
The first day he came to a village,
but the unfriendly villagers drove him off.
He simply said, "God knows best."
That night he camped by the roadside
and lit a candle to read his Bible,
but the wind kept blowing it out.
He curled up behind a bush, saying,
"God knows best." An hour later, he awoke,
looked around, and discovered that someone
had taken his rooster and donkey.
Again, he said, "God knows best."
The next day he learned that during
the night, soldiers had slain the people
and seized all their property.
When the rabbi learned this,
he didn't have to say, "God knows best."

How does this story apply to me right now?

Behind the dim unknown,
Standeth God within the shadow,
keeping watch above his own. James Russell Lowell

Jesus said,
"Take my yoke and put it on you. . . .
For the yoke I will give you is easy,
and the load I will put on you is light."
                                      Matthew 11:29–30

Eleven-year-old Joe had a crooked back.
When his shirt was off as it was now,
it looked ugly. Joe hated his back.
The doctor examining Joe sensed
how the boy felt and did something unusual.
He cupped Joe's chin in his big hands,
looked gently into his eyes, and said, "Son,
do you believe in God?" Joe sputtered,
"Yes." "Good!" said the doctor.
"The more you believe in God,
the more you believe in yourself."
Then with Joe looking on, he wrote
on the chart under "Physical Characteristics":
"Joe has an unusually well-shaped head."
That moving episode taught Joe a lesson
he would never forget: If you believe in God
and focus on the *best* in yourself,
nothing can defeat you—nothing!

How deeply do I believe in God? In myself?
What is the "best" in myself,
and how well do I focus on it?

People are made by their beliefs.
As they believe, so they are.   Bhagavad Gita

FRIDAY
WEEK 15 _____ ORDINARY TIME

*Jesus said, " 'It is kindness that I want,
not animal sacrifices.' "*   Matthew 12:7

Anne Herbert was sitting in a restaurant
in Sausalito, California. Suddenly, she took
a pencil from her purse and wrote down
a phrase she'd been mulling over for days.
Now you see the phrase on bumper stickers,
business cards, and at the bottom of letters.
One woman saw it spray-painted
on a warehouse 100 miles from her home.
When she got home, she tried to recall it
to write it down, but it wasn't quite right.
So she drove all the way back to copy it.
The phrase that appeals to so many reads:
"Practice random kindness
and senseless acts of beauty."
Anne believes that "random kindness"
can trigger a tidal wave of good in the world,
just as "random violence" triggers evil.
Maybe that's why the phrase is so popular.
It touches something deep in the heart;
it appeals to the very best in us.

What "random kindness" or
"senseless act of beauty"
might I recklessly "commit" today?

*Like all revolutions, guerrilla goodness
begins slowly, with a single act.
Let it be yours.*   *Glamour* magazine

[Jesus fulfilled what Isaiah foretold:]
"He will not break off a bent reed,
nor put out a flickering lamp."

Matthew 12:20

A mother had just attended a lecture
on the importance of dealing creatively,
compassionately, and affirmatively
with children. A few days later,
her son's report card arrived in the mail.
She opened it and was shocked to find
that it contained 3 Ds and 2 Fs.
With a card like that, she wondered,
how can I deal creatively, compassionately,
and affirmatively with my son, Jason?
Then she got an idea.
When her son arrived home that night,
she presented him with the card, saying,
"One thing is in your favor, Jason.
With a report card like this,
you certainly aren't cheating.
And for that I congratulate you.
Now let's see if we can start studying."

How sensitively do I deal with people,
especially children like Jason,
so as not to "break off a bent reed"?

Someone may never be
as good as you give them credit for being,
but they'll try harder thereafter. Anonymous

[Jesus told a story about an evil person
who sowed weeds in a farmer's wheat field.
When they appeared, the farmer
told his workers not to pull them up,
lest they harm the wheat. Instead, he said,
"Leave them until harvest.]
Then . . . pull up the weeds . . .
and burn them."   Matthew 13:30

Some time ago, the *Wall Street Journal*
carried a front-page story on hell, saying,
"Hell went into eclipse in the late 60s. . . .
Now it is popping up again . . .
in cafe conversations, Hollywood movies,
books and college classrooms."
What's going on?
Ted Hondrick of the University of London
suggests: "As the world gets to be
a lousier and lousier place,
the idea of divine providence,
of punishment in hell for evil doers,
starts to look quite attractive."

What is my reaction to the "weeds" of evil
growing tall and fast
in the wheat field of today's world?

We'll never stop crime
until we get over the idea
that we can hire or elect people to stop it.
                                    Anonymous

[Jesus rebuked some Jewish authorities
for failing to repent their sins, saying,]
"On the Judgment Day
the people of Nineveh
will stand up and accuse you,
because they turned from their sins
when they heard Jonah preach;
and I tell you that there is something here
greater than Jonah!"   Matthew 12:41

Edward Wilson was the physician
on the ill-fated British expedition
to the South Pole. The team of five men,
led by Captain Robert Scott,
froze to death on their way home,
just ten miles from shelter and supplies.
During Wilson's final hours on earth,
in preparation for his appearance
before the judgment seat of God, he wrote:
"This I know is God's truth,
that pain and troubles and sorrows . . .
are either one thing or another.
To all who love God, they are love tokens. . . .
To all who do not love God . . .
they are [just the opposite].

Why do/don't I find it hard to see sorrows
and troubles as "love tokens" from God?

Salvation: Don't leave earth without it.

Author unknown

TUESDAY
WEEK 16 _____ ORDINARY TIME

Jesus said, "Whoever does
what my Father in heaven wants
is my brother, my sister,
and my mother." Matthew 12:50

There's a dramatic scene
in the movie *The Ice Man Cometh*
where Lee Marvin preaches
to some of his old barfly buddies, saying:
"If anybody wants to get drunk—
if that's the only way
they can be happy and feel at peace
with themselves—
why the hell shouldn't they?
Don't I know the game from soup to nuts?
I wrote the book.
The only reason I quit is—
well, I finally had the guts to face myself
and throw overboard
all that damned lying pipe dream
that was making me so miserable
and do what I had to do
for the happiness of all concerned.
Then, all at once, I was at peace with myself,
and I didn't need booze any more."

When did I, perhaps, say yes to God's will
and find true peace for the first time?

Nothing can bring you peace but yourself.
Ralph Waldo Emerson

Jesus . . . went to the lakeside,
where he sat down to teach.
The crowd that gathered around him
was so large that he got into a boat
and sat in it,
while the crowd stood on the shore.
He used parables to tell them
many things. . . .
Jesus concluded, "Listen, then,
if you have ears!"   Matthew 13:1–3, 9

A new clergyman gave a great first sermon.
The next Sunday his congregation returned
filled with anticipation and expectation.
To their surprise, he repeated the sermon.
He did the same thing the next two Sundays.
Finally, the congregation sent a committee
to ask for an explanation.
He told them:
"As far as I can see my words have had
no impact on your lives.
I plan to keep repeating that sermon
until I see it producing some results."

Why do/don't I think Jesus' message is
having a great impact on many people today?

To preach to people who are not ready,
that is a waste of time.
But not to preach to people who are ready,
that is a waste of human beings.   Confucius

THURSDAY
WEEK 16 _____ ORDINARY TIME

Jesus said, "How fortunate you are! . . .
Many prophets and many of God's people
wanted very much to see what you see,
but they could not, and to hear what you hear,
but they did not."   Matthew 13:16–17

On a beach at Kitty Hawk, North Carolina,
in 1903, Orville and Wilbur Wright
flew the first "flying machine" 850 feet.
Wilbur died in 1912 without seeing
the impact his invention had on the world.
Years later John Kennedy cleared the way
for flying to the moon and back,
but he died before seeing the goal realized.
In a different field but in a similar way,
Martin Luther King Jr. pioneered civil rights
but died before seeing the fruit of his work.
And long before any of these events,
Moses led the Israelites to the Promised Land
but died before entering it himself.
History shows that leader after leader
die before seeing the fruit of their labors.

What are some things I am striving for
but will probably never see accomplished?
What motivates me to keep striving?

It isn't a calamity
to die with dreams unfulfilled,
but it is a calamity not to dream.
Benjamin E. Mays

*Jesus said, "Learn what the parable
of the sower means. . . . The seeds
that fell among thorn bushes stand for those
who hear the message; but the worries
about this life and the love for riches
choke the message."* Matthew 13:18, 22

In his youth the French novelist
Honoré de Balzac was practically starving
in a one-room apartment. One night
a thief entered and was trying to pick the lock
on his desk. Suddenly, a loud laugh
totally shattered the thief's composure.
It was de Balzac. He had been lying in bed,
watching the thief work.
When the thief recovered from shock,
he asked, "Why do you laugh?" Balzac said,
"I'm laughing at the risk you're taking
to try to find money in my desk by night,
when I can't find any in it by day."

Are worries about money or other things
choking God's word in me?
If so, what might I do about this situation?

*I refuse to worry about the future.
When I was a little kid, one of the
surprising things my father told me—
and it has really worked for me—
was that it was a sin to worry too much.*
                                    Actor Mel Gibson

SATURDAY
WEEK 16 _____ ORDINARY TIME

[Jesus told a story about an evil person
who sowed weeds in a farmer's wheat field.
The farmer told his workers not to pull them up,
lest they pull up wheat along with them.
Instead, he said, "Leave them until harvest.]
Then . . . pull up the weeds . . .
and burn them."   Matthew 13:30

James Michener wrote an introduction
to A. Grove Day's book *Rascals in Paradise*.
In it he tells how a learned Australian
saw World War II coming.
He checked a world atlas
for a safe haven to be when war came.
He chose an obscure island in the Pacific.
One week before Hitler invaded Poland,
he moved to his safe haven, Gaudalcanal.
As fate would have it, it was destined
to become the site of one of the bloodiest
battles of the war. The point? In today's
world there are no more safe havens.
The darkness of evil will shadow us
no matter where we go.

The pervasive presence of evil
leaves us with two options:
to curse the darkness or to light a candle.
What candle might I light?

Don't bunt. Aim out of the ballpark.
                    David Ogilvy

*Jesus said, "The Kingdom of heaven
is like this. A man happens to find a treasure
hidden in a field . . . and sells everything he has,
. . . and buys that field."* Matthew 13:44

Abraham Lincoln was a great storyteller.
He said that he told stories for two reasons.
First, he used them to avoid a long,
useless discussion on some point or topic
that would be difficult to put
briefly and clearly in words.
Second, he said he used stories
to blunt the edge of a rebuke
or reprimand to some official.
Jesus told stories for similar reasons.
For example, when someone asked him,
"Who is my neighbor?" Jesus avoided
a long, useless discussion by telling the story
of the Good Samaritan. Luke 10:25–37
Jesus also used stories to blunt the edge
of a rebuke or a reprimand. Thus, to show
Simon the Pharisee the error of his ways,
he told him a story. Luke 7:36–50

Robert Frost once said,
"Society can never think things out.
It has to see them acted out by actors."
How do stories do this?

*I am always ready to learn, although I do not
always like being taught.* Winston Churchill

MONDAY

*Jesus said, "The Kingdom of heaven
is like this. A man takes a mustard seed
and sows it in his field. It is the smallest
of all seeds, but when it grows up,
it . . . becomes a tree, so that birds come
and make their nests in its branches."*

Matthew 13:31–32

In 1990, Secretary of State James Baker
convened the Arab-Israeli peace talks
in Madrid, saying, "The road to peace
is very long and it is very difficult.
We have to crawl before we can walk
and we have to walk before we run,
and today I think we all began to crawl."
What Baker said about the road to peace
can be said about so many things in life:
success, holiness, happiness.
The road to them is long and difficult.
And the first step is always a "crawl."
But if we begin and persevere,
this mustard-seed beginning
will someday grow into a great tree.

At what stage am I
on the road to my dream:
crawling, walking, or running?

*The future belongs to those
who believe in the beauty of their dreams.*

Eleanor Roosevelt

[Jesus told a story in which he compared
a farmer's field to the world.]
"The good seed is the people
who belong to the Kingdom;
the weeds are the people who belong
to the Evil One. . . . [At harvesttime
the two will be separated by God's angel's.]
Then God's people will shine
like the sun in their Father's Kingdom."

Matthew 13:38, 43

Along a little-used road in Allen, Texas,
there's a small wooden cross.
Painted on it are the words "We Love You."
A clump of flowers grows at its base.
Occasionally, someone ties balloons
to the cross, and they flutter in the breeze.
Whenever I pass by the cross,
I wonder about the person who died there.
I also wonder about my destiny with death.

What will be the bottom-line concern
when it comes to my own hour of reckoning?

After we have brushed off
the dust and chips of life,
we will have left
only the hard, clean question:
Was it good or was it evil?
Have we done well—or ill?

John Steinbeck (slightly adapted)

WEDNESDAY
WEEK 17 _____ ORDINARY TIME

[Jesus compared God's Kingdom
to a man in search of fine pearls, saying,]
"When he finds one that is unusually fine,
he goes and sells everything he has,
and buys that pearl."　Matthew 13:45–46

Johnny Unitas was someone
in search of a dream: playing football.
But the colleges told him he was too small.
He kept searching; finally, a small college
gave him a chance. He excelled.
After college, he kept searching, but in vain.
He got a job, and played weekend ball
at six dollars a game to hone his skill.
In a surprise break, he tried out
with the Baltimore Colts and was signed.
When quarterback George Shaw was injured,
he got his chance. The rest is history.
He became a great star
and was voted into the pro Hall of Fame.

Jesus invites me to pursue God's Kingdom
as did the pearl buyer in the gospel
and as did the dreamer, Johnny Unitas.
He promises, not fame that will pass,
but eternal happiness that will never end.
How am I responding to Jesus' invitation?

The bitterest tears shed over graves
are for words left unsaid and
deeds left undone.　Harriet Beecher Stowe

Jesus said,
"The Kingdom of heaven is like this.
Some fishermen throw their nets out
in the lake and catch all kinds of fish.
When the net is full, they pull it to shore
and sit down to divide the fish:
the good ones go into the buckets,
the worthless ones are thrown away.
It will be like this at the end of the age."
Matthew 13:47–49

Albert Schweitzer was a great theologian,
respected historian, concert pianist,
and outstanding missionary doctor.
A committee representing 17 countries
voted him the "man of the century."
Schweitzer maintained that it is not enough
to be a good parent and good spouse, saying,
"That's all very well.
But you must do something . . .
for those who have need of help,
something for which you get no pay
but the privilege of doing it. For remember,
you don't live in a world all your own."

What am I doing "for those who have need
of help" apart from my family and friends?

[On Judgment Day,] God will not
look you over for medals, degrees
or diplomas, but for scars.   Elbert Hubbard

FRIDAY
WEEK 17 _____ ORDINARY TIME

Jesus said,
"A prophet is respected everywhere
except in his hometown
and by his own family." Matthew 13:57

There's a moving Ray Bradbury story
about a little girl called Margot. If memory
serves me, she's part of an "Earth colony"
on a planet where it rains nonstop—
except for seven minutes every seven years.
Margot loved the sun and was excited
beyond belief when the "sun" day came.
That day, the other school kids
(who doubted the sun would shine)
started teasing her. During recess,
they jokingly locked her in a closet.
Seconds later, the rain stopped and the sun
came out. For seven delirious minutes
the kids danced and sang joyfully.
Then the clouds closed, the sun vanished,
and the rain fell again. All of a sudden,
someone remembered Margot.
They unlocked the closet and let her out.

Why do you think "prophets" are often
rejected by others—and often deprived
of enjoying the fruit of their labor?

The Don Quixote of one generation
may live to hear himself called the savior
of society by the next. James Russell Lowell

[When John the Baptist confronted Herod,]
Herod had him . . . put in prison.   Matthew 14:3

Edith Cavell was famous for her work
as a nurse in the slums of London.
A Belgium surgeon invited her
to set up a medical clinic in Brussels.
When war engulfed Belgium in 1914,
her clinic secretly treated some 200
Allied soldiers and helped them to escape.
The Germans learned this and arrested her.
She admitted everything, saying,
"My job as a nurse is to save lives,
not destroy them."
She was sentenced to be shot.
A chaplain describes her last moments:
"We partook of Holy Communion together.
At the close of the little service,
I began to repeat the words, 'Abide with me,'
and she joined. . . . Then I said good-bye. . . .
She smiled and said, 'We shall meet again.' "
At that point she was shot.

How ready am I to stand by my principles,
even when it will cost me dearly?

Do not be surprised at the painful test
you are suffering. . . . Rather be glad
that you are sharing Christ's sufferings,
so that you may be full of joy
when his glory is revealed.   1 Peter 4:12–13

*Jesus left . . . in a boat and went
to a lonely place by himself.*   Matthew 14:13

Author Anne Morrow Lindbergh loved
going off by herself to a deserted beach
and walking along it.
The rhythmic sound of the waves,
the soothing sun on her bare back,
and the mist from the sea spray in her hair
gave her a feeling of peace and well-being.
She especially enjoyed walking into
the surf and out again, like a sandpiper.
In her book *Gift from the Sea,* she writes:
"These are among the most important times
in one's life—when one is alone.
The artist knows he must be alone to create;
the writer, to work out his thoughts;
the musician, to compose; the saint to pray."

If I cannot go off to a beach to be alone
and meditate, what are my alternatives?

*Because I am a woman involved
in practical cares, I . . . must meditate
when I can, early in the morning and
on the fly during the day.
Not in the privacy of a study—
but here, there and everywhere—
at the kitchen table . . . on my way
to and from appointments.*
Dorothy Day in *House of Hospitality*

MONDAY

[The disciples got caught in a storm at sea.
Suddenly, Jesus appeared walking on
the waves. They all grew terribly afraid.]
Then Peter spoke up. "Lord, if it is really you,
order me to come out on the water to you."
"Come!" answered Jesus. [Peter came.] . . .
But when he noticed the strong wind,
he was afraid and started to sink. . . .
Jesus . . . grabbed hold of him. . . . They both
got into the boat, and the wind died down.

Matthew 14:28–32

In 1544, 46 Dominican friars left Spain
for Mexico. Father de la Torre kept a journal.
One entry describes a great storm.
Waves hit the ship with such force that
the crew thought each blow might be the last.
All went to confession and commended
themselves to God. Then the bishop prayed
over the sea, ordering it in the name of Jesus
to be silent. It obeyed. Father de la Torre
wrote that he hesitated to call it a miracle,
but that's the only way he could describe
the calm sea that ensued.

What are my thoughts as I read this story?

We die on the day when our lives cease
to be illumined by the steady radiance,
renewed daily, of a wonder, the source
of which is beyond reason. Dag Hammarskjold

TUESDAY
WEEK 18 _____ ORDINARY TIME

Jesus went up a hill by himself to pray.
When evening came, Jesus was there alone. . . .
[The next day Jesus went to Gennesaret,]
where the people . . . begged him to let
the sick at least touch the edge of his cloak;
and all who touched it were made well.

Matthew 14:23, 35–36

Corretta Scott King said: "When you think
of what some black women have gone
through, and then look at how beautiful
they still are, it is incredible that
they still believe in the values of the race,
that they still feel the deepest compassion,
not only for themselves
but for anyone who is oppressed;
this is a kind of miracle, something that
we have to preserve and pass on."

Quoted by Alice Walker in *In Search of Our Mother's Gardens*

The "miracle" to remain "beautiful"
in spite of oppression
sprang from the same source of power
that enabled Jesus to work miracles: prayer.
What miracle might prayer work for me?

I will not let prejudice . . . and injustices
bear me down to spiritual defeat.
My inner life is mine, and
I shall defend and maintain its integrity
against the powers of hell. James Weldon Johnson

[A pagan woman kept shouting to Jesus,]
"My daughter has a demon. . . ."
His disciples . . . begged him,
"Send her away! She is following us
and making all this noise!"
[Jesus tried to explain to her
that his mission was to the Jews.
But she refused to take no for an answer.]
So Jesus answered her,
"You are a woman of great faith!
What you want will be done for you."
And at the very moment her daughter
was healed.   Matthew 15:22–23, 28

Lew Kraft used to drive his horse, Paddy,
from store to store selling cheese.
In spite of long hours and hard work,
sales remained low—very low.
One day a friend told him bluntly,
"Lew, you're licked; admit it."
But Lew continued to visit stores and talk
to his horse, Paddy, about his dream.
Today the multimillion-dollar Kraft Company
is a monument to a man
who refused to take no for an answer.

What is one area of my life that tends to
discourage me? What might I do about it?

The thing to try
when all else fails is again.

THURSDAY
WEEK 18 _____ ORDINARY TIME

Jesus said, "Peter: you are a rock,
and on this rock foundation
I will build my church. . . . I will give you
the keys of the Kingdom of heaven;
what you prohibit on earth
will be prohibited in heaven,
and what you permit on earth
will be permitted in heaven."

Matthew 16:18–19

Michelangelo was hired by Pope Paul III
to paint *The Last Judgment* in the Vatican.
As it neared completion,
a minor papal official kept pestering
the artist for a private sneak preview of it.
His patience at an end, Michelangelo
decided to teach the official a lesson.
He painted him among the sinners
being punished in hell.
When the official learned about his fate,
he complained to the pope, who said,
"As Peter's successor,
Jesus gave me the authority to prohibit
and to permit on earth and in heaven,
but he said nothing of authority over hell.
So I'm afraid the matter is out of my hands."

How do I react to slights or humiliations?

He who stays not in his littleness
loses his greatness. Saint Francis de Sales

Jesus said,
"You must forget yourself,
carry your cross, and follow me.
For if you want to save your own life,
you will lose it."   Matthew 16:24–25

John Updike
wrote a popular novel called *Rabbit Run.*
It's about a man named Harry Angstrum.
Harry got the nickname "Rabbit" as a child
because of a nervous flutter of his nostrils.
The name stayed with him as he grew up,
and it became symbolic of a character flaw.
Harry couldn't handle problems or "crosses."
He ran from them, like a scared rabbit.
As a result his life was filled with tragedy.
He became the kind of person
Jesus had in mind when he warned us,
"If you want to save your own life,
you will lose it."

Harry's tragic life invites me
to inventory how well I face up
to problems or "crosses," such as
a personal problem or a personal difficulty
with a family member.

What is it about human nature
that makes it easier
to break a commandment than a habit?
                                        E. C. McKenzie

SATURDAY
WEEK 18 _____ ORDINARY TIME

Jesus said,
"If you have faith as big as a mustard seed,
you can say to this hill, 'Go from here
to there!' and it will go."   Matthew 17:20

A woman was near despair. In spite of a life
of poverty and pain, she'd picked up
her cross daily and followed Jesus.
But now a deep darkness enveloped her.
She even began to question God's existence.
She wrote: "I come to this time in life
gasping for God as if for air,
needing desperately some tangible sense
of God's presence with and in me."
Then one day a tiny spark of hope
flickered—ever so faintly. She wrote:
"Although I am still afraid to trust
the fragile reality of this experience,
I think that God's love is being kindled
again at the core of me. Oh, may it be so."
Quoted by John F. Kavanaugh in *America* magazine

Can I recall a time when my own faith
seemed to flicker and almost go out?
Why does God allow such things?

Through the dark and stormy night
Faith holds a feeble light . . .
In a patient hope I rest,
For the full day-breaking.
                    John Greenleaf Whittier

Jesus went up a hill by himself to pray.
Matthew 14:23

On the National Day of Prayer in 1994,
USA Today carried a full-page ad showing
the famous bronze bas relief of George
Washington in prayer at Valley Forge.
Next to it was a plaque reading:
"In this hour of darkness . . .
when every human prospect . . .
was disheartening, he retires to
a sequestered spot, and there laid the cause
of his bleeding country at the throne of grace."
The ad reads: "There have been few times
in our history when America needed prayer
more urgently than today. . . . Great men
who have gone before us have understood
the power of a nationwide call to prayer.
This led [to] . . . a National Day of Prayer . . .
over 200 years ago.
It was later proclaimed by . . .
many other presidents. Congress made it
a permanent observance . . . in 1952."

Do I feel the call to pray for our nation?
How might I do it?

Oh, help me, Lord, to take the time
To set all else aside,
That in the secret place of prayer
I may with you abide.   Author unknown

MONDAY
WEEK 19 _____ ORDINARY TIME

Jesus said to his disciples,
"The Son of Man is about to be handed over
to those who will kill him." Matthew 17:22–23

A woman missionary visited
the tent of an Arab youth who was dying.
She asked if she might tell him a story.
When the mother nodded, the woman knelt
and told him how Jesus died for our sins.
The youth's eyes showed unusual interest.
The missionary returned the next day
and told him the same story.
Now his face reflected peace and love.
The missionary returned again the next day
and started telling him of Jesus' birth.
But he raised his hand and said, "No!
Not that! Tell me again how he died for us."
When the missionary returned the fourth day,
the boy's mother was weeping.
Her son had died. She told the missionary
that just before he died,
someone began reading prayers to him.
But he raised his hand and said feebly,
"No! Not that!
Tell me how Jesus died for my sins."

Why do I think the story of Jesus' death
had such a powerful impact on the youth?

Nothing in my hand I bring.
Simply to the cross I cling. August Toplady

Jesus said,
"Don't despise any of these little ones.
Their angels in heaven, I tell you,
are always in the presence of my Father
in heaven." Matthew 18:10

Author Joan Webster Anderson's son and
two other college students were en route
to Illinois in subzero, snowy weather.
They stopped in Fort Wayne to drop off
one of the students; then the other two
headed for the tollway by a rural route.
Suddenly, miles from nowhere,
the car stopped operating. The cold was
so intense that the two boys began to panic.
Just then two headlights appeared.
To their amazement a tow truck pulled up.
The driver returned them to Fort Wayne.
Joan's son ran inside to get money
to pay the driver. When he returned,
he stopped dead in his tracks.
Not only was there no tow truck,
but there were no tracks in the snow
except those of his own car.

Can I recall some episode from my own life
that might fit in the category
of the college students in the story?

God will put his angels in charge of you
to protect you wherever you go. Psalm 90:11

WEDNESDAY
WEEK 19 _____ ORDINARY TIME

Jesus said, "Where two or three
come together in my name,
I am there with them." Matthew 18:20

A. J. Gordon recounts a dream
that had a profound effect on his life.
It was Sunday, and he was just
mounting the pulpit to preach
when a stranger entered the church.
All during the sermon Gordon's eyes
kept drifting to the stranger.
He thought, "I must meet this person
after the service." But after the service
Gordon lost him in the crowd.
Gordon did, however, notice the person
who sat next to him, so he said, "I'm sorry
I missed the stranger sitting next to you.
Do you know who it was?"
"Why, yes," said the person.
"Didn't you recognize him? It was Jesus."
"Why didn't you detain him,"
said Gordon, "so I could speak with him?"
"Don't worry," said the person.
"He comes every Sunday; he'll be back."

How firmly do I believe that
where two or three gather in Jesus' name,
he is there?

"The Lord is here! He is in this place,
and I didn't know it!" Genesis 28:16

Jesus said,
"Forgive . . . from your heart."   Matthew 18:35

A moving scene from
All Quiet on the Western Front portrays
a German soldier in a shell hole,
taking cover from artillery fire.
Suddenly, an enemy French soldier leaps
into the same hole to take cover.
The German pounces on him and stabs him.
But the Frenchman doesn't die immediately.
The German—hardly more than a boy—
studies the French soldier's dying eyes.
Moved to pity, he makes him comfortable
and gives him a drink from his own canteen.
When the Frenchman dies minutes later,
the young German feels great remorse.
He says to the dead man,
"When you jumped in here,
you were my enemy—and I was afraid. . . .
But you're just a man like me,
and I killed you. . . . O God! Why did they . . .
send us out to fight each other?
If we threw away these rifles and
these uniforms, you could be my brother. . . .
You have to forgive me."

What are my thoughts on the above scene?

Forgiveness is the fragrance a violet sheds
on the heel that has crushed it.   Mark Twain

FRIDAY
WEEK 19 _____ ORDINARY TIME

Jesus said, "No human being must separate,
then, what God has joined together."

Matthew 19:6

Nguyen Quang Le
was a North Vietnamese radio operator.
The day he left home
he began a journal.
In it he wrote this moving passage:
"Departure takes place in a few hours.
Meanwhile, my wife, Ngoan,
sews a book bag for me."
Two weeks later he writes:
"It's hard to sleep tonight. . . .
Ngoan . . . receives all my love.
Even if she has a love child,
I will tolerate her. . . .
Such thoughts assault my mind,
and I toss and toss,
spending a wakeful night."

What are some of my thoughts
or doubts about my marriage
that occasionally assault my mind
to make me toss and toss
during a wakeful night?

In marriage,
being the right person is as important
as finding the right person.

Wilfred Donald Gough

Some people brought children to Jesus
for him to place his hands on them
and to pray for them,
but the disciples scolded the people.
Jesus said, "Let the children come to me
and do not stop them,
because the Kingdom of heaven
belongs to such as these." Matthew 19:13–15

Chantz Cottrell plays right field
"with the sublime indifference
of an eight-year-old.
His glove is perched like a big blackbird
on his left shoulder;
his cap is crashing down on his ears.
Runs are rolling up against his team
in waves, but his reverie is unshaken.
At times he appears to be singing.
He is happy to be out there
in the evening's last wink, playing."
Kevin Sherrington, *The Dallas Morning News* (June 16, 1994)
The amazing thing about Chantz
is that he is suffering from a disease
that makes becoming a teenager chancy.
Chantz knows this,
but "his reverie is unshaken."

What might I learn from Chantz's "reverie"?

Pray, and then start answering your prayer.
Deane Edwards

SUNDAY
WEEK 20 _____ ORDINARY TIME

[A] woman came and fell at Jesus' feet.
"Help me, sir!" she said. . . .
Jesus answered her, "You are a woman
of great faith! What you want
will be done for you." Matthew 15:25, 28

Sarah Bernhardt had a leg amputated,
yet continued to star on stage
until her death about ten years later.
Helen Keller, blind and deaf from age two,
wrote ten books and lectured widely.
Charles Steinmetz was born a hunchback,
yet became a celebrated engineer and inventor,
holding over 200 patents.
Franklin Roosevelt was paralyzed in both legs,
yet became president of the United States
for four consecutive terms.
Henry Viscardi was born without legs,
yet wrote nine books, became chairman
of the White House Conference
on the Handicapped, and received
thirteen honorary degrees.

What makes some people see adversity
as a stumbling block; others, a stepping-stone?

I have learned this secret,
so that anywhere, at any time, . . .
I have the strength to face all conditions
by the power that Christ gives me.
Philippians 4:12–13

*[One day when a young man asked Jesus
what he must do to receive eternal life,
Jesus said,] "Keep the commandments."*
Matthew 19:17

There's an story about a youth
who went through the streets shouting,
"We must keep the commandments!
We must keep the commandments!"
At first people cheered him on
and were happy someone was taking
a stand for the cause of goodness.
But soon they got use to his shouting
and went on with their business.
Then came the day when the shouts
began to annoy the people.
One day a woman said to the youth,
"Don't you know
no one listens to you anymore?
Why do you keep shouting?"
The youth said, "I keep shouting
not so much to remind others
what they should be doing, but to keep
reminding myself what I should be doing."

What do I do to keep reminding myself
of what I should be doing?

*You cannot just go on being a good egg.
You must either hatch or go bad.*
C. S. Lewis

Jesus said, "It will be very hard
for rich people to enter
the Kingdom of heaven. . . .
Many who now are first will be last."

Matthew 19:23, 30

"Column 8" is an extremely popular
daily newspaper column in Australia.
It features human interest stories.
For example, one story concerns a man
in economy class on a plane. He objects
to sitting next to a woman of color.
Since the economy class section is full,
the man demands that the flight attendant
check to see if there is an open seat
in the business class section.
The flight attendant comes back smiling.
As the man begins to unbuckle his seat belt
to prepare to move to the more expensive
section of the plane, the flight attendant
says to the woman of color,
"Madam, please follow me
and I'll take you to the business section."

Why would/wouldn't this be something
that Jesus might have done
had he been the flight attendant?

Creating all people free and equal
isn't enough. Some means must be devised
to keep them free and equal. E. C. McKenzie

*Jesus said, "The Kingdom of heaven
is like this. . . . [A man went out five times
in one day to hire workers. At day's end,
he paid them all a full day's wage.
When the first workers complained, he said,]
'Are you jealous because I am generous?' "*

Matthew 20:1, 15

One day Henry Tyson heard glass breaking.
Running outside with a portable phone,
he saw two boys next to the house
throwing stones at bottles. Seeing Henry
on the phone, they thought he was calling
the police and started throwing stones at him.
He dropped the phone and cornered the boys.
To their surprise, he told them,
"I was planning to clean up the lot anyway,
and I'll pay you $5 apiece to help me."
They saw he was serious and agreed.
An hour later two more boys joined them.
When they finished, Henry paid each boy $5.
To his surprise, the first two boys complained
that this wasn't fair. Henry said later,
"It was a repeat of the gospel story;
people haven't changed in 2,000 years."

How might the point of Jesus' parable
apply to me in my life, right now?

*The only person worth envying
is the person who doesn't envy.* E. C. McKenzie

THURSDAY
WEEK 20 _____ ORDINARY TIME

Jesus said, "The Kingdom of heaven
is like this. Once there was a king
who prepared a wedding feast for his son. . . .
The king went in to look at the guests
and saw a man
who was not wearing wedding clothes.
[The king expelled him.]"   Matthew 22:2, 11

Ignace Lepp became a Communist, saying,
"I felt no need of God."
Then two things happened: Communism
turned sour, and he began to question
the meaning and purpose of life. He writes:
"It didn't seem logical that beings endowed
with a capacity for thinking and loving
could be thrown into an absurd universe,
where there was nothing to think,
nothing to love, and nothing to hope for."

The story of Ignace Lepp's conversion
helps us better understand Jesus' parable.
The wedding feast stands for God's *Kingdom;*
the wedding garment stands for *repentance*
(conversion accompanied by *good works*)—
the conditions for entry into the Kingdom.
What keeps me from complete conversion?

"How does one become a butterfly?" she asked.
"You must want to fly so much that you are
willing to give up being a caterpillar."
                    Trina Paulus, *Hope for the Flowers*

Jesus said,
"'Love your neighbor as you love yourself.'"
Matthew 22:39

One evening during rush hour,
a man was running to get in line for a bus.
Suddenly, a large woman
pushed in ahead of him,
almost knocking him down.
In mock apology he said, "Pardon me.
I didn't mean to smash into you like that."
The woman did a double take and said,
"I'm sorry! How can you be so kind
after what I did?"
Now he did a double take—the woman
actually thought he was sincere.
He groped for a reply, saying something like,
"It doesn't hurt to be nice to people."
Riding home, the man felt embarrassed
and humbled by his pettiness and insincerity.
"Lord," he prayed, "what are you telling me?"
Back came the reply:
"I'm trying to tell you what I've been trying
to tell people for centuries:
Love releases a chain reaction of love
just as hate releases a chain reaction of hate."

What chain reaction do I usually release?

No one needs love more than someone
who doesn't deserve it.   Author unknown

SATURDAY
WEEK 20 _____ ORDINARY TIME

Jesus said,
"Whoever makes himself great
will be humbled,
and whoever humbles himself
will be made great."   Matthew 23:12

Cardinal Bernardin of Chicago
was vacationing far from the city.
One day, while casually dressed,
he went shopping in a local supermarket.
Suddenly a stranger rushed up and said,
"I can't believe it! It's really you!
Could I impose on you just one minute?
My wife's outside in the car.
It would mean so much to her
if you'd go out and say hello."
The cardinal smiled and followed the man,
past the checkout counter, out the door,
and into the parking lot. He wondered,
"How did he recognize me way up here?"
When they got to the car, the man opened
the door and said excitedly,
"Helen, look who's here! It's Dr. Kresnick!"

How do I react when I am imposed upon,
or when I'm put in an embarrassing or
humbling situation by another's error?

The person with true humility
never has to be shown his place;
he is always in it.   E. C. McKenzie

[One day Jesus asked his disciples,]
"Who do you say I am?"
Simon Peter answered,
"You are the Messiah." Matthew 16:15–16

An old story concerns an innocent fugitive
fleeing hostile government soldiers.
Some friendly villagers fed and hid him.
The next morning the soldiers showed up
and threatened to destroy the village by noon
if the fugitive's hideout was not revealed.
Some villagers went to the old rabbi's cave
outside the town to seek his advice.
The old man opened his Bible for an answer.
His eyes fell on the words, "It is better
for one man to die than for all to perish."
He told the villagers to hand over the man.
Later an angel appeared to the rabbi and said,
"What have you done?
That young man was the Messiah!"
The rabbi wept, saying, "How was I to know?"
The angel said, "You should've met
with him and looked into his eyes.
Then you would have known."

To know that Jesus is the Messiah
I must meet with him personally
and look into his eyes. How might I do this?

Turn to the LORD and pray to him,
now that he is near. Isaiah 55:6

MONDAY
WEEK 21 _____ ORDINARY TIME

Jesus said, "How terrible for you,
teachers of the Law and Pharisees! . . .
You lock the door to the Kingdom of heaven
in people's faces, but you yourselves
don't go in, nor do you allow in
those who are trying to enter!" Matthew 23:13–14

The movie *The Ox-Bow Incident*
concerns town leaders who bypass the law
and hang three people without a trial.
Later they learn the terrible truth:
The three people were innocent.
Before being hanged, one young man
asks to write a letter to his young wife.
After he is hanged, someone reads it.
A portion of it says:
"I suppose there's some good men
[in this crowd] . . . only they don't realize
what they're doing.
They're the ones I feel sorry for,
'cause it'll be over for me in a little while,
but they'll have to go on remembering
the rest of their lives."

What strikes me most about the attitudes
of Jesus and the young man?
What would probably have been
my own attitude?

It wasn't the nails that held Jesus on the cross
but his love for us. Anonymous

[Jesus said, "You observe minor teachings,]
but you neglect to obey
the really important teachings of the Law,
such as justice and mercy." Matthew 23:23

The film *Teahouse of the August Moon*
is about postwar Okinawa under the Americans.
In one scene an old villager makes
a moving appeal to the American commander.
He points out that there are lovely teahouses
in the big cities, but the men of his village
have never been inside them
because they are too poor to visit them.
Then he says, "All of my life
I have dreamed of visiting a teahouse
where paper lanterns cast their shadows
on the lotus pond and where
the bamboo bells hanging in the pines
tinkle as the breezes brush them.
But this picture is only in my heart.
I may never see it. I am an old man, sir. . . .
Give us our teahouse, sir.
Free my soul for death."

Jesus' words to the Jewish leaders and
the old villager's words to the commander
invite me to ask: Am I so hung up on little
details that I miss life's bigger picture?

Life is short! . . .
Make haste to be kind. Henri Amiel

WEDNESDAY
WEEK 21 _____ ORDINARY TIME

Jesus said, "How terrible for you,
teachers of the Law and Pharisees! . . .
You are like whitewashed tombs,
which look fine on the outside
but are full of bones and decaying corpses
on the inside. In the same way, on the outside
you appear good to everybody, but inside
you are full of hypocrisy and sins."

Matthew 23:27–28

A Japanese soldier testified
that in the final months of World War II,
ammunition was scarce in the Osaka region.
As a result, aircraft guns fired
mostly blanks at United States planes.
The reason for the blanks?
The military wanted to give the impression
that they were defending the people.
"Even when real shells were used,
the Japanese soldiers knew they could not reach
the high-flying B-29 bombers.
They risked their lives to keep up
the appearance of defending their homeland."

Edward Hays, *Feathers on the Wind*

Is there an area of my life where, perhaps,
I'm firing blanks for impression's sake?

When you try to make an impression,
that is the impression you make.

Sydney J. Harris

Jesus said, "If the owner of a house
knew the time when the thief would come,
you can be sure that he would stay awake
and not let the thief break into his house.
So then, you also must always be ready,
because the Son of Man will come
at an hour when you are not expecting him."

Matthew 24:43–44

A retired woman invested her life's savings
in a business deal presented to her
by a clever young con artist.
When she discovered the awful truth,
she phoned the Better Business Bureau.
The spokesperson for the bureau asked,
"Why didn't you consult us
before handing over your money?
Didn't you know that's why we exist—
to identify these thieves for you?"
"Yes, I knew," said the woman,
"but the young man looked so honest
that I didn't think it necessary in this case."

Jesus used the example of the "thief"
to dramatize the need for me to be ready
for the end of the world or
for the end of my own life in the world—
whichever comes first. How ready am I?

Get ready for eternity. You are going
to spend a lot of time there.   E. C. McKenzie

314

FRIDAY
WEEK 21 _____ ORDINARY TIME

Jesus said, "Watch out, then,
because you do not know
the day or the hour
[of the Son of Man's return]."　　Matthew 25:13

Paul Auster was eight years old
when he saw his first baseball game.
His favorite team (then the New York Giants)
was playing. After the game,
Paul and his parents and some friends
sat and talked about the game
while waiting for the stands to empty out.
Finally, they left by the center field exit.
Just then, Willie Mays, Paul's hero,
emerged from the dressing room.
Paul was thrilled and said,
"Mr. Mays, could I have your autograph?"
"Sure," said the great star. "Got a pencil?"
Paul did not. He asked the others with him.
Not one of them had a pencil either.
Willie said sadly,
"Sorry, kid, I don't have one either."
Paul cried all the way home.
He said, "After that, I carried a pencil
everywhere I went—just to be prepared."

Paul's story makes me ask, How prepared
am I to meet my hero when he comes?

If it's going to be, it's up to me.
　　　　Robert Schuller

[Jesus said, "The Kingdom of heaven
is like an owner who gave money
to three servants to invest.
Two turned a profit; the third did not.
So the owner told the other servants,]
'Now, take the money away from him and . . .
throw him outside.'" Matthew 25:28, 30

General William "Gus" Pagonis directed
the movement of troops and supplies
during the Gulf War. The operation
was called "the greatest logistical feat
in modern military history."
"Gus" began by shining shoes
in his dad's restaurant.
He said, "My father taught me
to ask the customer if I had done a good job
and to offer to reshine the shoes
if the customer wasn't satisfied."

How do I understand Jesus' parable?
Why am I, perhaps, more willing
to work harder to win a temporal crown
than an eternal one?

The dictionary is the only place
where success comes before work.
Hard work is the price we pay for success.
I think you can accomplish almost anything
if you are willing to pay the price.
Coach Vince Lombardi

SUNDAY
WEEK 22 _____ ORDINARY TIME

Jesus said, "I must go to Jerusalem
and suffer much. . . ."
[Peter said,] "God forbid it, Lord! . . ."
Jesus said, "If any of you want to come with me,
you must forget yourself, carry your cross,
and follow me." Matthew 16:21–22, 24

An old story concerns a moth collector
who saw the cocoon of a rare moth on a branch.
He clipped the branch and brought it home.
As the days passed, he noticed movement
inside the cocoon, but no moth emerged.
So he slit the cocoon slightly
to make it easier for the moth to emerge.
The moth emerged, but to his dismay
it was sickly looking and soon died.
When he told a friend of it, the friend said,
"Nature has arranged it so that the moth
must struggle to break out of the cocoon.
It's this daily struggle that enables it
to develop its wings.
When they're strong enough to break
the cocoon, they're strong enough to fly.
When you tried to help it,
you killed its chances to mature and fly."

How are Jesus' words and this story linked?
What motivates me to pick up my cross daily?

Out of suffering have emerged
the strongest souls. Edwin Hubbel Chapin

[Jesus got up in the synagogue at Nazareth]
and found the place where it was written,
"The Spirit of the Lord . . . has chosen me
to . . . announce that the time has come
when the Lord will save his people." . . .
[Then Jesus said,] "This passage of scripture
has come true today, as you heard it. . . ."
[The people were shocked and said,]
"Isn't he the son of Joseph?" . . .
They rose up [against him,] but he walked
through the middle of the crowd
and went his way.   Luke 4:17–19, 21–22, 29–30

Raymond Fosdick writes:
"The only life worth living
is a life that is unafraid and adventurous.
It thinks its own thoughts . . .
and is governed by its own conscience.
The herd may graze where it pleases
or stampede when it pleases,
but he who lives the adventurous life
will remain unafraid
when he finds himself alone."

Jesus' witness and Fosdick's words invite me
to ask: In what sense is my life of faith
"adventurous" and "unafraid"?

Be careful how you live; you may be
the only Bible some person ever reads.
                                          N. I. Toms

TUESDAY
WEEK 22 _____ ORDINARY TIME

Then Jesus went to Capernaum . . .
where he taught the people. . . .
They were all amazed
at the way he taught. . . .
And the report about Jesus spread.
Luke 4:31–32, 37

To plant a seed is to plan for a year.
To plant a tree is to plan for 10 years.
To teach people is to plan for 100 years.
To plant a seed is to harvest once.
To plant a tree is to harvest 10 times.
To teach people is to harvest 100 times.
To write on paper is to teach 100 years.
To write on stone is to teach 1,000 years.
To write on the heart is to teach forever.

The 19th-century French poet, dramatist,
and novelist Victor Hugo said,
"Whoever opens a school door, closes a prison."
What can I do concretely to emulate Jesus
by teaching people and writing the "good news"
of God's love on human hearts?

A school should be the most beautiful place
in every town and village—
so beautiful that the punishment
for undutiful children should be
that they should be debarred
from going to school the following day.
Oscar Wilde

At daybreak Jesus left the town
and went off to a lonely place.
The people started looking for him.   Luke 4:42

Dorothy Day worked among New York's poor.
Together with Peter Maurin,
she founded the Catholic Worker Movement.
When she died in 1980, the *New York Times*
did not hesitate to call her one of the most
influential Christians of our time.
Dorothy Day used to pray daily
in a small, deserted neighborhood church.
When her work made this impossible,
she prayed whenever she found time
and wherever she found herself—
on a bus, walking down the street,
or waiting for an appointment in some office.
Like Dorothy Day, we all have periods
of waiting in our lives. These periods can be
used as opportunities for privacy and prayer.
They can become opportunities for touching
base with ourselves and listening
to inner voices that we never knew existed
until we started to listen for them.

What are some periods of waiting in my life?
How might I turn them into prayer times?

In prayer, the important thing
is not to think much but to love much.
                                    Saint Teresa of Avila

THURSDAY
WEEK 22 _____ ORDINARY TIME

[Jesus told Simon Peter,]
"Let down your nets for a catch."
"Master," Simon answered, "we worked hard
all night long and caught nothing."　Luke 5:4–5

Edward Hays wondered why circus elephants
chained to a small wood peg in the ground
never tried to pull the peg up. He writes:
"Recently I learned the answer. . . .
A baby elephant is trained by being chained
to a concrete post buried deep in the earth.
Should a young elephant tug at the post
with all its might,
it couldn't pull it out of the earth.
The result of such childhood training
is that later in life
it will never attempt to pull up the post
to which it is chained."　*Feathers on the Wing*

Peter made the same mistake
the elephant did.
His fishless night made him think
another try at fishing was useless.
As the elephant failed to factor in
the change that adult strength makes,
so Peter failed to figure in "the Jesus factor."
Am I, perhaps, making this same mistake?

Jesus said,
"I am the vine, and you are the branches. . . .
You can do nothing without me."　John 15:5

[Some people opposed Jesus
because his disciples did not observe
some of the traditional dietary laws.
Jesus responded,] "New wine
must be poured into fresh wineskins!
And you don't want new wine
after drinking old wine.
'The old is better,' you say."   Luke 5:38–39

Italian astronomer Galileo Galilei
was ridiculed for proposing
that the earth revolved around the sun—
rather than the other way round,
as many people believed.
Scottish physician Sir James Simpson
was opposed for advocating
the use of chloroform
to make medical operations less painful.
English surgeon Joseph Lister was opposed
for pioneering the use of antiseptics
to make surgery safer.

Examples like these invite me
to evaluate my opposition to things.
Have I simply closed my mind to truth?
How do I decide if this is the case or not?

Instead of letting their light shine,
some people spend their time
trying to put out the lights of others.
                    E. C. McKenzie

SATURDAY
WEEK 22 _____ ORDINARY TIME

Some Pharisees asked [Jesus' disciples],
"Why are you doing what our Law says
you cannot do on the Sabbath?"
Jesus answered . . . "The Son of Man
is Lord of the Sabbath."   Luke 6:2–3, 5

Paul Waldemann came from a Jewish family.
One day a "startling question"
popped into his mind:
Could Jesus really be God?
He tried to dismiss the thought,
but it kept returning to him.
And so he began to read up on the matter.
But reading only confused him more.
Finally, he asked a priest—a former Jew—
to help him reach clarity. The priest said,
"Speak to God in your own words.
Ask him to lead you." Waldemann writes:
"For weeks on end . . . I pleaded with God,
'Please show me what you want me to do.'
But he remained silent. . . .
[Then one evening God answered my prayer.]
I was filled with a peace . . .
I had never known before."
Richer Than a Millionaire: One Man's Journey to God

What is the link between study and prayer,
and how do I decide when to do what?

When Jesus teaches me to sing his song,
how can I keep from singing it?   Author unknown

Jesus said, "Where two or three
come together in my name,
I am there with them." Matthew 18:20

On October 12, 1972,
a plane carrying a Uruguayan rugby team
crashed high up in the Andes.
Plunging into deep snow,
the plane skidded and broke into pieces.
Incredibly 28 young men survived.
Eventually 12 more died, leaving a total
of 16 survivors. Rescue came 70 days later.
One thing that gave the survivors strength
during this period
were nightly prayer sessions together.
During these sessions,
even boys who had never been religious
felt God's presence as never before.
For example, as one of these sessions
came to an end,
one of the boys began weeping softly.
"Why are you crying?" someone asked.
"Because," he said, "I feel so close to God."

Can I recall feeling God's presence
during a group prayer service
or experience? When?

When they call to me, I will answer them;
when they are in trouble,
I will be with them. Psalm 91:15

MONDAY
WEEK 23 _____ ORDINARY TIME

[Some religious leaders] wanted a reason
to accuse Jesus of doing wrong,
so they watched him closely to see
if he would heal on the Sabbath.
But Jesus knew their thoughts.   Luke 6:7–8

Franklin Pierce Adams was a journalist,
humorist, and charter performer
of the radio program *Information, Please.*
He was also a member of a poker club.
One of the members was Herbert Ransom,
a refreshingly transparent individual.
When he got a good hand,
his face lit up like a Christmas tree.
This led Adams to suggest that the club
adopt the following rule:
Looking at Ransom's face after he is
dealt a hand is regarded as cheating.

This humorous story recalls
how the gospels frequently refer
to Jesus' ability to read hearts.
A parent of six children
said she would be surprised
if Jesus had *not* been able to do this—
even from a purely natural point of view.
To what was she probably referring?

We can't always trust what we hear
with our ears, but we can always trust
what we hear with our heart.   Anonymous

*Jesus went up a hill to pray and spent
the whole night there praying to God.*

Luke 6:12

Author Arthur Gordon
tells how one night in his boyhood
his father woke him from his sleep,
took him by the hand,
and walked him outside into the night.
As they stood looking up at the sky,
Arthur saw a star streak across it.
Then he saw a second and a third.
"What's going on?" he asked his father.
"It's a shower of shooting stars,"
his father explained.
"Showers like this don't happen often.
I thought you'd like to see it."
Arthur said he never forgot that night.
And he always counted himself blessed
to have a father who felt that a shower
of shooting stars was more important
than a night of unbroken sleep.

What important message might a sky full
of shooting stars give a child? Give me?

*Two things fill the mind with ever new
and increasing wonder and awe—
the starry sky above me
and the moral law within me.*

Immanuel Kant

WEDNESDAY
WEEK 23 _____ ORDINARY TIME

Jesus said, "Happy are you poor. . . .
Happy are you who are hungry. . . .
Happy are you when people hate you . . .
because of the Son of Man! . . .
Dance for joy, because a great reward
is kept for you in heaven."   Luke 6:20–23

Viktor Frankl writes:
"We who lived in concentration camps
can remember those who walked
through the huts comforting others,
giving away their last piece of bread.
They . . . offer sufficient proof
that everything can be taken from a person
but one thing—the last freedom—
to choose one's attitude
in any given set of circumstances."
Jesus makes the same point, saying
to the poor, the hungry, and the hated,
who trust in God and refuse
to return evil for evil,
"Be glad . . . dance for joy"   (Luke 6:23),
for you have used your *last freedom*
to make your plight in this world
a stepping-stone to God,
rather than a stumbling block.

How do I use my "last freedom"
in situations that I can't control?

We are our choices.   Jean-Paul Sartre

Jesus said, "Love your enemies,
do good to those who hate you,
bless those who curse you,
and pray for those who mistreat you."
Luke 6:27–28

A grief-stricken father
slumped down into a chair after learning
that his son was brutally murdered.
His grief and that of his family
weighed down on his heart like rock.
For a long time he didn't move.
Then he picked up a pencil and wrote:
"O God,
we remember not only our son
but also his murderers . . .
because through their crime we now
follow thy footsteps more closely
in the way of sacrifice. . . .
So when his murderers
stand before thee
on the day of judgment,
remember . . . and forgive."

Can I compose a similar prayer to God
concerning the sorrow I feel?

All which I took from thee
I did but take not for thy harms,
But just that thou might'st seek it
in My arms. Francis Thompson

Jesus said, "One blind man
cannot lead another one; if he does,
they both fall into a ditch." Luke 6:39

Once there were two men: a blind man,
called "Bear" because of his strength,
and a crippled man,
called "Bug" because of his size.
They tried to get along on their own.
"Independence is a good thing," people said.
But "Bear" and "Bug"
didn't find this to be true in their cases.
So "Bear" stayed home because he'd always
end up in a ditch, and "Bug" stayed home
because—well, he couldn't walk at all.
They both lived lonely lives. Then one day
they happened to meet and talk.
That's when "Bear" got an idea.
"Bug," he said excitedly,
"you sit on my shoulders and be my eyes,
and I will be your legs."
From that day forward, "Bear" and "Bug"
were never lonely and traveled far together.

For whom might I serve as "eyes" or "legs"?

Why can't we build our orphanages
next to homes for the aged?
If someone's sitting in a rocker,
it won't be long before a kid
will be in his lap. Cloris Leachman

Jesus said, "Anyone who hears my words
and does not obey them
is like a man who built his house
without laying a foundation;
when the flood hit that house it fell."

Luke 6:49

A young man applied to teach religion
in a Christian school in India.
When the principal asked him
if he were a practicing Christian, he said,
"No, but I have studied Christianity
and completed a doctorate thesis on it.
I'd gladly take a test to demonstrate
my knowledge of the teachings of Jesus."
The principal explained
that the important thing about Christianity
was not knowing the teachings of Jesus,
but living them. Christianity is a thing
not only of the mind but also of the heart.

What teaching of Jesus do I most often
fail to put into practice in my own family?
What might I do
to improve this situation?

Lord, help me
not only to hear your word
but to implement it,
not only to love it but to live it,
not only to profess it but to practice it.

SUNDAY
WEEK 24 _____ ORDINARY TIME

[Jesus told a story about a servant
who owed a huge debt to a king.
When the servant begged for mercy,
the king forgave the entire debt.
But the servant then went out and refused
to show similar mercy to a fellow servant.
When the king heard about this, he punished
the unforgiving servant severely, saying,]
"You should have had mercy
on your fellow servant,
just as I had mercy on you."   Matthew 18:33

A mother pleaded with Napoleon to pardon
her son a serious offense. Napoleon said,
"This is his second offense;
justice demands he be severely punished."
The mother said, "I'm not asking for justice;
I'm pleading for mercy." Napoleon replied,
"Your son does not deserve mercy."
"Sir," the mother said, "if he deserved it,
it wouldn't be mercy. I'm asking for mercy."
At this, the French general said,
"I will show him mercy."

What keeps me from being more merciful
in my thoughts, words, and actions?

Teach me to feel another's woe,
To hide the fault I see;
That mercy I to others show,
That mercy show to me.   Alexander Pope

[A pagan Roman officer had a servant
who was near death. He begged Jesus
to give the order for his servant to be well.]
Jesus was surprised when he heard this;
he turned around and said to the crowd
following him, "I tell you, I have never found
faith like this, not even in Israel!"   Luke 7:9

Theologian Avery Dulles says:
"Jesus constantly does
the most unexpected things,
revolutionizing the accepted norms of conduct.
He praises pagans and prostitutes,
draws near to Samaritans and lepers.
He attacks the most respected classes,
and insults his hosts at dinner. . . .
He finds time to welcome little children. . . .
He rebukes the wind and the waves,
and falls silent before his accusers. . . .
Men would never have fabricated such a . . .
religious leader, and precisely for this reason
the Gospels have undying power
to convert humble hearts."
Apologetics and the Biblical Christ

Which "unexpected thing" that Jesus did
surprises me most? What might Jesus
be saying to me by this action?

I know men, and I tell you that Jesus Christ
is no mere man.   Napoleon Bonaparte

TUESDAY
WEEK 24 _____ ORDINARY TIME

Jesus went to a town named Nain. . . .
A funeral procession was coming out.
The dead man was the only son of a woman
who was a widow. Luke 7:11–12

"No bands played; no flags waved.
A car honked. My son picked up his bag
and kissed his mother.
Then he shook my hand and said,
'So long.'
'Good luck, son!' I said.
We walked him to the door.
We waved, and the car drove away.
Our son was off to war.
I wish I could have told him
how much I really loved him.
Later I thought to myself
how foolish we are with our children,
always wanting them to fit our dreams,
never accepting them for what they are."
Retold in the first person
Howard O'Brien
never saw his son again;
he died in battle.

What might this story be saying to me?

We are all dreaming of some magical
rose garden over the horizon—instead of
enjoying the roses that are blooming
outside our windows today. Dale Carnegie

[Jesus told some people, "You are like
ill-tempered children.] John the Baptist . . .
fasted and drank no wine,
and you said, 'He has a demon in him!'
The Son of Man came,
and he ate and drank, and you said . . .
'He is a glutton and wine drinker.' " Luke 7:33–34

Sue and Sam were married for five years.
After a good beginning,
their relationship deteriorated.
If Sue made a suggestion, Sam objected;
if Sam made a suggestion, Sue objected.
Neither could do anything to satisfy the other.
One night Sam came home and found Sue
packing. "I can't stand it anymore," she said.
"We are like two mean-spirited children.
All we do is bicker, complain, and fight."
Sam stood bewildered as Sue walked
out of the house, down the street to a motel.
Running to the closet, he threw a few things
in his suitcase and ran after Sue, shouting,
"I can't stand it any longer either.
I'm going with you!"

Jesus' words and the story of Sam and Sue
invite me to inventory my relationships.
Which are thriving? Which need attention?

Anger is the wind that blows out
the lamp of the mind. Robert Ingersoll

THURSDAY
WEEK 24 _____ ORDINARY TIME

[A sinner washed Jesus' feet with her tears.
When a Pharisee complained, Jesus said,
"Two people owed debts they couldn't repay:
one, a large sum; the other, a small sum.
The man erased both debts." Jesus asked,]
"Which . . . will love him more?"
[The Pharisee said,] "I suppose . . .
the one who was forgiven more."
"You are right," said Jesus. . . .
Then Jesus said to the woman,
"Your sins are forgiven."   Luke 7:42–43, 48

In 1984 Velma Barfield was the first woman
to be executed in 22 years in the U.S.
In prison, she had a true conversion.
She says: "I wept and as I lay there weeping,
I questioned could Jesus love me,
someone who had hurt so many people?
And it was then it seemed He appeared . . .
saying, 'Yes, I do love you
and I died on the cross for your sins, too.' . . .
Right then and there
I asked Him to come into my life. . . .
Ever since I've been telling others of His love.
I can't hide it—I have to share it."
Velma Barfield, *Woman on Death Row*

How do I tell others of God's love for me?

Evangelism is one beggar telling another beggar
where he found bread.   D. T. Niles

Jesus traveled through towns and villages,
preaching . . . about the Kingdom of God.
The twelve disciples went with him,
and so did some women who . . . used
their own resources to help.   Luke 8:1–3

Young Samuel Clemens (Mark Twain)
was returning home one night.
He saw what looked like a page from a book
blowing along the sidewalk.
Catching up with it, he saw it was a page
from a story about a certain Joan of Arc.
He'd never heard of her,
but reading the page attracted him to her.
Years later he wrote
Personal Recollections of Joan of Arc.
It was called "the loveliest story" ever written
about the martyred peasant girl.
Her holiness and valor revitalized
the morale of the French army and changed
the course of European history.

What are my thoughts about God's choice
of unlikely people, like a peasant girl,
to play such a key role in history?

God selects his own instruments,
and sometimes they are queer ones;
for instance, he chose me
to steer the ship through a great crisis.
                                        Abraham Lincoln

SATURDAY
WEEK 24 _____ ORDINARY TIME

Jesus said,
"The seeds that fell among thorn bushes
stand for those who hear;
but the worries and [concerns] . . .
of this life . . . choke them,
and their fruit never ripens."   Luke 8:14

During World War II Corrie ten Boom
risked her life helping Jews escape
into the Dutch underground.
When someone asked her if she worried
about being detected and arrested, she said:
"Worrying is carrying tomorrow's load
with today's strength. . . .
It is moving into tomorrow ahead of time.
Worrying does not empty tomorrow
of its sorrow—it empties today of its strength."
Eventually she was arrested, but survived.
After the war and her release,
she lectured throughout Europe on the need
for reconciliation and forgiveness.

Edith Bunker said of her husband:
"Archie doesn't know how to worry
without getting upset."
How might I handle worry better?

Worry is like a rocking chair.
It gives you something to do,
but it doesn't get you anywhere.
                    Author unknown

*[Jesus told about a man who went out
at different times of the day to hire workers.
At day's end he paid each the same wage.
When some protested, he said,]*
*"Don't I have the right to do as I wish
with my own money? Or are you jealous
because I am generous?"* Matthew 20:15

Imagine there are four houses on your street.
Yours is valued at $400,000.
The house next to you, at $300,000.
The third, at $200,000. The last at $100,000.
One day a buyer offers you $500,000
in cash for your house.
You are delighted and you sell it.
The next day you learn
that the other three owners were given
the same price by the same buyer.
You're dismayed
that they received the same price as you.
So you call the buyer and tell him off.
He responds,
"Weren't you delighted at the sale?
Why are you angry now?
Is it because I cheated you?"

How would I respond to the buyer and why?

*Until you make peace with who you are,
you'll never be content with what you have.*
Doris Mortman

MONDAY
WEEK 25 _____ ORDINARY TIME

Jesus said, "Be careful . . . how you listen;
because those who have something
will be given more, but whoever has nothing
will have taken away from them
even the little they think they have."   Luke 8:18

New Zealand probably has more nonflying birds,
like the penguin and the kiwi,
than any other nation. Why is this?
"Scientists say that long ago these birds
could fly, but because they had an endless
supply of food and no natural predators,
they had no reason to exercise
that God-given ability.
Eventually their great gift was lost!"
Edward Hays, *Feathers on the Wind*
This sheds light on
the warning Jesus issues in today's gospel
to the people of his day.
The Jerusalem Bible explains it this way:
"For those of good will,
what they have learned from the old covenant
will be added and perfected by the new.
The ill-disposed will even lose
what they have, namely, that Jewish Law,
which without the perfection Christ brings to it,
is destined to become obsolete."

How well am I using God's gifts to me?

I alone control the inner switch.   Anonymous

*Jesus said, "My mother and brothers
are those who hear the word of God
and obey it."*   Luke 8:21

There's a provocative story about
an unchurched man who, when need arose,
helped out the local funeral director.
Only on such professional occasions
did he ever venture near a church.
On one such rare occasion,
he was standing outside a church.
Nearby several parishioners
were outdoing one another
in saying how sorry they felt for the widow,
who was now the sole support
of her young family.
The man went over to the group and said,
"I couldn't help but hear how sorry you felt
for the widow, and I know you'll join me
in a concrete expression of our sorrow."
With that, he gave $50 to the group leader
to begin a collection for the young widow.

What is one way the practice of my faith
may not quite match my profession of it?

*One sacrifice . . .
is worth all the mere good thoughts,
warm feelings, passionate prayers
in which idle people indulge themselves.*
                                    John Henry Newman

WEDNESDAY
WEEK 25 _____ ORDINARY TIME

*[Jesus sent out his disciples to preach
and to heal,] saying to them,
"Take nothing with you for the trip . . .
no food, no money,
not even an extra shirt."*   Luke 9:3

Jesus tells his disciples to trust in God
and to focus on their life's *purpose,*
not their life's *style.* This invites meditation.
There's a story about a tourist who saw
an islander lying on a beach "enjoying life."
"You should spend your time more profitably,"
said the tourist. "For example, get a boat and
fish. Then you could sell the fish for money."
"What would I do with the money?"
asked the islander. "Save it and buy a motor
for your boat and purchase nylon nets.
Then you could earn even more money."
"What would I do then?" asked the islander.
"Well," said the tourist,
"you could retire early and enjoy life."
"But I'm doing that right now,"
said the islander.
Adapted from a story by Anthony de Mello, S.J.

To what extent am I focusing more
on my life's style than my life's purpose? Why?

*When we begin to live more seriously inside,
we begin to live more simply outside.*
                      Ernest Hemingway

When Herod, the ruler of Galilee,
heard about all the things that were
happening, he was very confused. . . .
Herod said . . . "Who is this man
I hear these things about?"
And he kept trying to see Jesus.   Luke 9:7, 9

A little girl
came back home after her first class
in religious education in her new parish.
"How did your first class go?"
her mother asked.
The little girl said, "I had no idea
who everyone was talking about."
"Do you remember the person's name?"
asked the mother.
"Yes," said the little child.
"They kept saying the name
over and over. It was Jesus!
Who was Jesus, Mother?
I don't know anything about him."

If the little girl asked me who Jesus was,
how would I respond to her?
How well do I really know Jesus—
in a personal, not a "bookish," way?

Today the greatest single deterrent
to knowledge of Jesus is his familiarity.
Because we think we know him,
we pass him by.   Winifred Kirkland

FRIDAY
WEEK 25 _____ ORDINARY TIME

One day [Jesus asked his disciples,] . . .
"Who do you say I am?" Luke 9:18, 20

One hot August Sunday in 1980,
Cordell Brown, a cerebral palsy victim,
spoke at a pregame chapel service
to the champion Philadelphia Phillies.
Why him? What could he—
from his world of pain and deformity—
say to superstars?
The Phillies were asking the same thing
as they sat to listen to him.
Cordell began by putting them all at ease.
He said, "I know I'm different,
but by the grace of God I am what I am."
Then for 20 minutes
he talked about God's goodness to him.
He concluded, saying in a loving way,
"You may hit .350 for a lifetime and get
$1 million a year, but when the day comes
that they close the lid on that box,
you won't be any different than I am.
That's one time we'll all be the same.
I don't need what you have, but one thing is
for sure: You need what I have: Jesus Christ."

What kind of an impact do you think Cordell
had on these superstars? Why?

Life with Christ is an endless hope,
without him a hopeless end. Anonymous

*Jesus said, "The Son of Man is going to be
handed over to the power of human beings."
But the disciples did not know
what this meant.*   Luke 9:44–45

Years ago, Lord George MacLeod shocked
his hearers, saying: "Is there any greater
pathos in our world than the number of youth,
miles outside our churches, who are longing
for a savior, looking pathetically toward
revolutionaries like Che Guevara, or the
student who burned himself alive in Prague?
Do you know the hush that comes down
when either of them is mentioned?
Why no hush for Jesus!
Because we have gotten him lost
in our violent Establishment in which
the Church is seen as 'part of the show.' "

A reporter asked Mother Teresa,
"What's wrong with the Church?" She said,
"You and I, Sir; we are what's wrong
with the Church, for we are the Church."
Why would/wouldn't I agree
that we've gotten Jesus lost,
and are seen as "part of the show"?
What can I, personally, do to help correct
the image some have of us?

*O God, forgive us for crucifying Christ
on earth again.*   Fred Kahn (adapted)

*[Jesus told a parable about a father
who said to his son,]* " *'Go and work
in the vineyard today.' 'I don't want to,'
he answered, but later he changed his mind
and went."* Matthew 21:28–29

The film *Tom Brown's School Days*
concerns a popular boy who lived with
about a dozen other boys in the dormitory
of a British boarding school.
One night a new boy innocently knelt
beside his bed to say his prayers.
Several older boys poked fun at him.
That night Tom lay awake thinking about
what had happened. He also thought about
how his mother taught him to pray nightly—
something he no longer did.
The next night several boys were planning
to poke more fun at the new boy.
When bedtime came, however, something
unexpected happened to change their plans.
When the new boy knelt down
to say his prayers, so did Tom.

How does Jesus' parable about the father
and the son act as a mirror parable?
What is one thing in my life
that I should change?

*When you're through changing,
you're through.* Bruce Barton

Jesus said, "Whoever welcomes this child
in my name, welcomes me."   Luke 9:48

William Purkey told a story about a mouse
that took up temporary residence
in the computer of a testing service.
It triggered a key that changed the scores
of Henry Carson, a so-so student.
When the school saw the printout of Henry's
phenomenal scores, they were delighted
to learn they had a genius in their midst.
They not only repented their misappraisal
of his talents but also reaffirmed his person
in ways that made Henry blossom.
And would you believe it, college recruiters
invited Henry and his parents out to dinner.
New worlds opened up for the exultant youth.
His confidence sang and his self-image soared.
To make a long story short, Henry went on
to become a leader of his generation—
all because of a clumsy mouse who took up
temporary residence in the computer
of a testing service.

What point does this modern parable make?
How might I apply it to my life right now?

Affirmation empowers people—
especially young people—
to see and become the beautiful person
God made them to be.

TUESDAY
WEEK 26 _____ ORDINARY TIME

[Some Samaritans refused to let Jesus
enter their village. James and John said,]
"Lord, do you want us to call fire down
from heaven to destroy them?"
Jesus turned and rebuked them.   Luke 9:54–55

High in the Andes, and visible
for miles and miles, is a statue of Jesus.
Called *Christ of the Andes,* it straddles
the border between Chile and Argentina.
According to M. Nassan, both nations
were preparing to war against each other.
On Easter Sunday, bishops of both nations
began a giant, aggressive peace initiative.
As a result, the people, who opposed war,
made their governments sit down
and settle the differences peacefully.
When an agreement was reached,
the big bronze guns being produced for war
were melted and recast into the present statue.

Jesus said, "Happy are those
who work for peace;
God will call them his children!"   Matthew 5:9
How peaceful a person am I?

These mountains shall fall and crumble to dust
before the people of Chile and the Argentine
shall forget their solemn covenant
sworn at the feet of Christ.

Inscription on *Christ of the Andes*

[Jesus asked some people to follow him.
One man said,] "I will follow you, sir;
but first let me go and say good-bye
to my family." Jesus said to him,
"Anyone who . . . keeps looking back
is of no use for the Kingdom of God."

Luke 9:59, 61–62

A farmer gave a poor boy a basket and said,
"You may pick the best ears of corn
in a given row in my field.
There is only one condition.
You must choose as you walk along and
not go back once you pass an ear of corn."
The boy began to walk. He was wide-eyed
at the big ears he saw as he walked down
the long row. But a bigger ear
always appeared just ahead of him.
So he kept walking down the row.
Suddenly the boy was horrified.
He had come to the end of the row—
without having put one ear of corn
in his basket.

How might Jesus' words to the man
and the story of the indecisive boy apply
to a situation I find myself in right now?

Whoever insists upon seeing
with perfect clarity before he decides,
never decides. Henri Amiel

THURSDAY
WEEK 26 _____ ORDINARY TIME

Jesus said, "There is a large harvest,
but few workers to gather it in.
Pray to the owner of the harvest
that he will send out workers
to gather in his harvest." Luke 10:2

One Sunday,
author Harry Paige walked into a church
and noticed large sections of pews
that were roped off
with signs reading "Reserved."
He figured special guests were coming
and wondered who they might be.
Mass began but no one showed up.
Then, in his homily, the priest explained:
"The roped-off sections were reserved
for family members and friends
who once knelt and worshiped with us,
but for some reason have ceased doing so."
The priest didn't say
what we should do about it,
but he didn't have to. We knew.

Do I know
what I am supposed to do about it?

I decided to call a friend
who hadn't been to church in years.
To my surprise, he accepted, almost as if
he had been waiting for my call.

Harry W. Paige

Jesus said to his disciples,
"Whoever listens to you listens to me."
                                            Luke 10:16

Kermit Long tells the story
of two men walking in a downtown area.
Suddenly, one of them stop dead and said,
"Listen to the lovely sound of that cricket."
The other listened but heard nothing.
Turning to his friend, he asked,
"How can you hear the sound of a cricket
in the midst of all this noise?"
His friend, a zoologist, said he had trained
himself to listen to the voices of nature.
But he didn't explain.
"He simply took a coin out of his pocket
and dropped it on the sidewalk,
whereupon a dozen people
began to look about them.
'We hear,' he said, 'what we listen for.'"

How well am I trying to train myself
to listen to Jesus' voice speaking to me
within my heart—
or through other people?

The more faithfully you listen
to the voice within you,
the better you hear
what is sounding outside of you.
                                            Dag Hammarskjold

SATURDAY
WEEK 26 _____ ORDINARY TIME

[Jesus told his disciples,] "I have given you
authority, so that you can walk on snakes
and scorpions and overcome all the power
of the Enemy, and nothing will hurt you.
But don't be glad because the evil spirits
obey you; rather be glad because your names
are written in heaven." Luke 10:18–20

The Little Flowers of Saint Francis is a
collection of old legends about the saint.
One story concerns a wolf that
used to terrorize the town of Gubbio, Italy.
One day Francis tracked it down and said,
"Brother Wolf, I order you in Jesus' name
not to harm me or anyone."
The wolf came forward like a pet dog
and lay gently at Francis's feet.
The saint then brought the wolf to Gubbio,
where he became a town pet.
Even the dogs treated him gently.
When the wolf died two years later,
the town mourned, because he had been
a reminder to them of the power of Jesus
and of the holiness of Francis.

What is one reason why this legend
has survived the centuries?
What truth does it enshrine?

Be glad and rejoice forever in what I create.
Isaiah 65:18

Jesus said,
" 'The stone which the builders rejected
as worthless turned out to be
the most important of all.' "   Matthew 21:42

In *Hinduism,* Paul and Susan Younger
tell the story of Panini.
One day an old man adept at reading palms
studied the boy's right hand carefully.
He shook his head and said sadly,
"You are a fine lad.
Your heart is sound. You have a good mind
and your life line is not bad.
But alas, there is absolutely nothing
where a career line should be!
You might end up as a nonentity
and a dunce."
Panini thanked the old man for his wisdom.
Then, taking a small knife, he drew it gently
across the place where his career line
was supposed to be. He promised himself,
there and then, that he would apply himself
and make his new career line a reality.
He did. He became one of the greatest
of all Indian grammarians.

How do the words of Scripture
and the story of Panini apply to me?

If God is for us, who can be against us?
                                            Romans 8:31

MONDAY
WEEK 27 _____ ORDINARY TIME

[Jesus told a story about a man
who was attacked by robbers and left half dead.
"A priest saw the man, but he walked on by.]
A Samaritan . . . saw him . . . and took him
to an inn, where he took care of him."

Luke 10:33–34

John Chrysostom lived for two years
in a mountain cave near Antioch.
There he memorized the entire New Testament.
Eventually, he won fame as a preacher.
His love for the poor, and his blunt preaching
of the obligation of the rich to them,
made him unpopular with the powerful.
Predictably, the empress silenced him
by exiling him to a remote region.
Here's a sample of his preaching style:
"Of what use is it to weigh down
Christ's table with golden cups,
when he himself is dying of hunger? . . .
Do not, therefore, adorn the church
and ignore your afflicted brother,
for he is the most precious temple of all."
John Chrysostom died in exile and
was eventually canonized as a saint.

What kind of love do I have for the poor?
How do I express it in action?

God does not want golden vessels
but golden hearts. Saint John Chrysostom

[Jesus was visiting Mary and Martha.
Martha rushed about doing things.
Jesus finally said to Martha,]
"You are worried and troubled
over so many things, but just one is needed.
Mary has chosen the right thing."   Luke 10:41–42

William Barclay, the Scottish theologian,
says one of his favorite stories concerns
the great American Bishop Quayle.
Quayle was a worrier. He used to sit up
half the night worrying. Then one night
an amazing thing happened. He said he
"heard God's voice as clearly as if it had
been someone sitting in the same room."
God said, "Quayle, go to bed.
I'll sit up for the rest of the night."
The impact of the experience on the bishop
was transforming. Barclay says,
"And thereafter there was in Quayle
a wonderful serenity, for he had learned
to cast his burden on the Lord."   *Daily Celebration*

What is one worry I have right now?
What advice would I give to another
who came to me about the same worry?

There is no need
to nervously pace the deck
of the ship of life when the Great Pilot
is at the wheel.   E. C. McKenzie

WEDNESDAY
WEEK 27 _____ ORDINARY TIME

One day Jesus was praying. . . .
When he had finished, one of his disciples
said to him, "Lord, teach us to pray."
[Then Jesus taught them the Lord's Prayer.]

Luke 11:1

A man named Spriggs recalls
his first night as a homeless person.
Someone directed him to a shelter.
There he found a lot of rough-looking men
waiting in line. Finally, the door opened,
and they all got beds—
about a hundred men in all.
Minutes later, they turned out the lights.
Spriggs writes: "I was terrified. . . .
Then out of the darkness a voice said,
'Our Father, who are in heaven . . .'
and the entire dormitory joined in.
At the end of the prayer another voice began,
'Now I lay me down to sleep . . .'
Even now I get goose bumps thinking about it.
That minute I realized that God . . .
seems to be closer to the homeless.
You could feel him in the shelter. . . .
My fears were replaced by peace."

The Catholic Standard, Washington, D.C.

Can I recall ever feeling God's presence—
perhaps when I was alone and frightened?

Go to sleep in peace. God is awake.   Victor Hugo

Jesus said, "You know how to give. . . .
How much more . . . will the Father . . . give
the Holy Spirit to those who ask!" Luke 11:13

Long ago, no rain fell, and all life was dying.
One day a girl went up a mountain
with a tin dipper to seek water
for her dying mother.
Returning, she gave a drink to a dying dog.
As she did, the dipper changed to silver
and refilled. Then she gave a drink to a man
who was so thirsty he could no longer speak.
The dipper turned to gold and refilled.
Arriving home, the girl gave the dipper
to her mother, who drank all she wanted.
Water still remained. The girl then gave
a drink to a stranger who came to the door.
One drop clung to the dipper.
As the girl took the dipper, the drop fell.
Where it hit the ground, a spring gushed up,
watering the whole land. In the excitement,
no one saw the stranger disappear.
But that night everyone saw
a "dipper of stars" sparkling in the sky.
It remains there to this very day.

In light of Jesus' words,
how might I interpret the "dipper" story?

God's gifts
put man's best dreams to shame. E. B. Browning

FRIDAY
WEEK 27 _____ ORDINARY TIME

Jesus said,
"Anyone who does not help me gather
is really scattering."   Luke 11:23

"I knew I was a convicted criminal,
but I was proud of my crime.
It was the crime of joining my people
in a nonviolent protest against injustice. . . .
It was the crime of desiring for my people
the inalienable rights of life, liberty,
and the pursuit of happiness.
It was above all the crime
of seeking to convince my people
that noncooperation with evil
is just as much a moral duty
as is the cooperation with good."
Martin Luther King Jr., *Stride toward Freedom*

How well am I helping Jesus "to gather"
rather than "scatter" in racial matters?

Before the ship of your life
reaches its last harbor,
there will be long drawn-out storms . . .
and tempestuous seas
that make the heart stand still.
If you do not have a deep patient faith
in God, you will be powerless to face
the delay, disappointment,
and vicissitudes that inevitably come.
Martin Luther King Jr., *Strength to Love*

Jesus said, "How happy are those
who hear the word of God and obey it!"
                                    Luke 11:28

Baltimore Oriole shortstop Cal Ripken
broke Lou Gehrig's record of playing
2,131 straight games on September 6, 1995.
When the game became official
in the fifth inning, a packed stadium
broke into a spontaneous celebration
for 22 minutes.
The celebration was so moving
that TV commentators kept quiet
the whole time, letting the camera tell the story.
Meanwhile, games around the country
stopped and players and fans alike applauded.
One reason for the tremendous outpouring
of fans across the country is Cal Ripken himself.
His quiet manner, personal integrity,
and loyal dedication to his family,
Baltimore fans, and baseball
make him a star and a role model
everyone can truly look up to and admire.

How would I rate my own personal integrity
and loyal dedication to my family,
friends, and associates?

If we are faithful,
God will look after our success.
                                    Author unknown

SUNDAY
WEEK 28 _____ ORDINARY TIME

Jesus said,
"The Kingdom of heaven is like this.
Once there was a king
who prepared a wedding feast for his son.
[When many invited guests failed to come,
he invited substitute guests.]"   Matthew 22:2

Like all of Jesus' parables,
this parable has two levels of meaning.
First, there is the *literal* meaning.
It's the story: a king holds a feast for his son.
When many invited guests don't come,
he replaces them with substitute guests.
The second level is the *intended* meaning.
A study of the parable shows
the king stands for *God;* the feast,
God's Kingdom in its final form in heaven;
the invited guests, *God's Chosen People;*
and the substitute guests, *the Gentiles.*
And so the second level of meaning shows
that God's Kingdom is now open to *all people,*
not just the Chosen People.
No one is excluded, *not even* the Gentiles.

Concretely, how am I showing my gratitude
to God for inviting me to his Son's feast?

Write it down for the coming generation
what the LORD has done,
so that people not yet born
will praise him.   Psalm 102:18

Jesus said, "On the Judgment Day
the people of Nineveh will stand up and
accuse you, because they turned from
their sins when they heard Jonah preach;
and I assure you that there is something here
greater than Jonah!" Luke 11:32

An ancient legend concerns a sinful woman
who died and showed up at heaven's gate.
She was told that she would be admitted
only on condition that she returned to earth
and brought back the gift God loved most.
She returned a week later
with a drop of blood of someone martyred
for the faith.
But she was told there was something
that God loved much more. A month later
she returned with the sweat from the brow
of an old missionary. Again she was told
that God loved something even more.
A year later she returned
with the tear of a repentant sinner.
When she presented it, there was great joy
in heaven. This was, indeed, the gift
that God loved most.

Like Jonah, Jesus called sinners to repentance.
How well am I heeding his call?

The greatest of all faults
is to be conscious of none. Thomas Carlyle

TUESDAY
WEEK 28 _____ ORDINARY TIME

[Jesus told a Pharisee who was surprised
he did not wash before eating,]
"Give what is in your cups and plates
to the poor, and everything
will be ritually clean." Luke 11:41

President Truman wrote notes to himself.
They form a kind of "White House diary."
Consider excerpts from two notes:
• "A couple of golden crowns with . . .
expensive jewels have been stolen. . . .
The crowns were on images of Jesus
and Mary, his mother. I have an idea
if Jesus were here his sympathies would be
with the thieves. . . . The only crown
he ever wore was one of thorns."
• "When the gates of heaven are reached
by the shades of the earth bound,
the rank and riches enjoyed on this planet
won't be of value. Some of our grandees
will have to do a lot of explaining
on how they got that way. Wish I could
hear their alibis! I can't, for the probabilities
are I'll be thinking of some myself."
Ralph Keyes, ed., *The Wit and Wisdom of Harry Truman*

How do the "notes" relate to today's gospel?

No one has had the courage to memorialize
his wealth on his tombstone.
It would not look well there. Cora May Harris

Jesus said, "How terrible . . .
for you teachers of the Law!
You put onto people's backs loads which are
hard to carry, but you yourselves will not
stretch out a finger to help them carry
those loads." Luke 11:46

Johann Wolfgang von Goethe,
the celebrated German philosopher,
listed eight requisites to a contented life:
"*health* enough to make your work a joy;
wealth enough to make ends meet;
strength enough to battle your difficulties
and overcome them;
grace enough to confess your sins
and forsake them;
patience enough to toil
until some good is accomplished;
charity enough to see good in your neighbor;
faith enough to make real the things of God;
hope enough to remove all anxious fear
concerning the future."

Which of these eight requisites
do I feel I am lacking to a crippling degree
and why?
What might I do to remedy my situation?

A second-class effort
is a first-class mistake.
William Arthur Ward

THURSDAY
WEEK 28 _____ ORDINARY TIME

[Jesus told the Pharisees and lawyers,]
"You have kept the key that opens the door
to the house of knowledge . . . and you
stop those who are trying to go in!" Luke 11:52

To help his flock understand the hostility
between Jesus and some religious teachers,
a preacher said, "Suppose a medical clinic
grew influential and wealthy because
of its work with AIDS patients.
Suppose it found the 'key that opens the
door' to a cure for AIDS, but suppressed it
so as not to lose its influence and wealth."
This example parallels
what some religious leaders were doing
in Jesus' day. They possessed
the "key that opens the door"
to knowledge of God and God's mercy,
but they deliberately withheld it
from the people to keep them dependent
on their own warped ideas of religion.
In other words, they were more interested
in feeding themselves than in feeding
the hungry flocks entrusted to them by God.

To what extent might I be blinded
to other people's needs
because of my selfishness?

Help another's boat across, and lo!
thine own has reached the shore. Old proverb

*Jesus said, "Even the hairs of your head
have all been counted. So do not be afraid."*

Luke 12:7

Actress Ann Jillian found a growth
on her body; she feared the worst.
Before going to the doctor,
she went to Saint Francis de Sales Church.
Over its entrance was this inscription,
which she had often seen
but never read until now:
"The same everlasting Father
who cares for you today
will take care of you tomorrow and every day.
Either he will shield you from suffering,
or he will give you unfailing strength
to bear it. Be at peace then and put aside
all anxious thoughts and imaginations."
Those words gave actress Ann Jillian hope
just when she needed it most.
Two weeks later she successfully
underwent a double mastectomy.

Did I ever have a similar experience
when words from Scripture
or elsewhere seemed addressed right to me?

*Trust the past to God's mercy,
the present to God's love, and
the future to God's providence.*

Saint Augustine

SATURDAY
WEEK 28 _____ ORDINARY TIME

*Jesus said, "Whoever says a word against
the Son of Man can be forgiven; but whoever
says evil things against the Holy Spirit
will not be forgiven."* Luke 12:10

A speaker kept insisting on the need
to continue to reach out to teenagers.
During the question-and-answer period,
a mother asked, "But what do you do
when you keep reaching out to teenagers
and they keep pushing you away and
even speak against you to their friends?"
This seems to be
what Jesus is referring to in today's gospel.
When people reject him
and speak against him, all Jesus can do
is to continue to reach out to them.
Hopefully, after he returns to the Father,
and the Holy Spirit comes,
they will see the light and accept salvation.
But if they also reject the Holy Spirit,
then even God's hands are tied.
Salvation—like love—is a gift. No one—
not even God—can force it on a person.

In what way might I be tying God's hands
when it comes to receiving salvation?

*If God is kept outside,
something must be wrong inside.*
E. C. McKenzie

*[Some Pharisees tried to trap Jesus
by asking if they should pay taxes to Rome.
Jesus foiled their plot, saying,]
"Pay to the Emperor what belongs
to the Emperor, and pay to God
what belongs to God."*   Matthew 22:21

Christians possess a dual citizenship:
earth and heaven. And as history shows,
it sometimes leads to a conflict
between God and country.
Take the case of Franz Jaeggerstatter.
When Hitler marched into Austria and held
a mock election to show that Austria
approved of his action, Jaeggerstatter was
the only person in his village to oppose it.
And when war came in 1939,
Jacggerstatter refused to report for duty.
He even refused noncombatant service.
His conscience wouldn't let him participate
in a war that he thought was unjust.
He chose to remain faithful to his primary
obligation as he understood it: God.
The Nazis executed him.

What is an example of a possible conflict
between God and government today?
What options are open to a Christian?

*Injustice expands in proportion
to our willingness to put up with it.*   Anonymous

366

MONDAY
WEEK 29 _____ ORDINARY TIME

[Jesus told a parable about a man
who stored up great worldly treasures.
God said to the man,]
" 'You fool! This very night
you will have to give up your life;
then who will get all these things
you have kept for yourself?' " Luke 12:20

The Associated Press carried this story
over its wire services on June 15, 1957:
"Three weeks ago
a frail little widow was found starving
in her dreary fire-charred Staten Island flat.
Today, it was learned she was worth
half a million dollars, $275,000 of it
in bills hoarded in her bedroom closet. . . .
Her wealth apparently had gone untouched
while she lived on 15-cent hot dogs
and saved boxes and wrappings
for her pot-bellied stove."

How do these words of Pope John Paul II
apply also to the widow in the AP story:
"It is not wrong to want to live better;
what is wrong is a style of life
which is presumed to be better
when it is directed
towards 'having' rather than 'being' "?

True wealth is the good we do in this world.
Muhammad

Jesus said,
"How happy are those servants
whose master finds them awake and ready
when he returns!"   Luke 12:37

Sandra, on an early lunch break,
was phoning from a restaurant.
An older woman was sitting nearby.
Sandra said, "Mr. Bell, please."
When Mr. Bell answered, Sandra said,
"I hear that you're looking for an assistant."
There was a pause. Sandra replied,
"Oh! You say you hired one two weeks ago?
And you're very pleased with her?
Thank you." With that, Sandra hung up.
The woman said, "I couldn't help but hear.
Sorry you didn't get the job."
Sandra replied cheerfully, "It's okay!
You see, Mr. Bell hired me two weeks ago
as his assistant, and I was wondering
what he thought of my work so far."

Jesus' words about his return
and the story of Sandra invite me to ask,
If I could ask Jesus right now
what he thought of my work
on earth so far, what might he say?

It is not only what we do,
but also what we do not do,
for which we are held accountable.   Molière

WEDNESDAY
WEEK 29 _____ ORDINARY TIME

Jesus said, "Much is required
from the person to whom much is given;
much more is required from the person
to whom much more is given." Luke 12:48

The Gold-Crowned Jesus
is a play by Korean poet Kim Chi Ha.
Kim is the artist who was sentenced to life
in prison by the Park Chung He regime
for denouncing its repressive measures.
In the play a leper discovers Jesus
in a state prison.
He asks Jesus, "Why do you stay in prison?
Why don't you use your divine power
to free yourself and
destroy evil in the world?"
Jesus surprises him, saying,
"My power alone can neither free myself
nor destroy evil in the world.
There's only one way I can do these things:
through people like you.
Without you I can do nothing.
With you, all things are possible."

What keeps me from placing myself
in Jesus' hands to be used by him
in any way he sees fit?

Blessed are they who place themselves
in the hands of Jesus. He will place himself
in their hands. Anonymous

ORDINARY TIME _____ WEEK 29

Jesus said, "I came to set the earth
on fire! . . . From now on a family
of five will be divided, three against two."
Luke 12:49, 52

Clarence Jordan was famous
for his *Cotton Patch Version* of the Bible.
In the 1960s he developed Koinonia Farm,
an interracial project in Georgia.
James McClendon says that one day
Clarence asked his brother Robert,
later a Georgia Supreme Court justice,
to help the farm with a legal matter.
Robert refused, saying it might hurt
his political future. Clarence was shocked.
He reminded Robert that as boys
they had both accepted Jesus together.
Robert replied that he still accepted Jesus:
"I follow him to the cross, but not onto it.
I'm not getting myself crucified like he did."
Clarence replied, "Robert, then you're not
a follower of Jesus; you're only a fan of his."

Which of the two brothers am I most like
in my following of Jesus—and why?

All I want is to know Christ . . .
and become like him in his death,
in the hope that I myself
will be raised from death to life.
Philippians 3.10–11

FRIDAY
WEEK 29 _____ ORDINARY TIME

*Jesus said, "You can look at the earth
and the sky and predict the weather;
why, then, don't you know the meaning
of this present time?"* Luke 12:56

On July 20, 1969, at 4:17 P.M. EDT,
Armstrong and Aldrin landed
the *Apollo 11* module on the Sea of Tranquility.
Six hours later, Armstrong became
the first human to walk on the moon.
Later, Aldrin wrote in *Life:* "It is difficult
for me to articulate my thoughts
about the significance of this flight. . . .
It was more than a team of people
and government and industry
working together. . . .
It is my hope that people
will keep this whole event in their minds
and see beyond . . . technical achievements
to the deeper meaning of it all:
a challenge, a quest, the human need
to do these things, and the need to recognize
that we are one mankind under God."

What deeper meaning do I see
in the moon landing and walking event?

*In the swift rush of great events,
we find ourselves groping to know
the full sense and meaning of these times
in which we live.* Dwight D. Eisenhower

*[Jesus told a parable about a man
who told his gardener to cut down a tree
because it failed to produce any figs.]
"But the gardener answered, 'Leave it alone,
sir, just one more year; I will dig around it
and put in some fertilizer.
Then if the tree bears figs next year,
so much the better; if not,
then you can have it cut down.'"* Luke 13:8–9

In *Uncommon Friends,* James Newton says
Thomas Edison and a team of assistants
had just finished improvements
on the first lightbulb. Edison gave the bulb
"to a young helper, who nervously
carried it upstairs, step by step.
At the last moment, the boy dropped it.
The whole team had to work
another 24 hours to make another bulb.
Edison looked around,
then handed it to the same boy.
The gesture probably changed the boy's life.
Edison knew
that more than the bulb was at stake."

In what sense is Newton's story of Edison
an application of Jesus' parable?
What might Jesus be saying to me through it?

*Sympathy is two hearts
tugging at the same load.* E. C. McKenzie

SUNDAY
WEEK 30 _____ ORDINARY TIME

Jesus said, " 'Love the Lord your God
with all your heart. . . .' This is the greatest
and the most important commandment.
The second most important commandment
is . . . 'Love your neighbor
as you love yourself.' "   Matthew 22:37–39

Actor Hume Cronyn was being interviewed
by a reporter. At one point he was asked
about his relationship
with his most important "neighbor," his wife.
He said: "I can bring almost any problem
I can think of—and a damned stupid one—
to her, and lay it in her lap,
and know I won't be laughed at,
and I won't be judged.
That's a line from a play: 'To love somebody
is to know that you can tell everything
and not be laughed at, or judged.'
I think that says a lot."

How would I describe my relationship
with the most important "neighbors"
in my life: my own family?

Two kids were screaming and yelling
at each other in a room. It was torrid!
Finally, the mother went in and asked,
"What in the world are you kids doing?"
They said,
"We're playing Mommy and Daddy."

A woman . . . was bent over
and could not straighten up at all.
When Jesus saw her, he . . . placed his hands
on her, and at once she straightened
herself up and praised God.   Luke 13:11–13

Peter Matthiessen was hiking in Asia.
He describes this pitiable sight:
"A child dragging bent useless legs
is crawling up a hill outside the village. . . .
She pulls herself along
like a broken cricket. . . . She gazes up,
clear-eyed, without resentment—
it seems much worse that she is pretty.
In Bengal, George Schaller says stiffly,
beggars will break their children's knees
to achieve this pitiable effect
for business purposes. . . . But the child . . .
is not a beggar; she is merely a child. . . .
I long to give her something—a new life?"
The Snow Leopard

Peter was unable to give the child
what Jesus was able to give the woman.
What might I be able to give a child like this
in exchange for what she gave by gazing up,
"clear-eyed, without resentment"?

Defeat may serve as well as victory
to shake the soul and let the glory out.
Edwin Markham

[Jesus said,
"The Kingdom of God is like this.]
A man takes a mustard seed
and plants it in his field. The plant grows
and becomes a tree."   Luke 13:19

A teacher told her class, "When I was a girl,
my grandma gave me a big cucumber
inside a bottle with a narrow neck.
She said she'd tell me a 'big secret'
when I figured out how
she got it into the bottle.
One day I was walking in grandma's garden,
and I saw a bottle into which she had
inserted a vine with a tiny cucumber on it.
Now I knew how she got the cucumber
in the bottle. She grew it there.
Then grandma told me her 'big secret.'
She said a 'good habit' formed in childhood
is like a tiny cucumber inserted in a bottle—
or like a tiny bit of yeast inserted in dough.
The habit grows so big and strong inside you
that no one can take it away from you."

What is one "good habit" formed in childhood
that has grown bigger in me?
What is one "bad habit" that I regret forming?

First we form habits, then they form us.
Conquer your bad habits,
or they'll eventually conquer you.   Dr. Rob Gilbert

[One day someone asked Jesus,]
"Sir, will just a few people be saved?"
Jesus answered them,
"Do your best to go in
through the narrow door;
because many people will surely try
to go in but will not be able."   Luke 13:23–24

A death scene in *The Magnificent Ambersons*
touches on Jesus' warning in today's gospel:
The narrator says:
"And now Major Amberson
was engaged in the profoundest thinking
of his life, and he realized
that everything that had worried
or delighted him during his lifetime—
all his buying and building and trading
and banking—that it was all a trifle and
a waste beside what concerned him now,
for the major knew now that he had
to plan to enter an unknown country
where he was not even sure
of being recognized as an Amberson."

What are my thoughts as I read the above?

When his cold hand touches yours . . .
he will lead you away from
your investments . . . and real estate,
and with him you will pass into eternity. . . .
You will not be too busy to die.   A. E. Kittredge

THURSDAY
WEEK 30 _____ ORDINARY TIME

Jesus said, "How many times I wanted
to put my arms around all [of you] . . .
as a hen gathers her chicks under her wings,
but you would not let me!"   Luke 13:34

John Cardinal Newman wrote:
"God beholds you. . . .
God calls you by name. . . .
God views you in your day of rejoicing
and in your day of sorrow.
God sympathizes
in your hopes and your temptations. . . .
God hears your voice,
the beating of your heart
and your very breathing.
You do not love yourself better
than God loves you.
You cannot shrink from pain
more than God dislikes your bearing it."

Why don't I better realize
God's love for me?

Escape from your everyday business
for a while. . . .
Enter your mind's inner chamber.
Shut out everything but God
and say with your whole heart . . .
"Lord, my God . . . teach me to seek you,
and when I seek you,
show yourself to me."   Saint Anselm

*[Jesus said to those present
  who opposed healing people on the Sabbath,]
"If any one of you had a child or an ox
that happened to fall in a well on a Sabbath,
would you not pull it out?"*   Luke 14:5

An elderly man lived in a poor neighborhood
in Liverpool. Kids played around his house.
One August night a thief entered
the man's house and stumbled over his body.
The man had been dead
for nearly six months.
A 70-year-old Portsmouth woman
was found dead in the kitchen of her home.
Her body was nearly decomposed.
Authorities estimated she had been dead
for about four years. No one ever came
to see her or check on her.

To what extent, perhaps, have I become
insensitive to the presence of the needy
around me—even unconsciously resenting
their claim on my help?

*No man is an island, entire of itself;
every man is a piece of the continent,
a part of the main. . . .
Any man's death diminishes me . . .
and therefore never send to know
for whom the bell tolls; it tolls for thee.*
                                John Donne

Jesus noticed how some of the guests
were choosing the best places [and said,] . . .
"Those who make themselves great
will be humbled, and those who humble
themselves will be made great."   Luke 14:7, 11

A symphony conductor was thrilled at
the enthusiastic ovation he was receiving.
He was especially impressed
that the ushers of the hall were leading it.
He thought to himself,
"They're probably musicians
working their way through school
and are more appreciative of good music
and good conducting than the holders
of some of the high-priced tickets."
Just then, a patron sitting in an aisle seat
overheard one of the ushers say to another,
"If we can keep this applause going
for another four minutes,
we'll qualify for overtime pay."

"Many would be scantily clad if clothed
in their humility." Anonymous Would I?

Bishop Clark . . . told of a dispute . . .
between two hot church members.
One said at last, "I should like to know
who you are." "Who am I!" cried the other.
"Who am I! I am a humble Christian,
you damned old heathen!"   Ralph Waldo Emerson

Jesus said, "The greatest one among you
must be your servant.
Whoever makes himself great
will be humbled,
and whoever humbles himself
will be made great."   Matthew 23:11–12

Coach Gary Barnett
surprised the entire sporting world
by winning "The Big Ten" title in 1995
and taking a Cinderella Northwestern team
to the Rose Bowl.
Later he surprised it again by something
he wrote in his autobiography, *High Hopes:*
Taking the Purple to Pasadena.
Describing a difficult adolescence, he wrote
with astonishing honesty and humility:
"My real distress came
from being a bed wetter."
Barnett broke the habit as a sophomore
before his first high school football game.
When asked by a reporter why he mentioned
such a humiliating thing in his biography,
he shrugged and said, "I am who I am,
and I'm comfortable with who I am."

What was a humiliating episode or period
in my adolescent life?

Humility and self-denial are always admired,
but rarely practiced.   E. C. McKenzie

MONDAY
WEEK 31 _____ ORDINARY TIME

Jesus said, "When you give a feast,
invite the poor, the crippled, the lame,
and the blind; and you will be blessed,
because they are not able to pay you back.
God will repay you." Luke 14:13–14

There's a scene in Frank Capra's movie
Mr. Deeds Goes to Town
in which Gary Cooper explains his concern
for the poor. He says:
"There will always be leaders and followers.
It's like the road out in front of my house.
It's on a steep hill.
And every day I watch the cars climbing up.
Some go lickety-split up that hill in high—
some have to shift into second—
and some sputter and shake and
slip back to the bottom again. . . .
And I say that the fellas who can make
the hill in high should help those who can't.
That's all I'm trying to do with this money.
Help the fellas
who can't make the hill in high."

Concretely, how am I showing concern for
"the fellas who can't make the hill in high"?

Happy are those
who are concerned for the poor;
the Lord will help them
when they are in trouble. Psalm 41:1

[Jesus told this parable:]
"There was once a man who was giving
a great feast. . . . When it was time . . .
he sent his servants to tell his guests,
'Come, everything is ready!'
But they all began, one after another,
to make excuses." Luke 14:16–17

Greg was a promising young businessman.
He had one serious flaw, however.
He found it impossible to give a clear-cut
yes or no on certain critical issues.
Finally, the company arranged for him
to see a psychiatrist.
After greeting Greg, the psychiatrist said,
"I understand you are having trouble
making decisions on certain critical issues."
Greg looked at the psychiatrist
somewhat puzzled and said,
"Well, yes—and no!"

Jesus' parable highlights the need
for clear-cut commitment to God's Kingdom.
There is no room for procrastination.
What keeps me, perhaps,
from clear-cut, total commitment
to Jesus and his work?

Jesus said, "Anyone who starts to plow
and . . . keeps looking back is of no use
for the Kingdom of God." Luke 9:62

WEDNESDAY
WEEK 31 _____ ORDINARY TIME

Jesus said, "None of you can be my disciple unless you give up everything." Luke 14:33

Archy and mehitabel is a book
of unique "poems" by Don Marquis.
Archy is a poet reincarnated as a cockroach;
mehitabel is Cleopatra come back as a cat.
As a cockroach, archy still retains
his love of poetry and writes poems
by throwing himself
against the typewriter keys.
Since he's not strong enough to depress
the shift key,
he writes everything lower case.
In one of his poems, archy asks a moth friend
why moths fly so closely to electric lightbulbs
and flaming candles,
risking incineration by the heat or the flames.
His friend explains that moths crave beauty
and excitement, saying that it is better
to live a short life and die in excitement than
to live a long time and die in boredom.
Archy doesn't buy this philosophy,
but he does say of his moth friend,
"i wish there was something i wanted
as badly as he wanted to fry himself."

What is one thing I want really "badly"?

*Strong lives are motivated by
dynamic purposes.* Kenneth Hildebrand

[Jesus said, "When you find a lost sheep,]
you are so happy
that you put it on your shoulders
and carry it back home."   Luke 15:5–6

George Vest's "Eulogy of a Dog" reads in part:
"He guards the sleep of his pauper master
as if he were a prince.
When all other friends desert, he remains.
When riches take wings . . .
he is as constant in his love as the sun
in its journey though the heavens.
If fortune drives the master forth an outcast
in the world, friendless and homeless . . .
the faithful dog asks no higher privilege
than that of accompanying him. . . .
And when . . . death takes the master . . .
there by his graveside will the noble dog
be found, his head between his paws . . .
faithful and true even to death."
Congressional Record (Oct. 16, 1914)

The loyalty of a dog and that of a shepherd
are faint images of Jesus' loyalty to me.
How well are they images of my own
loyalty and faithfulness to Jesus—and
to those to whom I owe much?

Never let go of loyalty and faithfulness.
Tie them around your neck;
write them on your heart.   Proverbs 3:3

FRIDAY
WEEK 31 _____ ORDINARY TIME

*Jesus said, "The people of this world
are much more shrewd in handling
their affairs than the people
who belong to the light."* Luke 16:8

In *In Pursuit of the Great White Rabbit,*
Father Edward Hays tells a story
of a man who was in grave difficulty.
He vowed that if God would save him,
he would sell his home
and give the money to the poor.
But when the problem was resolved,
he found himself bound by a vow
that he wished he hadn't made.
And so he set upon a solution.
He put his home up for sale,
stipulating that whoever bought it
must also buy his cat.
When the two items sold for $200,000,
the man kept his vow.
He banked $199,900 (the price of the cat)
and gave $100 (the price of the house)
to the poor.

Why is it that the people of this world
are much more shrewd
in handling their affairs
than the children of the light?

*Make sure the thing you're living for
is worth dying for.* Charles Mayes

Jesus said,
"Whoever is faithful in small matters
will be faithful in large ones;
whoever is dishonest in small matters
will be dishonest in large ones.
If, then, you have not been faithful
in handling worldly wealth, how can you
be trusted with true wealth?" Luke 16:10–11

Diogenes was walking through Corinth
in broad daylight, carrying a lighted lantern.
When asked what he was doing, he replied,
"I'm searching for a totally honest person."
Another story says that after Diogenes died,
he returned to earth to resume his search.
Holding his now-famous lantern,
he went from nation to nation
without success.
Finally, he came to the very last nation.
Again, he searched without success!
Worse yet, someone stole his lantern.

How honest am I in dealing with others?
What is the biggest cause of dishonesty?

An old Jewish rabbi asked his disciples,
"What most encourages people to steal?"
"Hunger," said young Benjamin.
"Debt," said Abraham. "Envy," said Joshua.
Young David answered best, saying,
"People who buy stolen goods."

SUNDAY
WEEK 32 _____ ORDINARY TIME

[Jesus said, "The Kingdom of heaven
will be like this.
Ten bridesmaids were waiting
at the bride's house to greet the groom.
He was tardy and night fell.
Five maids dozed and missed his arrival."]
Jesus concluded, "Watch out, then,
because you do not know the day or the hour
[of the Son of Man's return]." Matthew 25:13

The *Titanic* sank on April 14, 1912.
The *Washington Post* described this episode:
"In the wheel room, a nattily uniformed officer
hummed at his task. . . .
The phone rang. A minute passed!
Another minute! The officer was busy!
The third precious minute passed.
The officer, his trivial task completed,
stepped to a phone. From the 'crow's nest'—
'Iceberg dead ahead! Reverse engines!'
But too late. As he rushed to the controls,
the 'pride of the seas' crashed into
the iceberg amid a deafening roar.
Three precious minutes!
Attention to trivial details
and six hundred people paid with their lives."

Am I humming away precious minutes?

All the treasures of earth cannot bring back
one lost moment. French proverb

[Jesus said,
"How terrible for you if you]
cause one of these little ones to sin.
So watch what you do!"   Luke 17:2–3

An old story concerns
an elderly woman living with her son,
his wife, and their small daughter.
One day she began having accidents
at table, like spilling her coffee.
When the accidents became more frequent,
the son and his wife set up a little table
across the room in a corner.
There the woman ate alone off a bare table
that could be wiped easily after spills.
One day the couple saw their little daughter
building something.
When they asked her about it, she said,
"It's a little table for you to eat at
when I am a grown-up and married."
That night the couple
let the elderly mother return to the table.
And they were very kind to her,
even when she spilled her coffee.

How do I see the point of this ancient story
applying, perhaps, to my life right now?

The worst threat to the younger generation
is the example set by the older generation.
                                        E. C. McKenzie

TUESDAY
WEEK 32 _____ ORDINARY TIME

Jesus said,
"When you have done all you have been
told to do, say, 'We are ordinary servants;
we have only done our duty.'" Luke 17:10

Theoretical physicist Albert Einstein
echoed Jesus' words perfectly, saying:
"Strange is our situation here upon earth.
Each of us comes for a short visit,
not knowing why, yet sometimes
seeming to a divine purpose.
From the standpoint of daily life, however,
there is one thing we know.
That we are here for the sake of others . . .
for the countless unknown souls
with whose fate we are connected. . . .
Many times a day, I realize how much
my own outer and inner life is built upon
the labors of people, both living and dead,
and how earnestly I must exert myself
in order to give in return
as much as I have received."

From what three people
have I received much?
What was it? How can I return it?

Happiness will never be ours
if we do not recognize to some degree
that God's blessings were given us
for the well-being of all. Anonymous

[One day Jesus cured ten lepers,
but only a Samaritan
returned to thank him. Jesus said,]
"Why is this foreigner the only one
who came back to give thanks to God?"
And Jesus said to him, "Get up . . .
your faith has made you well." Luke 17:18–19

Many prisoners of war collapsed under
the terror of Nazi death camps, but not all.
Psychotherapist Viktor Frankl—
a prisoner himself—probed for the reason.
He concluded that the difference was faith.
Faith put them in touch with a power
that helped them maintain their humanity.
When freedom came,
some prisoners reacted bitterly;
others reacted gratefully.
Frankl was among the latter.
Shortly after his release,
he was walking through a field of wildflowers.
Overhead birds were circling and singing.
Instinctively Frankl knelt and prayed.
To this day, he has no idea how long
he knelt in prayer among the flowers.

How do I react to difficult situations?
How do they affect my faith in God?

When we do what we can,
God will do what we can't. E. C. McKenzie

THURSDAY
WEEK 32 _____ ORDINARY TIME

Jesus said,
"The Kingdom of God does not come
in such a way as to be seen.
No one will say, 'Look, here it is!' or,
'There it is!'; because the Kingdom of God
is within you." Luke 17:20–21

An old man lived in an old shack
at the end of the Street of the Lost Angel
in Krakow, Poland.
One night he dreamed about a treasure
hidden in an old shack under a bridge
in Warsaw. The dream was so real
that he went to Warsaw.
When he found the shack under the bridge,
a homeless youth was living in it.
The man told the youth about his dream,
planning to share the treasure with him.
"That's really weird!" said the youth.
"Last night I dreamed about a treasure
hidden in the shack of an old man
on the Street of the Lost Angel
in faraway Krakow. My dream was so real
that I planned to journey to Krakow
to find the treasure."

What is the treasure of my dreams?
Where has my search for it taken me?

The greatest treasure isn't far, far away;
it is closer to you than your own breath.

[Jesus compared his return in glory
to the suddenness and clarity
of lightning flashing across the sky.]
"On that day
someone who is on the roof of a house
must not go down into the house
to get any belongings;
in the same way
anyone who is out in the field
must not go back to the house."   Luke 17:31

Linda Taylor was shepherding
her three tiny tots upstairs to bed.
Peggy, who had just begun kindergarten,
stopped and said, "Mommy,
if the world ended right now . . ."
Linda gulped and said a quick prayer
to God for guidance.
"Yes, Peggy," she said, "go on."
Peggy completed her question, asking,
"Would I have to
take my library book back,
or would it be okay to leave it at home?"

How seriously do I take Jesus' teachings,
especially about the goal of this life?

What you possess in the world
will be found at the day of your death
to belong to another, but what you are
will be yours forever.   Henry Van Dyke

SATURDAY
WEEK 32 _____ ORDINARY TIME

[Jesus told a story about a woman
who badgered a judge to act in her behalf.
"Finally, the judge said to himself,]
'I will see to it that she gets her rights.
If I don't, she will keep on coming
and finally wear me out!' " Luke 18:5

In 1952 Mother Teresa
saw an abandoned woman in the street,
literally being eaten by ants and rodents.
She carried the woman to a hospital,
but it wouldn't accept the her.
Next, Mother Teresa carried the woman
to city officials, demanding action.
A discussion ensued.
Then, Mother Teresa demanded a shelter
where she could care for the woman
and other victims like her.
Glad to be rid of the problem,
they led Mother to an abandoned shelter,
once used by Hindu pilgrims.
Thus began Mother Teresa's first home
for the destitute and the dying.

Success is spelled "PpPpPpPp":
Prepare prayerfully. Plan prudently.
Proceed positively. Pursue perseveringly.
Which pair of P's do I stumble over most?

Working hard means going all out
until you're all in. E. C. McKenzie

Jesus said,
"The Kingdom of heaven will be like this. . . .
A man . . . was about to leave home on a trip;
he called his servants and put them
in charge of his property. He gave to each one
according to his ability. [At his return
he repaid each according to how well
he used the money.]" Matthew 25:14–15

In his book *Souls on Fire,*
Elie Wiesel invites us to think about
using our talents in a different way
than we ordinarily use them.
He says that when we meet our Creator,
we won't be asked,
"How well did you use the talents I gave you
to do great things for my people on earth?"
Rather, we'll be asked,
"How well did you use your talents
to become *you?*"

If my Maker asked me right now,
"How well are you using your talents
to become what I made you to be?"
what would I have to say?

A rose only becomes beautiful
and blesses others when it opens and blooms.
Its greatest tragedy
is to stay in a tight-closed bud,
never fulfilling its potential. Anonymous

[A blind man heard Jesus passing by.]
He cried out, "Jesus! Son of David!
Have mercy on me!" . . .
Jesus stopped . . . and asked him,
"What do you want me to do for you?"
"Sir," he answered, "I want to see again."

Luke 18:38, 40–41

Laura Bridgman was blind, deaf, and mute.
She was the first person to educate herself
by the raised-alphabet system of Dr. Howe
of the Perkins Institute for the Blind.
Louis Braille was blinded at age three.
He went on to become a teacher and
the inventor of the Braille system
of writing for the blind.
James Thurber lost the sight of one eye
early in life and the sight of his other eye
as he grew older.
Yet he kept writing and drawing cartoons
with the aid of a large magnifying glass—
until his sight vanished completely.

What keeps me from believing
that if I open my heart to Jesus,
he can work miracles
in and through me, also?

The greatest calamity
that could befall a person
is to have sight and fail to see.   Helen Keller

[Zacchaeus desired to get to know more
about Jesus.] But he was a little man and
could not see Jesus because of the crowd.
So he ran ahead of the crowd
and climbed a sycamore tree. . . .
When Jesus came to that place, he looked up
and said to Zacchaeus, "Hurry down, . . .
I must stay in your house today." Luke 19:3–5

A child saw an Indian holy person praying
by a river. When the holy person finished,
the child said, "Teach me to pray."
The holy person took the child's head,
plunged it under the water, held it there
for a while, and then released it.
When the child got its breath back,
it said, "Why did you do that?"
The holy person said, "I just gave you
your first lesson in prayer. When you want
to pray as badly as you wanted to breathe
while your head was under water,
only then will I be able to teach you."
The same is true in getting to know Jesus.
We must desire it
as much as Zacchaeus did.

How deeply do I desire to know Jesus?
What obstacles am I encountering?

Christ is not valued at all
unless he is valued above all. Saint Augustine

[Jesus said, "A man summoned his servants,]
gave them each a gold coin and told them,
'See what you can earn with this.' " Luke 19:13

A famous violin maker
said the best wood for violins
comes from the north side of a tree.
The reason is that it has been seasoned
by the cold north wind.
And that seasoning gives it a special sound.
The same is true of human beings.
Some of the world's greatest people
have been seasoned by suffering.
Take Beethoven, for example.
The son of an alcoholic father,
he lost his hearing at age 28.
When he conducted the first performance
of his Ninth Symphony, he couldn't hear
the music, except in his mind.
Nor could he hear the thunderous applause
that followed the performance.

People complain that some handicap
or obstacle keeps them from "earning more"
with the talent ("gold coin") God gave them.
How might just the opposite be true?

The "gold coins" God gives me
often include some handicap or situation
that can make me either bitter or better.
And I am the one who decides.

[Jesus drew closer to Jerusalem,] and when
he saw it, he wept . . . , saying, "If you only
knew today what is needed for peace!
But now you cannot see it!"   Luke 19:41–42

Sportswriter Bill Lyon wrote:
"One of the most important things
about the Olympics is that they remind us
of the cleansing, therapeutic value
of a good cry. . . .
You watch the gold medalists mount
the victory platform, turn to face their flags
and listen to their national anthems,
and in most every instance
their eyes begin to mist. . . . The sleek,
the strong, the swift, they all succumb.
And in doing so, in showing their humanity,
they become even more appealing."
Dallas Morning News

What Lyon said of gold medalists applies,
equally, to Jesus. He wept. And in weeping,
he showed his humanity and became
even more appealing to us. What brings tears
quickest to my eyes: joy or sorrow?
When was the last time I cried—and why?

There is a sacredness in tears.
They are not the mark of weakness,
but of power. They speak more eloquently
than ten thousand tongues.   Washington Irving

FRIDAY
WEEK 33 _____ ORDINARY TIME

Jesus went into the Temple
and began to drive out the merchants,
saying to them,
"It is written in the Scriptures
that God said,
'My Temple will be a house of prayer.'
But you have turned it into a hideout
for thieves!" Every day Jesus taught
in the Temple.   Luke 19:45–47

There's a poem called "Three Things"
by an unknown author.
One version goes like this:
"I know three things must always be
To keep a nation strong and free.
One is a hearthstone bright and dear,
With busy, happy loved ones near.
One is a ready heart and hand
To love, and serve, and keep the land.
One is a worn and beaten way
To where the people go to pray.
So long as these are kept alive,
Nation and people will survive.
God, keep them always, everywhere—
The home, the heart, the place of prayer."

How "worn and beaten" is my path
to prayer?

Life is fragile; handle with prayer.
                              E. C. McKenzie

Jesus said, "The men and women . . .
in the age to come . . .
will be like angels and cannot die.
They are the children of God, because
they have risen from death."   Luke 20:34–36

General Charles de Gaulle
was France's president from 1959 to 1969.
His private life was not without sorrow.
One of his three children, Anne,
was born subnormal after
a car accident involving his wife.
De Gaulle used to spend hours with Anne.
Eventually she died at the age of 20.
At the graveside, after weeping silently,
de Gaulle said softly to his wife, Yvonne,
"Come. Now she is like the others."

British TV celebrity Malcolm Muggeridge
said, "The only ultimate disaster
that can befall us . . . is to feel ourselves
to be at home here on earth."
What is his point,
and how does it relate to de Gaulle's story?

O Lord, . . . a thousand years to you . . .
are like yesterday, already gone,
like a short hour in the night. . . .
Teach us how short our life is,
so that we may become wise.
                                    Psalm 90:1, 4, 12

SUNDAY
WEEK 34 _____ ORDINARY TIME

[Jesus said, "At the Last Judgment
the King will say, 'Whenever you helped]
one of the least important . . . ,
you did it for me!' " Matthew 25:40

Millard Fuller came from humble origins.
He went to Auburn University
and the University of Alabama and became
a self-made millionaire before he was 30.
While his business prospered, however,
his health, marriage, and integrity suffered.
Deep soul-searching moved him
to reconcile with his wife, Linda, and
to renew his Christian commitment.
The Fullers sold everything,
gave the money to the poor,
and embarked upon a life of service to God.
In 1978 they and some close associates
created Habitat for Humanity International,
an organization to provide no-profit,
no-interest, quality housing for the poor.
Since then, HFHI and its army of volunteers
have built homes in over 1,300 U.S. cities
and 50 other countries.

What in the Fuller story strikes me most?

I see life both as a gift and a responsibility.
My responsibility is to use what God
has given me to help his people in need.
Millard Fuller, recipient of many service awards

Jesus . . . saw rich people
dropping their gifts in the Temple treasury,
and he also saw a very poor widow
dropping in two little copper coins.
He said, "I tell you that this poor widow
put in more than all the others.
For the others offered their gifts
from what they had to spare of their riches;
but she . . . gave all she had to live on."
Luke 21: 1–4

A bag of damaged and worn-out paper money
was sitting in the U.S. Treasury vault
waiting to be shredded. A $20 bill and
a $1 bill began talking about their lives.
"Wow!" said the $20 bill, "I've lived a wild life.
Excitement! Excitement! Excitement!
I was taken to all kinds of exotic places:
gambling casinos, country clubs,
and world cruises. How about you?"
The $1 bill sighed, "How I envy you!
All I ever did was go to church,
go to church, go to church."

How generously am I sacrificing
for the spread of God's Kingdom on earth?

It's amazing how big a dollar bill looks
in a church on Sunday morning
and how little it looks in a bar
on Saturday night. Author unknown

Jesus said,
"Kingdoms will attack one another.
There will be . . . terrifying things
coming from the sky.
[But the end is not yet.]"   Luke 21:10–11

Writing on scraps of scorched paper,
Dr. Michihibo Hachiya described Hiroshima
after the atomic bomb
killed a hundred thousand people
and left an equal number to die slowly.
Dazed people moved about
like scarecrows, their burnt arms
held away from their burnt body
to keep the two raw surfaces
from rubbing together painfully.
Blistering hot winds whipped
"dust and ashes into our eyes and noses.
Our mouths became dry, our throats raw. . . .
Coughing was uncontrollable."
Dead bodies were everywhere,
like "some giant had flung them
to their death from a great height. . . .
Hiroshima was no longer a city."
It had become a hell on earth.

What are my thoughts as I imagine myself
to be Dr. Hachiya?

Wrong rules the land,
and waiting justice sleeps.   Josiah G. Holland

[Jesus warned his followers,]
"You will be arrested and persecuted. . . .
You will be brought before kings and rulers
for my sake. This will be your chance
to tell the Good News."   Luke 21:12–13

England's Dr. Sheila Cassidy worked
among the very poor in Chile in the 1970s.
One day she treated a wounded man
who could not go to a hospital
for fear of the corrupt secret police.
She was informed upon, arrested,
and tortured for days
to get her to divulge information.
She says: "For the first time in my life
I thought I was going to die. . . .
I was experiencing in some slight way
what Christ had suffered. . . .
I suddenly felt enormously loved by God . . .
because I felt I had in a way
participated in his suffering."

What are my thoughts
as I imagine myself to be Cassidy
suffering for helping the poor?
What may have been Jesus' thoughts
after being condemned for my sins?

The LORD says, . . .
"I have swept your sins away like a cloud.
Come back to me."   Isaiah 44:21–22

THURSDAY
WEEK 34 _____ ORDINARY TIME

Jesus said, "There will be strange things
happening to the sun, the moon,
and the stars. . . . Then the Son of Man
will appear, coming in a cloud
with great power and glory.
When these things begin to happen,
stand up and raise your heads, because
your salvation is near." Luke 21:25, 27–28

Near the end of *The Great Dictator*,
Charlie Chaplin cries out:
"Hannah, can you hear me?
Wherever you are, look up, Hannah!
The clouds are lifting!
We are coming out of the darkness
into the light. We are coming
into a new world—a kindlier world,
where men will rise above their hate
and their greed and brutality.
Look up! Hannah!
The soul of man has been given wings,
and at last he is beginning to fly.
He is flying to the rainbow—
into the light of hope—
into the future—the glorious future
that belongs to you—to me—
and to all of us! Look up! Hannah! Look up!"

How eagerly do I await Jesus' return?

Come, Lord Jesus! Revelation 22:20

Jesus told them this parable: "Think of . . .
trees. When you see their leaves beginning
to appear, you know that summer is near.
In the same way, when you see
these things happening, you will know that
the Kingdom of God is [near]."   Luke 21:29–31

Over 1,900 years ago, the cities of Pompeii
and Herculaneum were buried under
volcanic ash when Mount Vesuvius erupted.
Decayed bodies of people trapped
in the disaster have left cavities
in the hardened ash.
By pouring liquid plaster into them,
archaeologists made casts of the victims.
One cavity in Pompeii reveals a man
holding a sword. His foot rests on a pile
of gold and silver. Scattered about him
are five bodies, probably would-be looters.
Excavations in Herculaneum reveal a row
of tenement houses. In a room of one house,
archaeologists found a cross on the wall,
a telltale sign that a Christian lived there.

If the eruption of a volcano buried me and
my room right now, and if archaeologists
excavated it 1,900 years from now,
what Christian "signs" would they find in it?

Jesus said, "Every tree is known
by the fruit it bears."   Luke 6:44

SATURDAY
WEEK 34 _____ ORDINARY TIME

Jesus said, "Pray always
that you will have the strength
to go safely through all those things . . .
and to stand before the Son of Man."

Luke 21:36

A very young man in a military hospital
had lost a leg and was sinking rapidly.
Lincoln happened by, saw him, and
offered to write a letter to his mother.
When the boy finished dictating it,
Lincoln added this postscript:
"This letter was written by A. Lincoln."
When the boy read the finished letter
and saw the postscript,
he gazed at Lincoln and asked,
"Are you our president?"
Lincoln nodded and then asked,
"Is there anything else I can do for you?"
The boy said feebly, "I guess you might
hold my hand and see me through."

What struck me most in this story?

I shall pass through this world but once.
Any good therefore that I can do,
or any kindness that I can show
to any human being, let me do it now.
Let me not defer it or neglect it,
for I shall not pass this way again.

Attributed to Stephen Grellet

NOTES _____

NOTES _____

NOTES _____

_____ **NOTES**

NOTES _____

NOTES